Yngve R. Skarsten
Pickerington, Ohio
May 5, 2002

Interpreting the
Promise of America

The Norwegian-American Historical Association

Lawrence O. Hauge, President

BOARD OF PUBLICATIONS

Odd Sverre Lovoll

Interpreting the Promise of America

Essays in Honor of Odd Sverre Lovoll

Edited by
Todd W. Nichol

Northfield, Minnesota
Norwegian-American Historical Association
2002

Contents

✻ ✻ ✻ ✻ ✻

Preface   ix

Odd Sverre Lovoll as Historian
Rudolph J. Vecoli   3

Boundaries and Linkages: Norwegian Immigrants,
the United States, and Norway
Jon Gjerde   13

Interdisciplinary Approaches in American Immigration
Studies: Possibilities and Pitfalls
Øyvind T. Gulliksen   31

Fram, Fram, Cristmenn, Crossmenn! The Battle of Stiklastaðir
beyond the Sagas
Jan Ragnar Hagland   53

Swedish Americans and the Viking Discovery of America
H. Arnold Barton   61

Letters as Links in the Chain of Migration from Hedalen,
Norway to Dane County, Wisconsin, 1857–1890
Orm Øverland   79

America as Symbol in the Plays of Marcus Thrane
Terje I. Leiren   105

Traveling on His Trade: Martin Tranmæl's Stay in the
United States and the Radicalization of the Norwegian
Labor Movement
Jorunn Bjørgum   119

The Story of the Bergsten Brothers in Canada:
Ethnic Barriers, Unfavorable Sex Ratios, and the
Creation of Male Households
Sune Åkerman   137

American, Norwegian, or North Norwegian? Dilemmas
of Identity for Immigrants from Northern Norway in the
United States, 1900-1930
Einar Niemi   149

Reading Norwegian-American Cookbooks: A Case Study
Deborah L. Miller   175

Landstad in America
Todd W. Nichol   193

A Selected Bibliography of the Writings of
Odd Sverre Lovoll   211

The Authors   219

Preface

ODD SVERRE LOVOLL IS AN ACTOR in the story of emigration and immigration he has studied so deeply. Like his parents before him, he hails from Sunnmøre, Norway, although his father Alf Løvoll had at the age of eighteen moved to the United States and lived there for eleven years before returning to Norway. In 1930 Alf Løvoll married Astrid Elise Aase. The couple had two sons, Magnar and Odd, born in 1931 and 1934, and a daughter, Svanhild, born in 1937. In the fateful month of April 1940, Alf Løvoll was at sea with the Norwegian whaling fleet and was unable to return to Norway for the duration of World War II. This left Astrid Løvoll with three small children to care for without the help of her husband for five years. In 1946 the Løvoll family moved to Seattle, Washington where the father became a fisherman. Odd Lovoll, who eventually changed his surname into a form manageable for American friends, later returned to Norway where he studied at the Universities of Bergen and Oslo. After taking examinations in Norwegian at Bergen and in history at Oslo, he worked for a time as a teacher in Norway before returning to the United States along with his wife, Else Navekvien Lovoll, and their two children, Audrey and Ronald, in 1967. *"Norrønnafolket det vil fare, det vil føre kraft til andre,"* says the the poet Bjørnson of such courageous and venturesome folk as Odd Lovoll and his family. "The people of the north want to travel, they want to bring vitality to others."

In 1969 Odd Lovoll received the M.A. degree from the University of North Dakota, where he also taught from 1967 to 1970. In 1970 he began teaching at St. Olaf College in Northfield, Minnesota and in 1973 he completed the Ph.D. at the University of Minnesota with a specialization in immigration history. His doctoral dissertation, a study of regional associations among Norwegian-American immigrants, was later published by the Norwegian-American Historical Association as *A Folk Epic: The* Bygdelag *in America.*

During his thirty years of service at St. Olaf College, Odd Lovoll served the institution in several capacities. A member of both the Norwegian and history departments, he was for a time chairperson of the Norwegian department. Throughout these busy years at St. Olaf, he was tireless in his work on behalf of the Norwegian-American Historical Association. While the organization is independent of St. Olaf College, it has throughout its history been located at the college and closely associated with it. When Odd Lovoll became the association's editor in 1980, this followed a precedent established in 1960, when Professor Kenneth O. Bjork of St. Olaf's history department had assumed the post succeeding Theodore C. Blegen, Dean of the Graduate School of the University of Minnesota. As editor, Lovoll assisted in the creation of a new relationship between the association and St. Olaf College when the editorship was linked to a professorship in the college's history department by the terms establishing the endowment of the King Olav V Chair in Scandinavian-American Studies. In 1992 Odd Lovoll became the first occupant of the King Olav V Chair and held this appointment until his retirement in December of 2000. Testimony to his gifts as a teacher are the full classes he continues to meet during the January interim as an emeritus member of the faculty at St. Olaf. He also regularly teaches in Norway where he holds a part-time appointment in history at the University of Oslo. He is in constant demand as a public lecturer on both sides of the Atlantic.

In his capacity as editor of the Norwegian-American Historical Association, Lovoll edited and supervised the production of thirty-three books. They are listed in the bibliography included in the present volume. Among the most notable of his own publications for the association are his investigation of the *bygdelag* and his study of Norwegian-American life in a large metropolitan area, the first of its kind, *A Century of Urban Life: The Norwegians in Chicago before 1930,* which appeared in 1988. Kenneth O. Bjork, Lovoll's predecessor as editor, considered the latter work to have opened a new era in Norwegian-American studies and his judgment has since been sustained.

Lovoll's activity as an author and editor has not been confined to the work of the association. In 1983, for example, the University of Oslo Press published his comprehensive history of Norwegian America, *Det løfterike landet. En norskamerikansk historie.* An English version followed in 1984, *The Promise of America: A History of the Norwegian-American People,* published by the University of Minnesota Press in cooperation with the Norwegian-American Historical Association. The order of languages was reversed when Lovoll produced *The Promise Fulfilled: A Portrait of Norwegian-Americans Today,* published by the University of Minnesota Press and the association in 1998. A Norwegian translation, *Infridde løfter. Et norskamerikansk samtidsbilde,* followed in 1999. His many articles are further evidence of interest and competence in a broad array of fields.

Odd Lovoll's work as a scholar has attained wide notice. He was decorated with the Knight's Cross First Class of the Royal Norwegian Order of Merit in 1986 by King Olav V and in 1989 he was inducted into membership in the Norwegian Academy of Science and Letters. In this group he occupies one of nine chairs reserved for foreign historians. Among the many honors that have come to him in the United States are awards from the state historical societies of both Illinois and Wisconsin.

It is a privilege for his friends and colleagues to present this book of essays to Odd Sverre Lovoll on the occasion of his retirement both from the King Olav V Chair of Scandinavian-American Studies at St. Olaf College and from the editorship of the Norwegian-American Historical Association.

Todd W. Nichol
St. Olaf College
Luther Seminary

Acknowledgments

I AM GRATEFUL TO THE AUTHORS for contributing their essays to this volume in honor of our colleague, Odd Sverre Lovoll. I thank them as well for their patience and efficiency in responding to queries from the editor.

Thanks are also due to three other individuals. Professor Odd Lovoll provided biographical information, bibliographical data, and photographs at my request. He knew that something was afoot, but kindly did not ask questions. Alice Loddings prepared illustrations. Sylvia Ruud readied the entire manuscript for publication.

TWN
28 December 2001

Interpreting the Promise of America

Odd Sverre Lovoll as Historian

Rudolph J. Vecoli

IT WAS AN AUTUMN DAY in 1969 when Kenneth Bjork came to my office in the Social Science tower at the University of Minnesota accompanied by Odd Lovoll, fresh from the University of North Dakota where he had recently earned a master's degree in history. Although born and bred in Norway, Lovoll came to the United States at the age of twelve with his mother and siblings to join his father who was a halibut fisherman in Seattle. He returned to Norway in 1952 where he remained for fifteen years as a university student and teacher. Coming back to the United States, he initiated the studies of Norwegian immigration that were to carry him to the pinnacle of success as the first holder of the King Olav V Chair in Scandinavian-American Studies at St. Olaf College.

My first impression of Odd Lovoll was of a shy, even diffident, person. Although he was always respectful and modest, I soon learned that in spite of the young Lovoll's formal demeanor he was a genial and gregarious person with a clever sense of humor. To his intellectual work, he brought a high degree of self-confidence, determination, and intellect. Bjork had chosen him as his protégé and hoped to see Lovoll succeed him both as editor of the Norwegian-American Historical Association and as a member of the faculty at St. Olaf College. Bjork chose well.

Among immigrant groups, Norwegian Americans have been particularly blessed with a succession of excellent scholars who have dedicated themselves to the study of the history and heritage of the Norwegians in the United States. In addition to the generation including Ole Edvart Rølvaag and Thedore C. Blegen that founded the Norwegian-American Historical Association in 1925, a later generation including Einar Haugen, Kenneth O. Bjork, Carleton Qualey, Lloyd Hustvedt, and Carl Chrislock, among others, established Norwegian-American studies as a reputable field of scholarship. Under their leadership, the Norwegian-American Historical Association would become a model for ethnic historical societies.[1] While not immune to empathy with their forebears, in itself more a virtue than a vice, these scholars have avoided the filiopietism that has often marred the publications of other such organizations. The thirty-five volumes of *Norwegian-American Studies and Records,* the title of which was shortened to *Norwegian-American Studies* in 1970, constitute an invaluable body of historical literature documenting and interpreting the Norwegian-American experience. In addition to articles and monographs, these volumes contain extensive translations of letters, diaries, and other primary sources.

It was this formidable legacy that Odd Lovoll inherited, one which he was to nurture and embellish. Such a task might have made a lesser person tremble, but he was more than up to the challenge. But why, one might ask, would an aspiring student of Norwegian-American history have chosen to study with Vecoli? I certainly had no claim to expertise in the field. Besides, Norwegians and Italians were at odds over who first discovered America! Certainly the University of Minnesota has a distinguished tradition in American immigration history. Two pioneers in the field, George Malcolm Stephenson and Theodore Blegen, respectively historians of Swedish and Norwegian immigration, were members of its faculty.[2] However, I joined the history faculty under different colors, as an historian of Italian immigration and director of the Immigration History Research Center, which focused on the southern and eastern European immigrations. Subsequently, I learned a great deal about Scandinavian-Americans from my students Jon Gjerde, Joy Lintelman, and, of course, Odd Lovoll.

Having been invited in 1969 by Bjork to write the history of the *bygdelag* [regional associations], Odd Lovoll made short work of his graduate studies and dissertation. He began his doctoral work in the fall of 1970, received the Ph.D. in the spring of 1973, and published his first book, *A Folk Epic: The* Bygdelag *in America,* in time for the sesquicentennial of the Norwegian-American Historical Association in 1975. This impressive record reflects characteristics that have distinguished Odd Lovoll's scholarly career: focused labor, exhaustive research, and disciplined writing. He always makes deadlines.

In 1971, Lovoll began his academic career as assistant professor of Norwegian and some time later of immigration history at St. Olaf College. He was appointed to the King Olav V Chair in Scandinavian-American Studies in 1992. Recently he has also taught a portion of the year at the University of Oslo. He began publishing in the late sixties and early seventies with several articles based on his master's essay on the Norwegian-American press and initial findings regarding the *bygdelag* movement. *A Folk Epic,* the published version of his doctoral dissertation, is a study of the parochial identities and loyalties of Norwegian immigrants. It is "history from the bottom up," focused on the thoughts and emotions of common folk. (My own modest contribution to the study was to coin the term Norwegian-American *"campanilismo"* or "parochialism.") The first of a number of works that established Lovoll as the premiere historian of Norwegian Americans, it reflects the influence of the "new social history." Subsequently, he

Odd Lovoll at work on A Folk Epic: The *Bygedelag* in America.
Photo by Else Lovoll.

focused on various neglected dimensions of Norwegian-American history, not simply adding to the bibliography on the subject, but bringing it into the mainstream of American historiography.

Writing in 1985, Lovoll observed that while during "the 1920s and 1930s Scandinavian-American historians represented the 'mainstream' in American immigration studies," they subsequently had become "too parochial and specialized." To overcome this intellectual isolation and the "rural bias in Norwegian-American historiography," he called for more study of the urban experience and for comparative study of Norwegians with other immigrant groups.[3] Taking his own advice, Lovoll authored a monograph titled *A Century of Urban Life: The Norwegians in Chicago before 1930.* In this wide-ranging volume published in 1988, he traces the patterns of migration and settlement and records the religious and associational life of the Norwegians as well as their economic adaptation to an urban environment, giving attention to both their business activities and working-class occupations. Their involvements in labor movements, including socialism, and mainstream politics are discussed extensively, as are women's occupations and associations. Lovoll also emphasizes the interaction of Norwegians with Irish, German, and other immigrant groups, but he especially accents the close relations among Swedes, Danes, and Norwegians, going so far as to speak of a "Scandinavian Melting Pot in Chicago."[4] Clearly Odd Lovoll was attuned to the new approaches to immigration history.

In addition to teaching and writing history, beginning in 1980 Lovoll has served as editor of the Norwegian-American Historical Association. When appointed, he was only the third person to have held this position, having succeeded Kenneth O. Bjork who served from 1960 to 1980. Bjork in his turn had followed Theodore C. Blegen who edited the association's publications from 1925 to 1960. Among the publications of the association is the series *Norwegian-American Studies* as well as several other series, including the Travel and Description Series, the Authors Series, the Biographical Series, Topical Studies, and Special Publications. When he was appointed, Lovoll had already researched and co-written with Bjork a history of the Norwegian-American Historical Association on the occasion of its fiftieth anniversary.[5] As editor, he acted upon his belief in the need to integrate Norwegian-American history with the new perspectives informing the social history of the United States. Thus, in the volumes of *Norwegian-American Studies* appearing under his editorship we find a number of articles and documents relating to Norwegian-American women and feminism, socialism among Norwegian-Americans, and Norwegian-American interaction with other racial and ethnic groups. An example of the latter is the article by Betty A. Bergland, "Norwegian Immigrants and 'Indianerne' in the Landtaking, 1838–1892." In his preface to this volume, Lovoll observed that Bergland's critique "finds much wanting in Norwegian-American scholarship on this score, not only negligence but a lack of understanding and on occasion even a prejudicial terminology in describing Native Americans."[6] His willingness to include revisionist studies, even if they stepped on the toes of the older generation of scholars, was also exemplified by

Odd Lovoll signing copies of A Century of Urban Life: The Norwegians in Chicago before 1930. *Photo by Else Lovoll.*

his reprinting of the article by April Schultz, "'The Pride of the Race Had Been Touched': The 1925 Norse-American Immigration Centennial and Ethnic Identity." As Lovoll noted in his prefatory remarks, this piece on the construction of a Norwegian-American identity, influenced by the new cultural studies, "faults earlier scholarship for being . . . overly assimilationist."[7] Knowing something about the character of ethnic historical societies, which have a predominantly lay membership, I marvel at Lovoll's bravery in publishing such innovative scholarship and at the sophistication of the NAHA leadership that supported his editorial position.

On the occasion of the symposium inaugurating the King Olav V Chair in Scandinavian-American Studies at St. Olaf College in 1992, Lovoll articulated the rationale for a pan-Scandinavian, rather than narrowly Norwegian, perspective. Moreover, the volume of proceedings, entitled *Nordics in America: The Future of Their Past,* published in 1993, stretched the fabric to include Finns. Further, the keynote speaker at the symposium was John Bodnar, by no means a specialist in Nordic studies. In his contribution, Lovoll clearly espoused an inclusive immigration history embedded in the larger history of the American nation. "None of these ethnic groups," he declared, "can . . . be seen in isolation. . . . Our nation's history can in fact be fully understood only by a consideration of the dynamics and the drama of the interaction of diverse types of humans, the mix of national heritages, the prejudices and the rivalries among them. These are the forces that have shaped our uniquely American social, cultural, and political environment."[8] He added: "the specific history of all segments of the American population must be considered in order to fully capture the pluralistic dimensions of our society and develop a multicultural interpretation of our national experience."[9]

In addition to *Nordics in America,* Lovoll organized other conferences and edited their proceedings, including *Scandinavians and Other Immigrants in Urban America,* appearing in 1985. His inclusion of John Higham, Kathleen Neils Conzen, and myself among the participants in this symposium was yet another example of his desire to incorporate Scandinavian- or Nordic-American studies into the broader discipline of American social history.

In his two major works of synthesis, the products of a mature scholarship, Odd Lovoll realized his aspiration of writing Norwegian-American history that would exemplify the highest form of contemporary ethnic and immigrant studies. *The Promise of America: A History of the Norwegian-American People* was first published in 1984 and in a revised edition in 1999. *The Promise Fulfilled: A Portrait of Norwegian Americans Today* appeared in 1998. The former was initially written in Norwegian and published in Norway. *The Promise of America* is a lavishly illustrated, well-written volume that might be termed a "coffee-table book" if that term did not carry derogatory connotations. Looks in this case are deceiving, because this is a work of synthesis based on substantial scholarship. While acknowledging his debt to the historical literature, Lovoll describes his research in archival collections and libraries throughout the United States and Norway and his numerous interviews with Norwegian Americans. Influenced, as many of us have been, by Frank Thistlethwaite's path-breaking essay on the Atlantic migration, Lovoll's work brings to bear a transnational perspective on the Norwegian immigration.[10]

While *The Promise of America* does not offer novel interpretations, it is a meat-and-potatoes presentation of the Norwegian-American experience, replete with micro-histories of communities, vignettes of important episodes, and biographical sketches of atypical and typical immigrants, often based on letters, diaries, and other primary sources. Although Lovoll recognizes the operation of "impersonal economic forces," he reminds us that "the expectations and the uncertainty the individual emigrant harbored . . . affected the emigrant's resolution."[11] This emphasis on the individual is given a human face by the many photographs in the book. While highlighting positive aspects, he does not shy away from the negative, such as prostitution among Norwegian immigrant women. The overriding theme of the work, however, is one of social mobility and success. He concludes that although assimilation was "an inevitable and natural development" many Americans of Norwegian ancestry still retained "a consciousness of a common historical past and an ethnic bond between [themselves] and their kinsmen in Norway."[12]

The Promise Fulfilled is an obvious sequel to *The Promise of America*. As the subtitle, *A Portrait of Norwegian Americans Today*, suggests, it is a panoramic, encyclopedic view of the contemporary condition and status of this ethnic population. The volume departs in striking ways from Lovoll's previous work. Its subject is not the past, but the present. As such it employs the methodologies and sources of sociology and ethnography, participant-observer fieldwork, questionnaires, and interviews. The scale and extent of the research is itself mind-boggling. It required several years, thousands of queries to individuals, and thousands of miles traveled. This is not a cream puff of a book designed to satisfy the insatiable appetite of all ethnic groups for flattery. Although its thesis is that the promise of America has indeed been fulfilled for most Norwegian Americans, now predominantly of the third generation plus, who have attained a middle-class or better standard of living, Lovoll does not shy away from controversial subjects such as racism, criminality, and homosexuality. Among the interviewees of Norwegian ancestry are leaders of the right-wing white supremacy militia movement, two incarcerated murderers, and a number of gays and lesbians. The latter section provides fascinating insights into the dynamics and the emotional tone of Norwegian-American families.[13] Predictably he received indignant protests from irate readers when "negative" topics were reported (not always accurately) by the media. While reporting on those incidents as indications of a defensive ethnicity, Lovoll does not censor or apologize for his research findings.

The principal question posed by *The Promise Fulfilled* is: "How do Norwegian Americans in the 1990s define their ethnic heritage?"[14] What is the content and salience of Norwegian Americanness among persons who are three or more generations removed from the immigrant experience and who have realized upward social mobility? Not long ago the question would have been regarded as frivolous. Of course, they simply became Americans. In these post-melting-pot days, however, we take it seriously. To my knowledge, Lovoll's is the first study to examine the ethnicity of one of the "old" immigrant groups in a systematic and multidisciplinary fashion. In contrast to recent sociological works dealing with European-American ethnic groups in an ahistorical and one-dimensional manner, *The Promise Fulfilled* also interprets contemporary Norwegian-American ethnicity against a richly realized historical setting.

More than in his other writings, Lovoll here engages the theoretical literature regarding ethnicity. The text is sprinkled with names such as Richard Alba, John Bodnar, Herbert Gans, John Higham, Mary Waters, and Werner Sollors. Although revealing his broad reading of the relevant works across disciplines, this is not a case of name-dropping. Lovoll applies, and on occasion challenges, their ideas in his interpretation of Norwegian-American ethnicity. Among the various theories, Lovoll finds "the invention of ethnicity" most congenial. Indeed, much of the volume is devoted to analyzing how the symbols and settings expressing the identity of Norwegian Americans have changed over time. The discussions of language, folk arts, sports, and other activities as markers of ethnic identity are among the most informative and entertaining in the book. (Although he seeks to remain the neutral observer, he cannot refrain from describing the use of "Uff da" and Viking regalia as "silly.")[15]

Although recognizing that certain expressions of Norwegian-American ethnicity have been commodified, incorporated into popular culture, and adopted by non-Norwegian Americans, Lovoll rejects notions that that ethnicity is in a "twilight" stage, that it has become simply "symbolic," or that it is a fiction woven out of whole cloth. Thus he takes exception to the theories of Sollors, Alba, and Gans, emphasizing instead the continuity of ethnic identity and affiliation for many Americans of Norwegian ancestry, based in "social and cultural realities" of family and community, organizational and cultural activities, historical memories, and ties to contemporary Norway. "Invention" for Odd Lovoll signifies the continuing adaptation and evolution of the forms of ethnic expression with changing circumstances, but he insists upon the rootedness of ethnic identity in the realities of historical experience. "Norwegian-American ethnicity," he concluded, "remains a vital and progressively changing factor of American life."[16] *The Promise Fulfilled* is an important book not only for Norwegian-American studies but also as a contribution to the broader discussion of the nature and role of ethnicity in American society.

Historians are grateful to Odd Lovoll for his many contributions to their craft, not only as author of significant works, but as editor, conference organizer, and mediator between Norwegian and American scholarship. He has succeeded in bringing Norwegian-American studies into the mainstream of American historiography. As his mentor, I have derived particular pleasure from his growth and achievements as an historian. Odd Lovoll's scholarly career is, indeed, a promise fulfilled.

NOTES

[1]Rudolph J. Vecoli, "An Outsider's View of the Association," *Norwegian-American Studies* 27 (1977), 272–279.

[2]John T. Flanagan, *Theodore C. Blegen: A Memoir* (Northfield, MN, 1977); Rudolph J. Vecoli, "'Over the years I have encountered the hazards and rewards that await the historian of immigration': George Malcolm Stephenson and the Swedish American Community," *Swedish American Quarterly* 51 (April, 2000), 130–149.

[3]Odd S. Lovoll, "Preface," *Scandinavians and Other Immigrants in Urban America. The Proceedings of a Research Conference October 26–27, 1984,* ed. Odd S. Lovoll (Northfield, MN, 1985), iii; "Preface," *Norwegian-American Studies* 31 (1986).

[4]Odd S. Lovoll, "A Scandinavian Melting Pot in Chicago," in *Swedish-American Life in Chicago: Cultural and Urban Aspects of an Immigrant People, 1850–1930,* ed. Philip J. Anderson and Dag Blanck (Urbana and Chicago, 1992), 60–67.

[5]Odd S. Lovoll and Kenneth O. Bjork, *The Norwegian-American Historical Association, 1925–1975* (Northfield, MN, 1975).

[6]Betty A. Bergland, "Norwegian Immigrants and 'Indianerne' in the Landtaking, 1838–1892," *Norwegian-American Studies* 35 (2000), 319–350; Odd S. Lovoll, "Preface," *Norwegian-American Studies* 35 (2000), x.

[7]April Schultz, "'The Pride of the Race Had Been Touched': The 1925 Norse-American Immigration Centennial and Ethnic Identity," *Norwegian-American Studies* 33 (1992), 267–308; Odd S. Lovoll, "Preface," *Norwegian-American Studies* 33 (1992), x.

[8]Odd S. Lovoll, "A Chair in Scandinavian-American Studies," in *Nordics in America: The Future of Their Past,* ed. Odd S. Lovoll (Northfield, MN, 1993), 213–214.

[9]Lovoll, "A Chair in Scandinavian-American Studies," 222.

[10]Frank Thistlethwaite, "Migration from Europe Overseas in the Nineteenth and Twentieth Centuries," in *A Century of European Migrations, 1830–1930,* ed. Rudolph J. Vecoli and Suzanne M. Sinke (Urbana, IL, 1991), 17–57. For an appreciation of Thistlethwaite's influence see Rudolph J. Vecoli, "Introduction," 1–14.

[11]Odd S. Lovoll, *The Promise of America: A History of the Norwegian-American People* (Minneapolis, 1984), 4.

[12]Lovoll, *The Promise of America,* 197.

[13]Odd S. Lovoll, *The Promise Fulfilled: A Portrait of Norwegian Americans Today* (Minneapolis, 1998), 131–136.

[14]Lovoll, *The Promise Fulfilled,* 219.

[15]Lovoll, *The Promise Fulfilled,* 76.

[16]Lovoll, *The Promise Fulfilled,* 256.

Boundaries and Linkages: Norwegian Immigrants, the United States, and Norway

Jon Gjerde

ODD LOVOLL IN THE PAST quarter century has published some six books in addition to many articles on the history of Norwegians in the United States and Norway. He has also edited numerous volumes of *Norwegian-American Studies.* Since the publication in 1975 of his first book, *A Folk Epic: The* Bygdelag *in America,* the field of immigration and ethnic history in the United States, not to mention the study of Norwegian immigrants as a part of that field, has been transformed. Lovoll has been a participant in that transformation.

The field of immigration history, of course, existed before Lovoll took his Ph.D. from the University of Minnesota, so it is useful to review the state of the field as it was when he came of age intellectually. The earliest writers and scholars who considered immigration to the United States in the late nineteenth and early twentieth centuries tended to be concerned with justifying the place of their various "peoples" in America. If the alternative to absolute assimilation was fostering an ethnic identity, it mattered that this identity was set in a positive light. These concerns were made even more urgent by the periodic nativist outbreaks that questioned the immigrant's place in the United States. As a result, much of the earlier literature on immigration tended to be filiopietistic, reverential, and uncritical in tone.[1]

When professional historians undertook the study of immigration in the early twentieth century, they also faced impediments. Much of their scholarship sought to make their subjects matter in the larger historical narrative. Many of the works of Marcus Lee Hansen, for example, were aimed at showing how immigrants were similar to Americans generally. His essay on "Puritanism and Immigration" attempted to illustrate how the story of religious development in Norwegian communities resembled in important ways the narrative of the Massachusetts Puritans some two centuries before. Likewise, his essay on migration, settlement, and expansion depicted the role that immigrants played in creating the American frontier. Perhaps they were not pioneers, Hansen suggested, but as "fillers-in" they enabled the American pioneers to move westward.[2]

As they made the immigrant story matter, however, the first generation of professional scholars of immigration was not as uncritical of its subjects as the filiopietists who preceded it had been. Rudolph J. Vecoli, for example, has illustrated the conflicts between George M. Stephenson and Swedish clergy.[3] Although Stephenson's parents were devoted members of the Augustana Synod, the major Swedish-American Lutheran body, he rebelled against much of his religious environment. Stephenson's *The Religious Aspects of Swedish Immigration* of 1932, which remains influential to the present, so antagonized the clergy that it apparently became anathema to many in the Swedish community and sold poorly as a result. Stephenson's journey ultimately would lead him toward alienation from the Swedish-American community as a whole. The scholarship of Marcus Lee Hansen, son of a Danish father and Norwegian-American mother, also was influenced by critical childhood memories. His "law" of the immigrant generations, the notion that the second generation rejected its ethnic origins whereas the next generation rediscovered them, was informed by his youth. As a boy, he experienced the small Middle Western towns peopled by second-generation ethnics as bleak places whose residents attempted to be more American than the Yankees themselves. Hansen remembered these towns, stripped of the trappings of their European past, as places "on which our childish eyes were fed—or starved."[4]

A sea change in the study of immigration occurred in the 1960s and 1970s, when a "new social history" asserted forcefully that history should be studied from the bottom up, that common people mattered as much as the elite, and that the people had agency in making their impact on society. Historians of immigration, influenced by this perspective generally, began to study people in cities and in the countryside and to work on the history of immigrants in packinghouses, textile mills, and farms. They studied their ethnic worlds and how they interacted with the larger American society. Odd Lovoll was among this group.

The "new immigration history" consisted of scholars reacting against the idea that immigrants lacked agency or that they were bewildered and alienated peasants in an imposing American world.[5] Put briefly, the revision of the "new immigration history" focused on at least three concerns. First, the new immigration history rejected the inevitability of assimilation to American life. Revising a model developed by the Chicago School of Sociology, which had posited a schematic model of assimilation, the new scholarship stressed the vitality of ethnic groups and the contingency of cultural change. Second, these historians rejected the alienation that had been associated with the immigrant experience. Immigrants left their homelands more in hope of improving their situation than out of abject despair. Third, as they discarded the notion of alienation, historians stressed instead an agency among immigrants, an agency developed in the homelands and a proximate cause of immigration in the first place. In sum, historians increasingly came to appreciate, and even to romanticize, the world that the immigrants made. They tended to lack the criticism that characterized earlier historians such as Hansen and Stephenson.

In recent decades, the field has continued to evolve. Scholars have been animated by the new immigrants from a variety of locations—most notably Latin America, Asia, and Africa—whose stories have differed from the European story of which the Norwegian migration is a part. They have also been increasingly interested in the homelands, placing the study of immigration into a "transnational" framework that considers the entire migration process, a concern that had spurred Hansen a half century before. Whereas Lovoll obviously has remained focused on the Norwegian and Norwegian-American story, his research has certainly reflected the transnational shifts apparent in the study of immigrants to the United States.

In sum, Lovoll as a scholar aptly represents the evolution of the field of immigration and ethnic history in the past quarter century. Because this is a volume that congratulates him for his past work, moreover, it bears emphasizing that he has ably focused on an array of issues within larger immigration history, each of which has concerned others in the field as well. First, his work has illustrated the divisions and cleavages that existed *among* Norwegian Americans. Too often scholars have reified an ethnic group and analyzed it as if all those who descended from a particular lineage identified with one another. In fact, as Lovoll illustrated in his study of the *bygdelag* [regional associations], immigrants and their descendents had a variety of overlapping identifications.[6] Second, Lovoll has remained cognizant of the international connections that linked Norway and Norwegian America. Reflecting recent work on transnationalism, his praiseworthy works on the outlines of the story of the Norwegian immigration, such as *The Promise of America,* have considered the Norwegian antecedents.[7] Perhaps because Lovoll was born in Norway, perhaps because of his continuing work at the University of Oslo, perhaps because of the influential presence of NAHA-Norway, linkages between Europe and North America have not been forgotten in his work. Third, the boundaries of Lovoll's curiosity have consistently changed so that he has seized on areas of research that have not been adequately studied previously. Hence he has analyzed Norwegian immigrants and their children in the city, in such works as his study *A Century of Urban Life,* and the recent immigration from Norway and the ethnic identifications of Americans of Norwegian descent in *The Promise Fulfilled.*[8]

Lovoll's work has influenced most of us who have toiled on aspects of Norwegian-American history. As a way of honoring him, I would like to explore here some of the linkages between his scholarship and mine with particular reference to the first two issues in immigration history mentioned above: his attention to the diversity of the Norwegian-American population and the transnational character of the Norwegian migration. The title of my essay reflects the sense that a variety of boundaries and linkages divided and bound Norwegian immigrants to a variety of self-constructed groups. The first part of my argument focuses on the life of Norwegian Americans in the United States. I want to suggest that Norwegian immigrants had a variety of attributes that fostered a way of imagining the larger meaning of their migration. Specifically, they were accorded rights in the United States by virtue of their race that were denied many other immigrants. Attaining citizenship and the right to vote for men was a relatively simple process in a state that was based on a republican form of government. Wages were higher than in Norway for both women and men, and land was more abundant. Amid all of these differences, Norwegians were also provided the possibility to reconstruct cultural forms carried from home such as their churches and their linguistic traditions. As a result, many Norwegian immigrants were struck both by the social and economic opportunity in the United States *and* by the chance to replant a Norwegian world within their new national home. To explain these new conditions, Norwegian immigrants tended to use the shorthand term "freedom," which enabled them both to celebrate life in the United States and to recreate aspects of Norwegianness. At the same time, they juxtaposed the "freedom" of the United States with a past in Europe that often was characterized by a lack of freedom. The creation of a Norwegian-American identity in the United States was thus often linked to a larger American identity.

These notions of life in the United States returned to Norway, as I will suggest in the second part of the paper. Although the return migration to Norway was much lower than that of other national migrations from southern and eastern Europe and later from Asia and Latin America, the volume of the Norwegian migration dramatically informed perception of life in the United States. America letters, in addition to returned immigrants, told stories of how things were done in the United States and provided models of how Norway could be changed. The notion of "freedom," in sum, traveled back to Norway and immigrants were instrumental actors in changing a nation-state in which they no longer lived. In this case, linkages were created between Norwegian-Americans and Norwegians who remained at home.

"FREEDOM" AND COMPLEMENTARY IDENTITY IN THE UNITED STATES

The ethnic group of Norwegian Americans that formed out of the Norwegian migration to the United States conformed to a larger pattern of a nineteenth-century European migration generally, but was distinctive in two ways. For one, their volume of remigration was relatively small, so they were forced to develop ethnic group identities nested within a larger American identity.[9] Second, because they were deemed "white," the polity and society in the United States was relatively accessible to them.[10] These factors were critical in influencing the ways in which the ethnic group created identities and the ways in which these identities interacted with national identities. Because immigrants considered themselves permanent residents with rights of citizenship, their leaders were forced to balance the development of the ethnic group with that of integration into membership in the nation. Many immigrants from Norway did not long identify, or quickly lost their identity, as members of a group called Norwegian-American, in part because they might have married others of another ethnic or racial group and changed their identity. Immigrants who became ethnics, however, not only created myths of belongingness that fostered an ethnic identity, but they also merged their particularistic stories into larger narratives of nation. After all, those who did identify themselves as Norwegian American had other competing identities. They could maintain identities as workers or women or Lutherans or members of the Republican Party. They could also identify as American. As recent scholarship has suggested, there was often a relationship between a larger national identity and an ethnic one.[11] When they combined national and ethnic identities, they were central actors in creating what I will call complementary identities that fused multi-leveled identities in relation to one another.[12] As I will define it, complementary identity merged allegiance to national and ethnic group in a self-reinforcing dynamic that embedded pluralism into the national fabric as immigrants and their leaders understood it. This ingenious construction, however, had its risks for ethnic leaders: membership in nation could come to override ethnic membership, which in turn could endanger the allegiance of the ethnic leaders' clientele and foster the loss of identity as Norwegian American.

Norwegian ethnics and immigrants in the nineteenth-century United States merged the myths of America with those of their group. They quickly became aware of a common American tendency to celebrate the many ways in which their republic improved upon the tired systems of the old European states. As they were introduced to the rhetoric and institutions of American exceptionalism by their leadership, immigrants showed an inclination to celebrate the American political and social system itself. Mid-nineteenth-century European immigrants commonly praised the economic possibilities that defined the nation. They were also predisposed to esteem the nation's political institutions with their "natural freedom and equality." These identifications were powerful forces in encouraging recent arrivals to develop loyalties to the United States and to learn about its institutions.

A few examples of this rhetoric can give an indication of its content. Johan R. Reiersen in 1843, because the American government was unhampered by monarchical and aristocratic interests, argued that there was created a "spirit of progress, improvements in all directions, and a feeling for popular liberty and for the rights of the great masses exceeding that of any land in Europe." As a result, the republican government would not fail, in large part because "the masses" would never be "reduced, through the power of individuals or of capital, to the same slavish dependence that supports the thrones of Europe. Personal freedom is something the people suck in with their mother's milk," he concluded. "It seems to have become as essential to every citizen of the United States as the air he breathes. It is part of his being, and will continue to be until his whole nature is cowed and transformed in the bondage of need and oppression."[13] The letters from a Norwegian correspondence society of immigrants likewise stressed the spirit of freedom in the United States, which, they maintained, contained "the secret of general equality." As immigrants, they enjoyed tasting "the satisfaction of being liberated from the effect of all yoke and despotism."[14]

The absorption of national myths, however, did not mean that European leaders discarded cultural pasts. On the contrary, they seized on common national, linguistic, and religious traditions as cornerstones for fashioning their ethnic collectivities. These ethnic groups created boundaries from other ethnic groups, oftentimes reconfiguring common pasts that were instrumental for ethnic leaders in the pluralist society.[15] Ethnic institutions, based on common intellectual, geographical, or linguistic pasts originating in Europe, were created in the United States to support interest group associations in the polity and society. This process of "ethnicization" did not, however, nullify the development of loyalties to the United States. Rather than competing, the dual loyalties to nation and subgroup, invented under the auspices of an American creed, could be complementary.[16]

The ideological underpinnings of citizenship that privileged "freedom" and "self-rule" in fact enabled immigrants to nurture simultaneously their bond to nation and to ethnic subgroup. Tropes of "freedom" and "liberty," perhaps because their meaning was so pliant, proved to be malleable concepts that fostered an appreciation among immigrants of the responsibilities and rights of American citizenship. This frame of reference was used by immigrants to write their own foundation myths before the first Norwegian immigrant arrived in the United States, indeed even before the United States was a nation-state. In 1764, Christopher Saur, a Philadelphia German, would write: "[W]hether you are Englishmen, Germans, Low-Germans or Swedes, whether you are of the High Church, Presbyterians, Quakers, or of another denomination, by your living here and by the law of the land you are *free men, not slaves.*"[17] And Henry Miller, in a patriotic litany penned shortly before the Declaration of Independence was signed, reminded his readers, "Remember—and remind your families—you came to America, suffering many hardships, in order to escape servitude and enjoy liberty; Remember, in Germany serfs [*leibeigene*] may not marry without the consent of their master. . . . They are regarded as little better than black slaves on West Indian Islands."[18] A pliant use of the abstraction of freedom, set in a context of the unfreedom of the European world, was thus a useful rhetorical device for understanding life in the American republic.

Yet the very concept of freedom could also nurture the maintenance of old-world ties. One sense of "freedom," after all, implied a liberty to maintain patterns of life and practice conventions that varied from those of native-born Americans. Immigrants became citizens of the United States and theoretically performed the obligations as citizens, but basic rights inherent in their citizenship status allowed them to retain ethnic and religious allegiances carried from Europe. Immigrants and their children, then, could simultaneously—in a complementary, self-reinforcing fashion—maintain allegiances to the United States and to their former identities outside its borders.

These expressions of belonging within the complementary identity were American in conception and origin. They were also not exclusively Norwegian. In fact, nineteenth-century immigrants and their leaders invented and continually modified both a sense of allegiance to an imagined community composed of Americans and a reified notion of a common pre-immigration past.[19] These identities, when developed in tandem, modulated in relation to one another. Speeches made by ethnic leaders therefore would compare conditions in the United States with those in Europe and in biblical allusion they could stress how immigrants "had shaken the dust of Europe from their feet."[20] Or they would speak of their old country as a "land of tyranny."[21] Yet their reverence for their new country and their "patriotism" was often based on their freedom to be ethnically and religiously distinct. The cornerstone of a Catholic church edifice in rural Iowa contained a document that is an apt example of a mature dual identity. The document, composed in Latin, expressed "sentiments of thanksgiving of liberation of ten years of persecution abroad and for freedom here." Yet it also asked its descendants "to remain true Catholics and Germans." It solicited "God's abiding blessing" which it trusted the church would receive since the large, tall-steepled church manifested "the Catholic Faith and German sacrifice to Yankee materialism."[22] Some years before, a German-language newspaper reported that a rally of the Democratic Party manifested a "fire of patriotism" that "stirred the Americans up."[23] Patriotism, it was clear, was not dependent on being "American" nor was a European national identity dependent on remaining loyal to the old-world governments. And throughout all this, boundaries between groups and linkages with groups were central.

AMERICAN "FREEDOM" AS A MODEL FOR NORWAY

If complementary identities were developed by ethnic groups in the context of life in the United States, the immigrants' experiences in the United States had an impact on life in Norway as well. Because the contexts differed, the use of the image of the United States among Norwegians who stayed behind differed as well. Rather than using the notion of "freedom" to create a complementary identity, which by its very nature was pluralist, many Norwegians used the United States as an environment that allowed them to compare and criticize life at home. As Ingrid Semmingsen notes, members of the political opposition seized on the image of the United States. Ole Gabriel Ueland regarded America as Europe's teacher and Johan Sverdrup declared in the *Storting* that the United States was the "most flourishing nation on earth."[24]

Through what channels did these ideas diffuse? One powerful force was the influence of returned emigrants who made a great impact in changing Norway. I have noted above that the rate of return among Norwegians paled in comparison with that of other national groups. It is nonetheless true that nearly one out of six male immigrants *did* return to Norway in the first quarter of the twentieth century. It is also undoubtedly true, as I will argue below, that these people had an enormous impact on their home country. But we must not lose sight of the myths and ideas that coursed across the Atlantic Ocean and were not necessarily carried by returning immigrants. America letters, official reports, and newspaper articles broadened the Norwegian world and often provided models for doing things differently and ideas for change. Because the migration to the United States from Norway was so large, the volume of these ideas was significant as well. In sum, immigrants either became remigrants or remained in the United States, and people in both categories either sent ideas homeward or acted on those ideas when they returned permanently or temporarily as the case might be. And it is not surprising that these ideas often stressed "freedom" in a variety of forms ranging from political rights for the less powerful to the possibilities of individual initiative.

Although there are myriad factors that we might consider, I will briefly explore how the idea of the United States affected Norway with particular reference to social class and reform, religion, and nationhood.[25] In many ways, life in the United States provided a yardstick with which to evaluate conditions in Norway and to critique Norwegian life. On the one hand, the United States was for many a symbol and often a refuge for radical political movements.[26] It served as a model of a nation with greater freedoms and rights for the people. As a result, many reform-minded were among the immigrants. For example, Marcus Thrane advocated emigration as he strove to change the conditions of workers in Norway. After his arrest and incarceration, he moved to the United States and attempted to bring about political reform there. A journalist and a playwright in the United States, his theater productions were often indictments of the stratified class structures of Norway and the possibilities enabled by migration to the United States.[27] Søren Jaabæk, editor of *Folketidende* [*Peoples' Times*] for fifteen years beginning in 1873, repeatedly used the United States as a yardstick for where Norway was and how far it had to go. As Ingrid Semmingsen points out, he used "America letters" to illustrate life in the United States among immigrants and he used these texts to comment on Norwegian life. After printing one letter, he observed, "There is an American spirit through the entire letter—that is astonishingly free—but strange for Norwegian ears. . . . It will be long before we are imbued with the concept of freedom."[28]

It is true that remigrants played a significant role in Norwegian leftist politics. Martin Tranmæl, Norwegian labor leader and editor of the socialist periodical *Arbeiderbladet* [*The Workers' Paper*], who was a dominant figure in twentieth-century labor politics, learned ideology and tactics from the International Workers of the World in the United States.[29] Yet, like Ueland or Jaabæk, many learned of America without traveling there. And countless Norwegian expatriates observed developments in Norway with interest from their American homes. On the other hand, Norwegian immigrants, as Orm Øverland reminds us, remained attentive to Norwegian politics: it was immigrants in the United States who funded the Venstre [Liberal Party] in its early years shortly after a parliamentary government was established in Norway.[30]

If radicals criticized Norwegian life from an American perspective, others used the United States as a gauge to illustrate the benefits of individual industry. Ernst Beckman, a member of the Swedish Riksdag, evinced his liberal beliefs in 1883 when he argued that Swedes should "'move America over to Sweden' in the best sense of the term" by creating greater opportunities for landowning and removing restrictions on religious freedom among other reforms in Sweden.[31] One way to move America to Sweden or Norway was to encourage emigrants, who had been changed by their journey, to return. Norwegians displayed a hope that returnees would bring with them an initiative and spirit of enterprise. Utvandringskomiteen [the Norwegian commission on emigration] illustrated its certainty in 1912 that the returnees changed their home communities. "The returned Americans put their stamp upon it all," the commission wrote. "The rural districts are hardly recognizable. The farmers are not so burdened with debt as before; people live better, eat better, clothe themselves better,—thus the population itself improves. All those who come from America begin to till the soil better than it was tilled before. . . . Crop rotation is introduced, machinery is acquired, the buildings of the farm, dwellings as well as others, are improved, more rational dairy methods are practiced, and gardens are laid out. . . . [Returnees] bring home with them much practical experience and understanding, which redounds to the advantage of the whole region. Furthermore, they have a will to take hold, and have in America learned a rate of work, which is different from what people are accustomed to here at home."[32] In sum, returned emigrants changed their homes. But bringing America to Norway did not necessarily mean remigration: ideas could return as well to transform the homeland.

If the United States provided a staging ground for political change in Norway, it also influenced the structures of Norwegian Lutheranism. As Vidar Haanes has shown, the democratic impulses carried from the United States influenced the Norwegian church.[33] When Georg Sverdrup spoke in 1875 from Minneapolis, for example, he noted on the one hand that the United States was a place where there existed "a free people, in a free congregation, with Christ among us." In contrast, he said, there "lies a distant land, Norway" where there was a struggle and that "there too it is all about freedom or bondage for the Church of Christ." In the audience were members of the Norwegian clergy who likely were moved by Sverdrup's sermon. In any case, they were instrumental in church reform. Religious movements in Norway outside of Lutheranism also had the American stamp placed on them, in this case by remigrants. O. P. Petersen, who returned from the United States in 1849 to his hometown of Fredrikstad, founded the Methodist Church in Norway. The Norwegian Baptist church enjoyed economic support from America as well and was connected to the American Baptist movement in 1892.[34] This transatlantic exchange has two implications. First, the congregational freedom and sentiments of a church free from the state, and churches different from Lutheranism that had matured in the United States returned to Norway. Second, it is perhaps not coincidental that these religious efforts were connected to political ones. Georg Sverdrup's uncle was Johan Sverdrup, a leading political figure on the left who served as prime minister in the 1880s.

Perhaps the most notable example of homeland communities influencing the fatherland was the nationalism that developed in the United States. As Norwegians in the United States were constructing an ethnic nationalism, they also remained loyal to their old nation. In this, they were not alone: many ethnic groups from Irish in the nineteenth century to Chinese in the twentieth used the United States as a sort of staging ground to labor for national hopes and dreams. Norwegian Americans were especially active in the years that culminated in Norwegian independence. In the year of crisis of 1895, for example, Norwegians in Chicago raised funds to strengthen Norway's military. They sent a telegram to the Storting [Parliament] expressing "warm participation in the fatherland's fight for might." When inde-

pendence was achieved ten years later, the *Storting* expressed its gratitude to Norway's "emigrated sons and daughters for their work for
the National Cause."[35]

This understanding in Norway of the importance of "overseas
Norwegians" was related to the development of romantic nationalism. When people developed notions of an organic nation, of people
connected to one another because they all possessed a part of national soul, place of residence became less important. Proponents of
this idea, from O. E. Rølvaag in the United States to Bjørnstjerne
Bjørnson in Norway, stressed the commonalities of Norwegian America and Norway.[36] Not inconsequentially, this idea increased the power
of Norway. Bjørnson, in calling on Norwegians to "make Norway
larger," saw the potentialities of what he called "encouraging all possible cooperation between Norwegians at home and abroad." Similar
developments were occurring in Sweden where the Allsvensk Samling
attempted to unite Swedes in Sweden and elsewhere.[37] Likewise,
Normanns-forbundet, which linked Norwegians together, was formed
shortly after Norwegian independence.[38] Although the idea of romantic nationalism receded over time, and in fact was discredited
during the Nazi era, the cooperation between the two nations in Norway and Norwegian America endured.

BOUNDARIES AND LINKAGES

As in Odd Lovoll's work, then, we profit from examining the boundaries and linkages that divide and connect social groups. Norwegians
in the United States simultaneously created an ethnic group that distinguished itself from those of other ethnicities and linked their ethnic group to membership in the American nation. Thus they created
boundaries between other groups but linkages between themselves
and the idea of membership in the United States. Pluralism and assimilation were inextricably linked. Norwegian Americans could celebrate their membership both in an ethnic group and a membership
in a larger nation, but they were forced to puzzle over how the boundaries of the group could be maintained over the long term.

Linkages were common in transatlantic communities as well. I
have tried to show that the exchange between the United States and
Norway involved not only people, but capital and ideas as well.
Significantly, the sense that the United States could be a model for a

new Norwegian nation-state was long in place before Norwegian independence in 1905. Perhaps the fabled returnee who put on airs and emphasized the wealth and the station that resulted from emigration both annoyed and amazed Norwegians. The ideas that returnees and non-returnees conveyed to Norway nonetheless profoundly influenced and undoubtedly changed it as well.

NOTES

[1]See Orm Øverland, *Immigrant Minds, American Identities: Making the United States Home, 1870–1930* (Urbana, IL, 2000), for a good overview of this process generally.

[2]Marcus Lee Hansen, *The Immigrant in American History,* ed. Arthur M. Schlesinger (New York, 1940). See Jon Gjerde, "The 'Would-be Patriarch' and the 'Self Made Man': Marcus Lee Hansen on Native and Immigrant Farmers in the American Middle West," in *On Distant Shores: Proceedings of the Marcus Lee Hansen Immigration Conference,* ed. Birgit Flemming, Henning Bender, and Karen Veien (Aalborg, 1993), 35–55.

[3]Rudolph J. Vecoli, "'Over the years I have encountered the hazards and rewards that await the historian of immigration': George Malcolm Stephenson and the Swedish American Community," in *Migration och Mångfald: Essäer om Kulturkontakt och Minoritetsfrågor,* ed. Harald Runblom (Uppsala, 1999), 171–188.

[4]J. R. Christianson, "The Letters of Marcus Lee Hansen," in Flemming, Bender, and Veien, *On Distant Shores,* 22.

[5]See Jon Gjerde, "New Growth on Old Vines: The State of the Field of the Social History of Immigration to and Ethnicity in the United States," *Journal of American Ethnic History* 18 (1999), 40–65, for an extended discussion of these issues.

[6]Odd Lovoll, *A Folk Epic: The* Bygdelag *in America* (Boston, 1975).

[7]Odd Lovoll, *The Promise of America: A History of the Norwegian-American People* (Minneapolis, 1994).

[8]Odd Lovoll, *A Century of Urban Life: The Norwegians in Chicago before 1930* (Northfield, MN, 1988); *The Promise Fulfilled: A Portrait of Norwegian Americans Today* (Minneapolis, 1998). It bears emphasizing that Lovoll maintained a critical perspective toward the Norwegian-American community in the late twentieth century in *The Promise Fulfilled,* which differs from the ro-

manticized characterizations of immigrants made by many historians of his generation.

[9]In the quarter century between 1899 and 1924, Scandinavian men re-migrated at a rate of 15.4% Only the "Hebrew," Irish, and German males had lower percentages. The percentage of remigration prior to 1899 was surely even lower.

[10]In this realm, we need to pay particular attention to rules of naturalization and citizenship for immigrating populations. In the United States, citizenship was based on *jus soli,* that is, people born in the country were citizens by law. Still, as early as 1790, the United States Congress adopted a liberal naturalization policy that enabled immigrants to be naturalized after two years' residence in the nation, a requirement that later would be lengthened to five years. Significantly, however, this right was guaranteed only to people defined as "white" immigrants. Whereas people of African descent were enabled naturalization in 1870, other immigrating groups—Asians in particular—were denied access to citizenship well into the twentieth century. Thus, citizenship law, as many scholars have pointed out, embraced contradictions of liberal definitions of birthright citizenship and relatively accessible and voluntary political allegiance, on the one hand, and racial and gendered ascriptions that belied these very liberal definitions, on the other.

[11]Much of the following is detailed in Jon Gjerde, *The Minds of the West: Ethnocultural Evolution of the Middle West, 1830–1917* (Chapel Hill, 1997). See also Orm Øverland, *Immigrant Minds, American Identities,* and April R. Schultz, *Ethnicity on Parade: Inventing the Norwegian American through Celebration* (Amherst, MA, 1994).

[12]The first explicit use of the term and concept of complementary identity that I have seen is Peter A. Munch, "The Church as Complementary Identity," in *The Scandinavian Presence in North America,* ed. Erik J. Friis (New York, 1976), 64. See also David M. Potter, "The Historian's Use of Nationalism and Vice Versa," in *History and American Society* (New York, 1973), 74–75; and Morton Grodzins, *The Loyal and the Disloyal: Social Boundaries of Patriotism and Treason* (Chicago, 1956).

[13]*Pathfinder for Norwegian Emigrants by Johan Reinert Reiersen,* trans. and ed. Frank G. Nelson (Northfield, MN, 1981), 176, 183.

[14]Lars Fletre, "The Vossing Correspondence Society of 1848 and the Report of Adam Lövenskjold," *Norwegian-American Studies* 28 (1979), 267.

[15]See Jonathan D. Sarna, "From Immigrants to Ethnics: Toward a New Theory of 'Ethnicization,'" *Ethnicity* 5 (1978), 370–378; and William L. Yancey, et al., "Emergent Ethnicity: A Review and Reformulation," *American Sociological Review* 41 (1976), 391–403.

[16]The subgroup in the complementary identity, as I shall outline it, could refer to class and status identification. It is very important to note, however, that divisions at midcentury tended to be based on racial, religious, and ethnic terms. See Kathleen Neils Conzen, et. al., "The Invention of Ethnicity: A Perspective from the U.S.A.," *Journal of American Ethnic History* 12 (1992), 8.

[17]Christopher Saur, *Eine zu dieser Zeit höchstnöthige Warnung und Erinnerung an die freye Einwohner der Provintz Pennsylvanien,* cited in Willi Paul Adams, "The Colonial German-language Press and the American Revolution," in *The Press and the American Revolution,* ed. Bernard Bailyn and John B. Hench (Boston, 1981), 180. My emphasis.

[18]Henry Miller, *Staatsbote,* 9 March 1776, cited in Adams, "The Colonial German-language Press," 209–210.

[19]If ethnic groups invented traditions in the United States, they often reformulated conventions carried from specific European homelands. As Kathleen Conzen points out, for example, nationalist rituals enacted in the German states were a basis for German-American institutions and ritual traditions that affirmed dual loyalties in the United States. As Dorothy Dohen argues, Irish nationalism in the United States was powerfully informed by Irish nationalism in Ireland. See Kathleen Neils Conzen, "Ethnicity as Festive Culture: Nineteenth-Century German America on Parade," in *The Invention of Ethnicity,* ed. Werner Sollors (New York, 1989), 44–76; Dorothy Dohen, *Nationalism and American Catholicism* (New York, 1967), 59–63.

[20]*Die Iowa,* 7 July 1881. The scriptural allusion illustrates how immigrants believed true faith could be created in the United States away from meddling European states. But it also suggests the division between true believers and those outside the faith. See Matthew 10:14; Mark 6:7–13, and Luke 9:1–6.

[21]*Die Iowa,* 30 May 1878. These expressions of distaste for Germany were made amidst the anti-Catholic *Kulturkampf.*

[22]"X," *Die Iowa,* 4 May 1882.

[23]*Dubuque National Demokrat,* 5 July 1858.

[24]Ingrid Semmingsen, *Veien Mot Vest: Utvandringen fra Norge til Amerika 1865–1915* (Oslo, 1950), 476–477.

[25]The following is considered in greater detail in Jon Gjerde, "Transatlantic Linkages: The Interaction between the Norwegian American and Norwegian 'Nations' During the Century of Migration, 1825–1920," *Immigrants and Minorities* 20 (2001), 19–34.

[26]Dirk Hoerder, Rudolph J. Vecoli, and Lars-Göran Tedebrand each argue that the myth of America as a land of freedom was being subjected to

systematic critique in the late nineteenth century. See Marianne Debouzy, *In the Shadow of the Statue of Liberty: Immigrants, Workers, and Citizens in the American Republic, 1880–1920* (Urbana, IL, 1992), 1–61.

[27]Theodore C. Blegen, *Norwegian Migration to America, 1825–1860* (Northfield, MN, 1931), 323–329; Ingrid Semmingsen, *Norway to America: A History of the Migration,* trans. Einar Haugen (Minneapolis, 1978), 126. See Terje I. Leiren, "America as Symbol in the Plays of Marcus Thrane," in the present volume.

[28]Semmingsen, *Veien mot Vest,* 478.

[29]B. J. Hovde, "Notes on the Effects of Emigration upon Scandinavia," *Journal of Modern History* 6/3 (1934), 273. See Jorunn Bjørgum, "Traveling on His Trade: Martin Tranmæl's Stay in the United States and the Radicalization of the Norwegian Labor Movement," in the present volume.

[30]Orm Øverland, *The Western Home: A Literary History of Norwegian America* (Urbana, IL, 1996), 187.

[31]Ernst Beckman, *Amerikanska studier* (Stockholm, 1883), cited in Hovde, "Notes on the Effects of Emigration," 257–258.

[32]*Utvandringskomiteen, 1912–13, Indstilling III,* "Om foranstaltninger til at lette nordmænd at flytte til Norge," 3, cited in Hovde, "Notes on the Effects of Emigration," 278.

[33]Vidar L. Haanes, "Pastors for the Congregations: Transatlantic Impulses," in *Crossings: Norwegian-American Lutheranism as a Transatlantic Tradition,* ed. Todd W. Nichol (Northfield, MN, forthcoming).

[34]Semmingsen, *Veien Mot Vest,* 485–486.

[35]For a discussion of the influence of overseas Norwegians on the independence movement, see Arlow W. Andersen, *Rough Road to Glory: The Norwegian-American Press Speaks Out on Public Affairs, 1875 to 1925* (Philadelphia, 1990), 102–112; and Semmingsen, *Veien mot Vest,* 490.

[36]April R. Schultz, *Ethnicity on Parade,* 95–104.

[37]H. Arnold Barton, *A Folk Divided: Homeland Swedes and the Swedish Americans, 1840–1940* (Carbondale, IL, 1994), 265–277.

[38]Semmingsen, *Norway to America,* 171; Semmingsen, *Veien mot Vest,* 490–491.

Interdisciplinary Approaches in American Immigration Studies: Possibilities and Pitfalls

Øyvind T. Gulliksen

IMMIGRANTS TO THE UNITED STATES often look back on their lives as having been divided into three parts: life in the old country, the voyage, and the years spent in the new country. The following passage is a vivid description of the second stage of the immigrant experience that invites the reader to join immigrants in steerage: "Below decks is the place, its usual dimensions seventy-five feet long, twenty-five wide, five and a half high. Descend. In the fitful light your eye will discover a middle aisle five feet wide. It will be a while before you can make out the separate shapes within it, the water closets at either end (for the women; the men must go above deck), one or several cooking stoves, the tables. The aisle itself, you will see, is formed by two rows of bunks that run to the side of the ship. . . . This was the steerage setting. Here the emigrants lived their lives, day and night. The more generous masters gave them access to a portion of the deck at certain hours. But bad weather often deprived the passengers of that privilege, kept them below for days on end."

This quotation merits a moment of reflection. Notice its emphasis on the visual: "your eye will discover," "you will see." It contains references to contrasts of light and darkness. Indeed, this image of poor immigrants on their way from Europe to the United States sometime during the era of mass immigration could be imagined as the text for Alfred Stieglitz's famous image, "The Steerage." Stieglitz's picture, a piece of early American social photography, leads in itself to an interdisciplinary approach to immigration studies. As a photograph it serves as a text, a documentary narrative, an historical report of an eyewitness, recorded in a flash of a second and saved for posterity.

Clearly, the passage quoted above is written by someone who, like Stieglitz, intended to make a lively picture of immigrants in steerage. Moreover, the writer invites the reader to join him in the bunks of the steerage. To make us feel part of the scene, he uses the present tense. It is so dark down there, it will take "a while before you" [the reader] can spot the dark figures of immigrant men and women. And in order to reveal the atmosphere of the steerage, the writer addresses the reader directly in the imperative: "Descend." He goes on to make up a story of how people lived in steerage and he uses the literary devices and metaphors that any writer of fiction would use. The term "masters" for the captains brings to mind slave owners in the South.

This is clearly not the actual story of one who came by steerage. It is rather a new story, an invented narrative, based on a genuine interest in the lives of immigrants traveling to their new country. Yet it is not an excerpt from immigrant fiction. It is a passage from the once best known and most used history of American immigration, Oscar Handlin's *The Uprooted,* the study of mass immigration to the United States that starts with the famous confession of its author, "Once I thought to write a history of the immigrants in America. Then I discovered that the immigrants *were* American history."[1]

Compare this passage from Handlin the historian with the following quotation. Here we are presented with the history of some Norwegian immigrants to Minnesota told in historical detail. It relates the basic facts of the life of Magnus Oleson, an immigrant from Norway. Oleson married a German-American immigrant in Minnesota and wrote letters about their life back to the old country. This is the brief account of their family and descendants in Minnesota: "Magnus and Katherine had three daughters before she died giving birth in 1871, so the Norwegian Bible was passed to the eldest girl, Hildur, and then to her daughter. Hildur married Oskar Tollefson after his first wife died, and they had seven children, including Amelia (b. 1885), who married Peter Ingqvist, begetting nine, including Esther (b. 1906), who married Gustaf Bunsen, by whom she had four children, including Clarence (b. 1925), who now has the Bible, his sister Eva having given it to him as a wedding present when he and Arlene were married, after Eva learned she could not have children."

The story has all the typical features of an immigrant family saga. Although biblical in tone, the prose is dull and to the point. It contains little more than factual information likely to be of little interest to those outside of the family. The common changes from Norwegian names to American names in the third generation are there, as well as the story of the old-country Bible, kept as a family treasure. In form it purports only to give us accurate information about one immigrant family. Yet this passage is pure fiction. It is created out of whole cloth from the author's imagination. Magnus Oleson is a fictional character, and the excerpt is from a novel that topped bestseller lists across the United States in 1985, *Lake Wobegon Days* by Garrison Keillor.[2]

I have used these two examples by two American writers, neither of whom were immigrants themselves, to illustrate a point about immigration studies: historians sometimes write immigrant literature of high quality and authors of fiction sometimes write excellent immigration history. Handlin, the historian, may show us something about the literary character of immigrant history. Keillor, the novelist, has a word or two to say about the historicity of literature. Handlin's prose uses the devices of a storyteller to give us what he perceives as the facts of the immigrant voyage. Keillor adopts a style known to readers of history. Both writers use their knowledge and their research in American immigration, even if their purpose in writing and their choice of genre is different.

To test the possibilities and pitfalls of interdisciplinary approaches and in particular to see what historians and students of literature can learn from each other, I will consider here narrative approaches to the lives of first-generation Scandinavian immigrants to the United States during the period of mass immigration, from the 1820s to the 1920s. This, of course, is not a new enterprise. Immigration studies is already a common denominator for a number of scholarly activities. Scholars who frolic in the literature of American immigrants, who compile and study their music, their languages, their arts and crafts, have long worked together under the rubric of "immigration studies." Historians, both of local and national reputation, experts and amateurs who gather and scrutinize countless sources in order to compose their histories of immigration, as well as sociologists of immigrant communities, all fit the category of immigration studies. Generally this is a happy cooperation, but it is not without its methodological difficulties.

LITERATURE AND HISTORY

An episode from the history of Scandinavian-American immigration studies comes quickly to mind. The two contenders were Kristian Hvidt, a Danish historian of emigration to the United States, and Dorothy Burton Skårdal, a scholar of Scandinavian-American immigrant literature. Reino Kero, a Finnish scholar of American immigration studies, played a minor role in what turned out to be a heated dispute. The confrontation between Hvidt and Skårdal, one a historian and the other a literary scholar within immigration studies, illustrates a possible pitfall of interdisciplinary approaches. The two participants were both front-runners in the field: Kristian Hvidt had published two classic histories of Danish emigration to the United States, first his *Flight to America* and then *Danes Go West*.[3] Skårdal's study *The Divided Heart: Scandinavian Immigrant Experience through Literary Sources* was published in 1974, a decade before she entered the fray mentioned above.[4] Skårdal had analyzed an astonishing amount of fiction written by Scandinavian immigrants to provide a social history "through literary sources." The book is generally regarded as a major contribution to immigrant studies and is mentioned several times by Werner Sollors in his *Beyond Ethnicity*.[5]

Both historians and literary scholars returning to the Hvidt-Skårdal contest will soon discover that the premises have changed since then. Both historians and literary scholars will today more readily acknowledge the literary character of the texts they study and of the texts they produce. It is not now an uncontested move to jump from either traditional documents or literary texts to sweeping conclusions about historical facts or social experience. The New Historicism has since then taught us more about the nature and history of texts.[6] In his essay entitled "Fact and Fiction: A Case for the Complementary Study of History and Literature," Hvidt argued that the historian of immigration had much to learn from immigrant fiction, if not necessarily from critical studies of immigrant fiction.[7] Immigrant fiction, he contended, could not be used by the historian as source material, but to add additional flavor to his or her historical analysis, it can be "a *complementary* discipline to history. Fiction *cannot* be used to reconstruct facts outside this area. What I am trying to say is that the [immigrant] novel or the short story can be used as an illustration of reality but that it cannot be used as a historical source."[8] Rølvaag's famous immigrant novel *Giants in the Earth* (1927) can perhaps be used to illustrate Hvidt's point. The novel dramatizes the immigrant experience on the frontier, but it cannot be used as a source for immigrant life as it was actually lived on the South Dakota prairie during the 1870s.[9]

This is still a tenable position. The problem is that Hvidt, the historian, does not seem to doubt that he as historian can "reconstruct" the facts of immigration. On the other hand, immigrant fiction cannot, according to Hvidt, "be used to reconstruct facts." It was above all this argument which caused Skårdal in her essay "'Hard' Facts and 'Soft' Sources: Literature as Historical Source Material?" to deliver a blow against the Danish historian. Skårdal insisted that literature, in this case immigrant literature, contained "much more historical evidence than Hvidt allows."[10] Skårdal called his position "nonsense."[11] Not only is the historian mistaken, but "Hvidt's kind of history is so deadly dull because it has deliberately abandoned all aspects of art in the name of exactness, and thereby falsified the human life that it is trying to 'reconstruct.'"[12] According to Skårdal, immigration history "can't afford to reject any sources."[13] She claimed that immigrant literature described "the historical life of that group . . . vividly and accurately. I have spent years testing it against traditional historical accounts and materials, and it holds true."[14]

Here, however, Skårdal falls into the same ditch into which she is trying to push the Danish historian. First, her argument functions as an attempt to convince the opponent by the authority of her experience. Second, there is no discussion of the nature and validity of "traditional historical accounts." Skårdal has tested immigrant literature against historical accounts and found this literature to be "true." That is, immigrant fiction matches facts related to us by historians. Immigrant fiction may be used not just to illustrate history but as "an historical source."[15] This, in my opinion, is not today a tenable position. Indeed, it is a very tricky business for scholars of literature to use the term "source" in this way at all. The term "source," as used by the historians, is rarely used in literary scholarship. Again Rølvaag may provide an example. Literary scholars may point to the fact that in *Giants in the Earth* Rølvaag applied stories told by his parents-in-law in South Dakota. But Rølvaag's novel about immigrants in South Dakota can never rightly be used as a source for immigrant life on the prairie. The novel may just as much be a reflection of agrarian myths of the 1920s.[16] In his reply, Hvidt argued that "literary sources are secondary because they are not intended as descriptions of reality," and he accused Skårdal of settling in "an area which is neither historical nor literary."[17]

If we take a closer look at the kind of interdisciplinary work we find in Skårdal's *The Divided Heart,* it is evident that Hvidt may have a point here. Skårdal's section devoted to the immigrant church may serve as an example.[18] Her purpose in this section is to find out how immigrant church life, and particularly such features as organization, finance, doctrinal controversies, and faith, are reflected in Scandinavian-American immigrant literature and how this literary portrait compares to that drawn in church histories. To do that the literary scholar needs the help of the church historian and perhaps even of the theologian. The stumbling blocks are many.

Skårdal first presents her views on how the church functioned in the old country: "When pietistic Lutherans undertook more active expressions of their faith, they often suffered both persecution and ostracism."[19] Here and elsewhere in Skårdal's study it is not entirely clear if this statement is based upon conclusions of other historians, or whether it is meant as a summing up of her own findings in immigrant literature. As a valid statement about the mid-nineteenth-century religious background of Norwegian emigrants, Skårdal's assertion is certainly open to debate. The author, however, presents her statement as uncontestable historical truth, for which she can find quantifiable evidence in immigrant fiction. This is a risky business, indeed.

To support her point she quotes an episode from an immigrant novel by N. N. Rønning, published in Minneapolis in 1928. The author of the novel is merely mentioned in a footnote, because neither the writer nor his text or the genre matters much in this type of argument.[20] To use this primary text as one of many "literary sources" for the "immigrant experience" is a questionable practice. The critical reader of Skårdal's study is ready to ask a number of questions here. Does Rønning's text claim to say anything about the immigrant experience? How does his text, or any other immigrant text, relate to the world outside the text? How does it relate to other texts? How can an American immigrant novel of the late 1920s serve as information about pietists and their situation in the old country? What was the writer's background? Why does he present the story the way he does? Here it is important to know that Rønning, who had emigrated as a seventeen-year-old in 1887, was a member of Hauge's Synod in America. He may have felt the need to create a fictional account of pietists' reasons to immigrate, but his story cannot be used as historical evidence for religious persecution in the home country. In his novel Rønning adopts a well-used American literary pattern of immigrants fleeing religious persecution at home to seek sanctuary in the new world. Various immigrant authors will turn to the matter of religion for different purposes. A thesis could be written on Rølvaag's theology or on the theology of the Russian-American immigrant writer, Abraham Cahan. One cannot, however, use their voices, or the voices of other less-known immigrant authors, to collect quantifiable textual evidence for general statements on the social history of immigrant religion.

Skårdal goes on to discuss the history of Scandinavian immigrant churches in the United States, their beginnings, their congregations, their schisms, and finally what she refers to as their "decline of faith," as it is reflected and discussed in immigrant fiction. Her portrayal of the history of immigrant churches is basically taken from what had already been written by church historians, such as E. Clifford Nelson and Eugene L. Fevold in their *The Lutheran Church among Norwegian-Americans*.[21] Like earlier scholars of immigrant church history, Skårdal argues that immigrants tried to keep their ecclesiastical rituals and sacraments as they had known them in the home country. This is most likely true and it is hardly surprising that one will find evidence of this in immigrant fiction. What is new here is not Skårdal's view of the immigrant church, but the fact that she uses immigrant fiction to back up her points, points which had also been made by historians of immigration. On the other hand, this can sometimes also mean that the most interesting statements about religion in immigrant fiction get lost. For instance, Rølvaag's rendering of a split in the local congregations in the beginning of his novel *Peder Victorious* is primarily not a description of how local controversies proved to be harmful to social life in local immigrant churches.[22] It is a reflection of the author's religious ideas. A student of immigrant texts must consider how the author's own ideas about the role of ministers and his own theology will color his depiction of a local religious debate. The passage from *Peder Victorious* in which Rølvaag describes the "period of storm and disruption [that] broke loose over *St. Luke's Norwegian Evangelical Congregation*" cannot be read to illustrate "facts" of religious experience in immigrant church history.[23]

In another section on the immigrant church, Skårdal shows that "fictional clergymen in low-church synods . . . who tended to come from families of lower-class origin, almost always were inspired to the service of God in the new world."[24] No literary source is mentioned to illustrate this point, but it is an interesting idea, which again leads to further questions. Why did immigrant writers of fiction so often provide their low-church ministers with such motivation? Do we find this sort of call or motivation in other kinds of immigrant texts? Here we need to note that immigrant literature is not limited to fiction, but contains a series of genres of texts, such as clergymen's auto-biographies, diaries, sermons, memoirs, letters: all texts which can be subjected to literary criticism. In the New Historicism, the student of literature and the student of history are both concerned with texts, all kinds of texts. Students of literature may include documents of real pastors in their textual analyses and compare these documents to narrative patterns, images, and statements found in stories of in-spiration from other immigrant groups. In such a way the literary scholar may, at the same time, end up making valid statements about cultural history. This reflects a desire on the part of the school of New Historicism to let various kinds of texts undergo the same liter-ary scrutiny.

In her introduction to *The Divided Heart,* Skårdal argued that most immigrant fiction writers "were too unskilled to be inventive" and that this left them less creative than the most artistically gifted writ-ers and dependent on a readership "dominated by naïve realism."[25] Therefore, Skårdal contends, we can read these immigrant writers as fairly reliable and realistic sources for our mapping of Scandinavian immigrant life and experience. As immigrant writers they were sup-posedly drawn "toward literal realism in recording the life around them."[26] Here, however, Skårdal's argument falters badly. First, no writer is too unskilled to be inventive. Second, the categories of "gifted" and "less gifted" writers are often arbitrary. Third, we cannot take any immigrant novel or short story as a realistic "recording of life around them."

The Norwegian-American writer Hans A. Foss may serve as a counterexample at this point. Foss is not generally regarded as the most skillful of writers. Yet his immigrant novel *Husmands-gutten* [*The Cotter's Son*], published in Iowa in 1885, does not at all reflect "realism in recording life" among immigrants.[27] His story about a poor farmer's son, who after years in the United States returns to Norway to win his love and buy a large farm, is a clever adaptation of a theme from popular literature adapted to the framework of an immigrant novel. Both Nils N. Rønning and Ole E. Rølvaag wrote immigrant novels on the motif of a sinful father who is saved by an innocent Christian daughter after years of self-effacing struggle. This is a basic theme in Rølvaag's *Paa glemte veie* [*On Forgotten Paths*] and in Rønning's *A Servant of the Lord*.[28] But from neither of these novels is it possible to infer anything about immigrant religious life. Rønning is a less well known writer than Rølvaag, but we cannot assume that his readership was more "dominated by naïve realism" than Rølvaag's. The fact that Rønning was a far less accomplished and skillful immigrant writer than Rølvaag does not make him more realistic or true to life. Their novels are not realistic renderings of immigrant religious life. Both writers were interested in religion as an intellectual and a literary pursuit. The depraved father who is saved by a pious daughter is a well-known device in American religious novels, of which the writers were well aware. It is cleverly adopted by both these writers into the plot of an immigrant novel from the classic contrivances of the American popular religious novel. Such a narrative is not a source for immigrant experience and it cannot be taken as historical evidence for anything outside of the textual world in which it exists. Texts interact with texts. Narrative is built on narrative.

THE NEW HISTORICISM AND IMMIGRANT NARRATIVES

It is above all the New Historicism that has made both Hvidt's and Skårdal's approach to immigrant studies appear outdated. In their 1984 debate, historical scholarship was regarded by both participants as the master discipline in immigrant studies. To contemporary historians literary criticism suggests other approaches to the past than those Skårdal used in *The Divided Heart*. Hvidt saw the study of immigrant literature as a source of useful illustrations. Skårdal regarded immigrant literature as source material for cultural and social history. Today, the scholar of immigration must constantly consider the literary character of the texts he or she is facing or producing. The question of historical representation is thus qualified. As the historian Lloyd S. Kramer has pointed out in his essay "Literature, Criticism, and Historical Imagination," it "is the pervasive influence of recent literary criticism, which has taught historians to recognize the active role of language, texts, and narrative structures in the creation and description of historical reality."[29]

Historians within immigration studies have also become more alert to their choice of metaphors. Writers of the great histories of immigration to the United States base their stories on epics of narration and are well aware of literary structures. Handlin's *The Uprooted* begins with the observation that "emigration started in the peasant heart of Europe" and ends with the alienated old immigrant parents in the United States who "could see the day ahead when there would be none of their kind left, when the country would be occupied entirely by natives, and when their own children or children's children would lose the very memory of immigrant antecedents."[30] Consequently, a notion of tragedy is basic to the narrative development of Handlin's book, which in the subtitle is explained as an "epic story." If the title of his book has an Old Testament flavor it is rather that of the diaspora than of the promised land.

Odd Sverre Lovoll, whose collected works now make up a great history of Norwegian immigrants, is not bound by the genre of tragedy in his immigration studies, and his Old Testament images are different than Handlin's, but they are there. His first survey of Norwegian immigration was called *The Promise of America* [*Det løfterike landet*]. His most recent work, a history of contemporary Norwegian Americans, is entitled *The Promise Fulfilled*.[31] At least in his titles, Lovoll clearly uses the sort of Old Testament images that were used to describe America already by the time the Puritans began writing the history of America. In fact, Lovoll's most recent title suggests a biblical prophecy fulfilled. At a dinner party in Minneapolis before the book was published, Lovoll admitted that the title should probably be followed by a question mark: Perhaps the promise was not really fulfilled? But this hesitation is left out in the final version. What does it mean in the context of American immigration studies to say that "promises" have been "fulfilled"? Some readers of immigrant studies may still be in doubt that what started with Rølvaag's *Giants in the Earth* is actually "fulfilled" with the *lefse*-and-*lutefisk* buttons of today.[32]

Jon Gjerde, another historian of American immigration, has used the concept of "complementary identity" to describe the immigrant mind: "Immigrants celebrated life in the United States because it enabled them to retain beliefs that originated outside of it."[33] Gjerde is talking about a possible "celebration" of life, rather than a sense of tragic uprooting. To arrive at this reading of immigrant experience, Gjerde also applies his reading of literature written by or about immigrants in the Midwest. He is not confined by inherited disciplinary structures and he uses different kinds of text material with ease and confidence. His study of the rural Middle West from 1830 to 1917 brings us to a new type of interdisciplinarity in immigration studies. His extensive anthology of texts related to American immigrant history includes a wide variety of essays and documents.[34]

In his discussion of "individual life chances within" the immigrant communities in the Midwest, Gjerde selects two Norwegian immigrant communities for investigation. He points out that sometimes "narrative and quantitative sources alike suggest that old structures of family underwent a process of profound change."[35] Gjerde has charted both "marriage prospects" and "marriage age" in the two communities through minute studies of statistical sources. He refers to all kinds of sources: memoirs, diaries, interviews, letters, historical scholarship of a wide variety: local and national, as well as Norwegian county books [*gards- og ættesoger*], American surveys of farm real estate values, immigrant church records, and ministerial reports. On this basis he adds plausible facts to fiction, when he concludes by saying: "Garrison Keillor's Norwegian bachelor farmers thus have a basis in fact."[36] Students of literature who have appreciated Keillor's portraits of Norwegian bachelor farmers in Minnesota will still continue to do so, but will now know that their reaction is both quantitatively and historically secured. This is a matter of reversing the method of *The Divided Heart*. Here history is used to prove the facts of fiction.

Above all, Gjerde has shown how a perusal of local and regional texts may add or give alternative perspectives to the "great" narratives produced by historians of immigration. From a close reading of the sources mentioned above, Gjerde affirms that Norwegian immigrant families in the Upper Midwest "reestablished the principles of the

European pattern of marriage. They continued to adhere to stem-household arrangements carried from Europe as their communities matured."[37] To explain what sorts of conflicts this way of life could provoke in rural Midwestern immigrant families, Gjerde includes an extensive analysis of Hamlin Garland's story "Among the Corn Rows," in which the stern old Norwegian immigrant father insists on putting his daughter back to farm work when she is tempted by an American suitor. The immigrant father figure here serves as an image of a "European patriarch." But Gjerde remains *within* a literary analysis of the fictional text and the genre he is confronting when he concludes: "Among the corn rows, Garland portrays the strict divisions between the exploitative European patriarch and the purported opportunities of autonomy in American life."[38]

THE IMMIGRANT LETTER IN AN INTERDISCIPLINARY CONTEXT

Perhaps the best way to ascertain the value of interdisciplinary approaches to immigration studies is to reconsider the scholarly use of a type of non-fiction, for example, the numerous immigrant letters. The immigrant letter home is the first chapter in the history of American immigrant literature. Many historians, including Theodore C. Blegen, have used such letters as historical source material.[39] As Orm Øverland and others have shown, however, with time we have come to regard these letters as what they truly are, an enormous body of folk literature.[40] Historians whose minds tend to work in quantitative ways may be tempted to accumulate information given in the immigrant letters, often detailed information about early Midwestern farming. Letters home will sometimes list the number of pigs, cows, and oxen the immigrants had acquired; how many bushels of potatoes and corn they had got; the price of wheat, etc. A quixotic mind with a sense for statistics could, of course, scrutinize hundreds of these letters, add up the number of cattle and then divide by the number of letters in order to find out the average number of cows on the immigrant farm, two or three years after arrival! A reader with a desire to count could, for instance, note the number of the episodes of expressed homesickness in these letters, add up, and come to a conclusion of how much homesickness affected the immigrants. This would be a dubious practice and not terribly interesting either. We must exercise care when we are tempted to extrapolate from letters to immigrant experience in general.

In an essay on "Learning to Read Immigrant Letters: Reflections towards a Textual Theory," Orm Øverland has reminded us that American immigrant letters "are a first-person record of a mass experience."[41] He poses two questions in which the historian may not typically have been interested: First, "How may we read them [the immigrant letters] so that we may even today catch some of the urgency with which they spoke to those they were written for?" And second, "How may we read them as texts that may yet have something to say to us in our own and present situations?"[42] In other words, he advocates both an historical and an existentialist reading which includes the present situation of the reader, whose world is different from that of those for whom the letters were originally written.

Øverland argues that "the immigrant letters available to us are in effect the canonized texts of the genre."[43] One such important collection in the canon of American immigrant letters is the group of letters that the immigrant woman Gro Svendsen (1841–78) sent from from Iowa to Norway during the 1860s and 1870s, collected and translated in the volume *Frontier Mother: The Letters of Gro Svendsen*.[44] A study of different approaches to this body of texts may teach us something about the validity and the benefits of interdisciplinary research in immigration studies.

A sketch of Gro Svendsen's life may help to set the stage for discussion of her letters. Gro and her husband, Ole, emigrated from Hallingdal, Norway, and settled in the northwestern part of Iowa in 1862. She was then a young woman of twenty-one. Just before the end of the Civil War, her husband Ole was drafted, but he returned safely in 1865. She went to school to learn English and she taught in the local Norwegian religious school. She died in childbirth at the age of thirty-eight, struggling to give birth to her tenth child. Over a period of fifteen years from the day she arrived in Iowa until shortly before she died, she wrote letters home about hardship on the frontier, weather conditions, the education of her children, and farm work.

Gro's letters have became well enough known to appear in recent anthologies of American writing from various immigrant groups. In a recent anthology entitled *Immigrant Voices: Twenty-four Narratives of Becoming an American,* letters of Gro Svendsen are included as the only Scandinavian-American immigrant voice.[45] In this work, six of

her letters are, oddly enough, printed next to a piece from the autobiography of an immigrant from Scotland, Andrew Carnegie. He
and Gro had precious little in common, except the fact that both had
emigrated from Europe. The juxtaposition of the two in the anthology becomes even more ironic when the editor, a professor of English
at the University of Wisconsin, Madison, introduces Carnegie by saying that he and his parents were driven out of Europe because of
poverty, whereas Gro is introduced as having been born into an
"upper class family" in rural Norway.[46] Gro's letters are also introduced as a selection "taken from her autobiography."[47] Here the editor has not attended to genre. *Frontier Mother* is not Gro Svendsen's
autobiography, but a collection of her letters, published some sev-
enty years after she died. She never wrote her autobiography. She
simply sent letters home.

In his study of immigrant letters, David A. Gerber returns to the
letters of Gro Svendsen alongside a number of other immigrant
letters from various nations.[48] He argues that the isolated, single immigrant letter may "help document social patterns," but he is more
interested in the immigrant letters that shape a kind of family correspondence over the years.[49] When these letters are put together they
constitute an important genre of folk literature. Gerber's focus is on
Gro, the correspondent. Here is the approach we have been looking
for: "She may or may not be *representative* whatever this may actually
mean and whatever its ultimate relevance but she emerges vividly
from her letters as a woman with a strong individuality, who created a
rich, dynamic and complex life for herself. This is the case not only
because of the content of her experience. One suspects, too, that
over many years she may well have grown in self-conception from a
woman with a need to report to thinking of herself as a reporter, as
she wrote the on-going narrative of her life in letter after letter to her
family in Norway."[50]

In his analysis of Gro's letters, Gerber is both an historian and a literary scholar. As an historian he is interested in the writer and the
text she produces. Notice his aside to other historians who have used
"representativity" as a criterion of interest. In his preface to Gro's letters, Blegen had already noted that she was "a born writer," but for
Blegen her letters epitomize his concept of "grassroots history."[51]
Gerber is more interested in the style and diction of this particular
immigrant writer of letters and how "she emerges" through her writ-

ing. In other words, she does not merely become an historical source, as most immigrant women writers have done. The scholar here is interested in the immigrant woman as a writer and the fact that, against all odds, she was able in her short life to define her life through her writing. Writing made a difference to her and to her family, as it does for readers of today. Gerber goes on to say: "As a writer, she succeeded in crafting a functional prose that allowed her to tell a great deal in the brief space of each letter and to achieve some sense of continuity between letters. We cannot precisely know the psychological functions writing these letters served for her, let alone the psychological processes to which they gave rise in her correspondents. It is certainly plausible to assume, however, that the act of writing each of them not only helped sustain her in the struggle to make a new life in America, and allowed her to preserve emotional links with family and friends in Norway, but gave her the opportunity for creative reflection on the person she was becoming as she endeavored to shape a new life in America. In such a life, writing and the growth of the self might become inextricably and dynamically bound. We are fortunate that she left behind for posterity these self-created artifacts of her life that open up to us the possibility of knowing her. But until we understand the nature of those artifacts, we cannot really claim to know Gro Svendsen."[52]

We need to know her as an immigrant and as a writer. In order to do so we must know more about the kind of text she was producing. Gro Svendsen did not, of course, save these letters for posterity. She needed a preserver and an editor of the treasures she left behind, someone who lifted these letters out of the immediate context and presented them to readers for whom they were not intended. Her collected letters function as a chronicle, composed over a few years, composed in moments of writing in which the writer does not know what will happen to her in the future, nor can she edit what she has earlier recorded and sent in the past. Indeed, Gro's letters must be read with the same kind of respect and inspiration for private writings which is exemplified in Elizabeth Hampsten's fine study *Read This Only to Yourself: The Private Writings of Midwestern Women, 1880–1910.*[53]

Let us finally turn to a participant in the interdisciplinary arena we often forget, the theologian. It is about time that he or she enters the field. Immigrant church history has been written by theologians, within the Norwegian-American immigrant context most notably by E. Clifford Nelson and Eugene L. Fevold. Combining history and doctrine, their *The Lutheran Church among Norwegian-Americans* (1960) is an interdisciplinary effort in itself. The two volumes combine church histories of two countries, the old and the new, in order to emphasize the double character of immigrant religion. The source material for their narrative is earlier church histories, church constitutions, histories of local congregations, publications of the Norwegian synods, church archives, immigrant church periodicals, letters of the early church leaders, congregational reports, and sermons. But it is almost entirely focused on the organizational history and on the biographies of leaders of the church. The immigrant church as it is treated in immigrant literature does not concern them at all. A still more interdisciplinary approach to church history is therefore long due. It must take into account the lives of local members of churches, not just the leaders. Historians of the church need to study the heaps of material published in church newspapers and periodicals and other archival sources in order to do full justice to the religious mind of immigrants.

When a church historian like Sidney Ahlstrom, in his classic study *Religious History of the American People,* includes a chapter on "Protestantism and Later Immigration," he does so by introducing the voice of whom else but Gro Svendsen.[54] To my knowledge, she does not appear in the histories of the Norwegian-American Lutheran churches. What happens to her texts, intended for family use in rural Norway in the late 1860s, when they are studied by a church historian a hundred years later? To Ahlstrom, Gro, the immigrant letter writer, becomes a central Protestant voice, even though she had no position in the apparatus of the immigrant church. For him Gro's letters become a reminder that the religious language of immigrant writing needs to be studied. It contains a reservoir of religious metaphors and conflicts, sometimes ignored or deleted by other scholars, who feel that religious language in immigrant letters is repetitious and full of clichés. To prove the opposite, Ahlstrom quotes from one of the first of Gro's letters where she writes about her voyage: "I am heavy-hearted. A silent prayer for comfort in my deepest sorrow and for strength and courage. . . . The captain led the worship. My heart was still heavy. My thoughts were with you, my dear ones, and of services at home. I could see you all in church. You know I was never absent—and now! O merciful God! . . . I shall never see my beloved

homeland. O God of mercy, my fatherland! Oh forgive me for caus-
ing my dear ones this anguish! O God, do not forsake us! Be our
comforter and give us patience and strengthen our faith."[55]

Ahlstrom uses this letter to "convey something of the grief that
millions of emigrants could never banish."[56] A literary scholar would
not have stopped there. It is tempting to compare Gro's religious language with that of the Puritan emigrants of the seventeenth century,
with how they interpreted the leaving of the old country through
their Protestant faith. In Gro's letter there is no relief at having left
an old country sunk into depravity. There is absolutely no sense of a
God-given mission of the immigrant. Her decision to emigrate gives
her a chance to live her own life, but at the same time she considered
her act to be a breaking away from duties severe enough to be felt as
a violation of the Fourth Commandment in the Lutheran catechism
she knew so well. Immigrant letters have their own theology.

Immigrant letters, including Gro's, are replete with religious language in which writers struggle to associate personal meaning with
traditional formulations. More than one letter-writer struggled with
the Christian dogmas and the biblical language he or she knew, to
bend language to reveal as much of the deeply personal as possible.
Nowhere is this more clear than in the religious language of immigrant letters. "By the grace of God" is not an empty phrase. And the
frequently expressed idea of heaven as a place where there is no
farewell, no parting, is immigrant theology supported by their own
experience of what to them was the almost unbearable moment of
farewell with the old folks at home. Even immigrant tombstones in
ethnic cemeteries may be read as remnants of a religious language.

Linguists may also contribute to the interdisciplinary effort here.
For too long linguists in immigration studies have traced remnants of
the old language in the ways immigrants and their descendants speak.
We need also to study the semantics of translated religious concepts.
Did immigrants feel that their old religious language was too personal
to be translated into American English, in which they seldom felt to-
tally at home? Did *tro* really mean *faith*, did *frelse* carry exactly the same
connotations as *salvation* for the authors of these letters?

THE "DOUBLE CONSCIOUSNESS" OF THE IMMIGRANT

I have argued that the New Historicism has reanimated an old connection between the disciplines of literature and history, without

turning back to the biographical-historical school of literary criticism. As such, the New Historicism may offer new insight into immigration studies. First, narrow concepts of what constitutes a literary text have been challenged. Even texts which appear at first glance to be mediocre or trifling may be subject to literary criticism. As Stephen Greenblatt has remarked, "New historicist methods are useful ways of constructing exchanges between diverse texts in a given historical period. Although in early new historicist work this exchange was often between literary texts and secondary historical sources, later it involved the construction of meaningful dialogues between many primary texts within the same period, including conduct books, penal documents, journal entries and travel narratives, as well as canonical literary texts."[58] Secondly, interest has moved from the use of such texts as sources to interest in the particular. This is perhaps best formulated by Greenblatt, one of the leading figures of the New Historicism. Confronting textual traces of the dead, he asks the reader: "How is it possible for those traces to convey lost life?"[59]

Immigration studies have also much to learn from other schools of American thought. The phrase "double consciousness" was first used by the Black scholar William DuBois in 1903 and has had a renaissance in African-American Studies.[60] It is frequently applied to how Blacks are able to look at themselves from a double perspective, both through their own eyes and the eyes of others. DuBois argued that the Black person entertains the idea of "a double self . . . two souls, two thoughts, two unreconciled strivings" in one body.[61] If this concept is added to the immigrant writers' talk of an old and a new self, their experience of "twoness," we have come to a center of American consciousness which should be confronted with Handlin's idea of a double alienation or with Gjerde's conclusion about a "complementary identity."[62] Based on his reading of DuBois, Henry Louis Gates, Jr. has argued that Black writers have a "two-toned heritage," that their texts are "double voiced."[63] Why is this knowledge so seldom transferred to the field of immigration studies?

NOTES

[1]Oscar Handlin, *The Uprooted*, 2d ed. (Boston, 1979), 3. The paragraph about life in steerage is from Chapter Two, "The Crossing," 45.

[2]Garrison Keillor, *Lake Wobegon Days* (New York, 1985), 96.

[3]Kristian Hvidt, *Flight to America: The Social Background of 300,000 Danish Emigrants* (New York, 1975). His next volume was published as *Danes Go West: A Book about the Emigration to America* (Skørping, Denmark, 1976).

[4]Dorothy Burton Skårdal, *The Divided Heart: Scandinavian Immigrant Experience through Literary Sources* (Oslo, 1974).

[5]Werner Sollors, *Beyond Ethnicity: Consent and Descent in American Culture* (New York and Oxford, 1986). Sollors takes issue with Skårdal when she argues that the poetry of Carl Sandburg falls outside the scope of her study. To Sollors, Carl Sandburg "would seem to be the perfect author for ethnic critics" (242).

[6]For a brief introduction to the contemporary school of thought called New Historicism, see Louis Montrose, "New Historicisms," in *Redrawing the Boundaries: The Transformation of English and American Literary Studies*, ed. Stephen Greenblatt and Giles Gunn (New York, 1992), 392–418.

[7]Kristian Hvidt, "Fact and Fiction: A Case for the Complementary Study of History and Literature," *American Studies in Scandinavia* 16/2 (1984), 67–71. I will also be referring to Hvidt's "Concluding Remarks" in the same volume, 98–101.

[8]Hvidt, "Fact and Fiction," 71.

[9]Ole E. Rølvaag, *Giants in the Earth: A Saga of the Prairie*, trans. Lincoln Colcord and Ole E. Rølvaag (New York, 1927).

[10]Dorothy Burton Skårdal, "'Hard' Facts and 'Soft' Sources: Literature as Historical Source Material?" *American Studies in Scandinavia* 16/2 (1984), 73.

[11]Skårdal, "'Hard' Facts and 'Soft' Sources," 76.

[12]Skårdal, "'Hard' Facts and 'Soft' Sources," 74.

[13]Skårdal, "'Hard' Facts and 'Soft' Sources," 75.

[14]Skårdal, "'Hard' Facts and 'Soft' Sources," 76.

[15]Skårdal, "'Hard' Facts and 'Soft' Sources," 77.

[16]See my essay "Ole E. Rølvaag, Thorstein Veblen, and the Independent Farmer," in *Performances in American Literature and Culture: Essays in Honor of Professor Orm Øverland on his 60th Birthday*, ed. Vidar Pedersen and Zeljka Sverljuga (Bergen, 1995), 74–84.

[17]Kristian Hvidt, "Concluding Remarks," *American Studies in Scandinavia* 16/2 (1984), 101.

[18]Skårdal, *The Divided Heart*, 166–186.

[19]Skårdal, *The Divided Heart*, 166.

[20]Skårdal is here referring to Nils N. Rønning's novel, *Lars Lee, the Boy from Norway* (Minneapolis, 1928). See Skårdal, *The Divided Heart*, 349.

[21]E. Clifford Nelson and Eugene L. Fevold, *The Lutheran Church among Norwegian-Americans: A History of the Evangelical Lutheran Church,* 2 vols. (Minneapolis, 1960).

[22]Ole E. Rølvaag, *Peder Victorious,* trans. Nora Solum and Ole E. Rølvaag (New York, 1929), 48–74.

[23]Rølvaag, *Peder Victorious,* 48.

[24]Skårdal, *The Divided Heart,* 148.

[25]Skårdal, *The Divided Heart,* 23.

[26]Skårdal, *The Divided Heart,* 23.

[27]Hans A. Foss, *Husmands-gutten. En fortælling fra Sigdal* (Decorah, 1885). Translated by Joel J. Winkjer, *The Cotter's Son* (Alexandria, MN, 1963).

[28]Ole E. Rølvaag (Paal Mørck), *Paa glemte veie* (Minneapolis, 1914), and Nils N. Rønning, *A Servant of the Lord* (Minneapolis, 1931).

[29]Lloyd S. Kramer, "Literature, Criticism, and Historical Imagination," in *The New Cultural History,* ed. Lynn Hunt (Berkeley, 1989), 97–98.

[30]Handlin, *The Uprooted,* 267.

[31]Odd S. Lovoll, *The Promise of America: A History of the Norwegian-American People* (Minneapolis, 1984). *The Promise Fulfilled: A Portrait of Norwegian Americans Today* (Minneapolis, 1998).

[32]Lovoll, *The Promise Fulfilled,* 68.

[33]Jon Gjerde, *The Minds of the West: Ethnocultural Evolution in the Rural Middle West, 1830–1917* (Chapel Hill, NC, 1997), 8.

[34]Jon Gjerde, ed., *Major Problems in American Immigration and Ethnic History: Documents and Essays* (Boston, 1998).

[35]Gjerde, *The Minds of the West,* 214.

[36]Gjerde, *The Minds of the West,* 213.

[37]Gjerde, *The Minds of the West,* 217.

[38]Gjerde, *The Minds of the West,* 219.

[39]Theodore Blegen, *Land of Their Choice: The Immigrants Write Home* (Minneapolis, 1955).

[40]Orm Øverland, "Learning to Read Immigrant Letters: Reflections towards a Textual Theory," in *Norwegian-American Essays 1996,* ed. Øyvind T. Gulliksen, et al. (Oslo: 1996).

[41]Øverland, "Learning to Read Immigrant Letters," 208.

[42]Øverland, "Learning to Read Immigrant Letters," 209.

[43]Øverland, "Learning to Read Immigrant Letters," 221.

[44]Pauline Farseth and Theodore C. Blegen, trans. and ed., *Frontier Mother: The Letters of Gro Svendsen* (Northfield, MN, 1950).

[45]Gordon Hutner, ed., *Immigrant Voices: Twenty-four Narratives on Becoming an American* (New York, 1999).

[46]Hutner, *Immigrant Voices*, 69.

[47]Hutner, *Immigrant Voices*, 70.

[48]David A. Gerber, "The Immigrant Letter between Positivism and Populism: The Uses of Immigrant Personal Correspondence in Twentieth-Century American Scholarship," *Journal of American Ethnic History* 16/4 (1997), 3–34. A version of this essay is also published in Rebecca Earle, ed., *Epistolary Selves: Letters and Letter-writers, 1600–1945* (Aldershot, England, 1999), 37–55.

[49]Gerber, "The Immigrant Letter," 3.

[50]Gerber, "The Immigrant Letter," 20.

[51]Farseth and Blegen, *Frontier Mother*, vii.

[52]Gerber, "The Immigrant Letter," 22.

[53]Elizabeth Hampsten, *Read This Only to Yourself: The Private Writings of Midwestern Women, 1880–1910* (Bloomington, IN, 1982).

[54]Sidney E. Ahlstrom, *A Religious History of the American People*, 2 vols. (Garden City, NY, 1975). The reference to Gro Svendsen's letters appears in 2:210–211.

[55]Ahlstrom, *A Religious History*, 2:210–211.

[56]Ahlstrom, *A Religious History*, 2:210.

[57]John Brannigan, *New Historicism and Cultural Materialism* (New York, 1998), 11–12.

[58]Stephen Greenblatt, *Shakespearean Negotiations: The Circulation of Social Energy in Renaissance England* (Oxford, 1988), 3.

[59]William E. B. DuBois, *The Souls of Black Folk* (New York, 1989).

[60]DuBois, *The Souls of Black Folk*, 3.

[61]See Handlin, *The Uprooted*, 254, and Gjerde, *The Minds of the West*, 8.

[62]Henry Louis Gates, Jr., introduction to DuBois, *The Souls of Black Folk*, xviii.

Fram, Fram, Cristmenn, Crossmenn! The Battle of Stiklastaðir beyond the Sagas

Jan Ragnar Hagland

WHAT COULD BE A MORE APPROPRIATE WAY to greet the recipient of the present collection of essays than to cite the proud motto inscribed in the emblem of St. Olaf College: *Fram, Fram, Cristmenn, Crossmenn!* [Forward, forward, men of Christ, men of the cross!]. These words, of course, echo Snorri Sturluson's famous description in *Heimskringla* of the Battle of Stiklastaðir in present-day Trøndelag, Norway. In Chapter 226 of the *Óláfs saga helga* [*Saga of Saint Olaf*], Snorri tells us, the *bœndr* [yeomen] attacked the king's army with their famous battle cry *Fram, fram, búandamenn!* [Forward, forward, yeomen!]. The king's men answered the challenge with their own war cry: *Fram, fram, kristmenn, krossmenn, konungsmenn!* [Forward, forward, men of Christ, men of the cross, men of the king!]. As is well known, the Battle of Stiklastaðir has been taken to symbolize the final stage of the Christianization of Norway. The Battle of Stiklastaðir in which King Óláfr Haraldsson was defeated and killed has symbolized the final victory over paganism that opened Norway to Christianity once and for all. It must consequently have seemed fitting for the founders of St. Olaf's School in 1874 to name the new educational enterprise after Saint Olaf, and it seems to have been considered equally appropriate to choose the battle cry quoted by Snorri Sturluson as the motto of the college when St. Olaf's School was made into St. Olaf College in 1889. Omitting the summons to obedience to the worldly king implied by the *konungsmenn* of the original text, the final version of the motto chosen for St. Olaf College fittingly emphasizes *Cristmenn* and *Crossmen*.[1]

Given the importance of this motto to generations of Norwegian-Americans and others, the historiographical background of the tradition behind it deserves to be looked at once again from a somewhat different point of view than that of the late-nineteenth-century reception of Snorri Sturluson's *Heimskringla* that provided the Norwegian immigrants in America with a kind of ideological basis upon which they could choose a motto for their new college. Compared with sources other than Snorri it is, perhaps, possible to see

Fram, Fram, Cristmenn, Crossmenn! The emblem and motto of St. Olaf College. Center for College History at St. Olaf College (Northfield, Minnesota).

the allegedly huge and magnificent Battle of Stiklastaðir depicted in *Heimskringla* in a somewhat different light.

One interesting source against which it seems relevant to assess Snorri's account of the battle is the old regional law of the Frostaþing, one of the four provincial areas of jurisdiction in medieval Norway before the 1270s when a new common law for all of Norway was passed by King Magnus the Lawmender (1263–80). It is relevant to the following that the area of jurisdiction covered by the Frostaþing law at the beginning of the middle ages was restricted to eight so-called *fylki* [districts] situated by the Trondheimsfjord in the inner districts of present-day Trøndelag. In the course of the High Middle Ages this area was gradually extended to cover most of what is at present termed Mid-Norway, including in addition to the Trøndelag area the county of Møre og Romsdal, the district of Helgeland, and perhaps even Jämtland in present-day Sweden.

As a point of departure for the present discussion, I want to take Chapters 50–52 in the section of the law that treats personal rights, the so called *mannhelgarbálkr,* of the Frostaþing law. Chapter 50 has the following wording in glossed translation: "No man shall make an onslaught on another man, neither the king nor any other man. If the king does this, the arrow shall be cut and be sent [i.e., as a declaration of war] through all [the eight] *fylki*. Men shall pursue him and kill him if they are able to seize him [the king]. If he escapes he shall never be allowed to return to the land. And whoever refuses to join in pursuing him shall pay a fine of three marks, and the same fine shall be due for failing to forward the arrow."[2] The two statutes or chapters following this deal with the same violation of the law if committed by a *jarl* [earl] or by a *lendmaðr* [baron]. In those cases the arrow was to be circulated in four and two *fylki* respectively. It is thus natural and correct to interpret, as has in fact been done, the wording *"fylki öll"* in Chapter 50 to refer to the eight *fylki innan fjarðar* [districts within the fjords], that is to say the territory which constituted the original area of jurisdiction. We shall return to this point. These statutes are commonly referred to as the Throndish law of resistance or the "law of resistance of the *þrændi.*" No parallel is known in Scandinavian or in Germanic legal systems and the statutes are consequently interesting per se for medieval studies in general.

The salient point here is the statute just quoted that concerns the king. According to recent work, including that by Jørn Sandnes in particular, this should be understood to refer to legal measures taken by the bœndr in order to prevent the exercise of violence by the king at an initial stage in the emergence of the kingdom of Norway.[3] The purpose of the statute was to oblige the bœndr to kill the king in case he offended against the law on this particular point. This has been interpreted as a reaction against the aggressive actions taken towards the þrœndir by Earl Hákon at Hlaðir near the estuary of the river Nið and the violence with which King Óláfr Tryggvasonr (995–1000) tried to christen the people. In consequence the statutes of resistance in the Frostaþing law, it has been suggested, should be dated in the years shortly after the turn of the first millennium. On this point, then, it seems possible, as convincingly pointed out by Sandnes, for us to go "beyond the sagas" and look at events transmitted to us by saga narratives from a different angle, based on a different kind of source. In this particular case the narratives to be considered are those in which the story of the Battle of Stiklastaðir is told, the most famous, of course, being Snorri Sturluson's Saga of Saint Olaf in the version of Heimskringla.[4] It is possible, in my opinion, to understand better what is said in the sagas about the size and importance of the Battle of Stiklastaðir when we bear in mind the importance of the Throndish law of resistance in the Frostaþing law, perhaps even more carefully than historians such as Sandnes and others.

In medieval historiography, the Battle of Stiklastaðir, as we have already seen, is presented as the definite turning point in the process of the Christianization of Norway. This is most likely one important reason that Snorri and other chroniclers depict the battle as a great and conspicuous event. Snorri goes over the top, so to speak, when he makes the army of the bœndr 120 times 120 [hundruð hundraða] men, which would yield a total of more than 14,000 men. The two other sagas to be considered here, the so-called Saga of Saint Olaf and Fagrskinna [The Fair Vellum] are somewhat more moderate about the size of the opposing army.[5]

According to the sagas, King Olafr Haraldsson had to flee the land in 1028 for political reasons when he encountered strong opposition and resistance from the chieftains of Trøndelag. In the summer of 1030 Olafr tried to return to Norway via Trøndelag. This might well have been interpreted at the time as an attempt by the king to "return to the land" [*koma i land aptr*], thus violating the statute in the Throndish law of resistance set out in chapter 50 of the *mannhelgarbálkr* in the Frostaþing law.

Given this context there was an explicit obligation for the *bœndr* to resist or oppose the king and even to kill him on his return to Norway from the east via Sweden. The violation of the law would, as we have seen already, result in heavy fines for the *bœndr*. Jørn Sandnes has made a point of the necessity of fines, for the *bœndr* mobilize army in the middle of the haymaking season.[6] Still the enormous size of the army mobilized by the *bœndr* and the *lendmenn* [barons] as described in the sagas may, on the basis of the law, legitimately be questioned. According to an estimate made Sandnes, the numbers given by Snorri Sturluson would have equalled the size of the entire population of the eight *fylki innan fjarðar*.[7] An army of one tenth of the number quoted by Snorri would seem more realistic in Sandnes's opinion. There is little reason, as far as I can see, to dispute this. There may be even more evidence to support this contention, as we shall see. It is, therefore, interesting to see how large is the number of warriors mobilized in the three kings' sagas that contain the story of the battle of Stiklastaðir, that is to say, the *Óláfs sögur* [*Olaf's Saga*] by Snorri Sturluson, the *Fagrskinna,* and the *Saga of Saint Olaf.* It may be possible better to understand the hyperbolic character of the saga narratives on this point if we look at them from the vantage point of the Frostaþing law. It is commonly agreed that these three sagas are dependent on common sources. To what extent any of the sagas are dependent on each other is somewhat more uncertain, especially where Snorri's account and *Fagrskinna* are concerned.

In Snorri Sturluson's *Óláfs sögur,* the army against which Olafr Haraldsson had to fight was recruited from areas reaching far outside that of the Frostaþing area. One, perhaps two, wings of the army consisted of *þrœndir* [men from Trøndelag] and *háleygir* [men from Hálogaland], Snorri tells us, whereas the third consisted of *rygir, hörðar, sygnir,* and *firðir* [men from western Norway, Rogaland, Hordaland, Sogn og Fjordane]. This is presumably to underscore the assumption that the *bœndr* disposed of an army of an enormous size, a hundred and twenty times a hundred and twenty men. The two other sagas may, I think, indirectly reveal how in its time a literary tradition on a particular point like this was created. Here the Frostaþing law seems to offer an opportunity for us really to look beyond the sagas.

It is a fact that the *Fagrskinna* as well as the *Saga of Saint Olaf* present us with an army of a somewhat more moderate size and also a more closely defined area from which the men were recruited. The *Fagrskinna* tells us, without quoting any number of men involved, that the *bonda herr* [the army of the *bœndr*] consisted of *háleygir, þrœndir,* and *mœrir;* the latter group, it seems, is vaguely specified as *alt fyrir norðan Stað* [everything north of Stad, that is to say, the area corresponding to the present-day Møre og Romsdal]. The *Saga of Saint Olaf* tells us that the *boanda herr* [army of yeomen] was composed of *þrœndir oc háleygir, naumdœler* [men from *Naumudalr* or present-day Namdalen] *oc mœrer* without confining the latter group to any particular part of the *Mœrir* district. This, indeed, seems to be as congruent as can be expected to the jurisdiction of the Frostaþing law as we know it in the late twelfth/early thirteenth century, that is to say, in the period when these saga narratives were composed. The *Saga of Saint Olaf,* interestingly enough, describes the size of the army in the following way: *Oc þeir bœndr er i þrondheimi varo samnadu saman liði miklu, xij. c. manna. En allz hafðu þeir .vij. þushundrad manna* [And the *bœndr* who were in Trøndelag gathered an army of twelve hundred men. But altogether they had seven thousand men]. The need here to specify the number of men provided by the *bœndr er i þrondheimi varo* [the yeomen in Trøndelag] may well reflect a genuine local tradition in Trøndelag that the battle was fought primarily by men from the eight *fylki innan fjarðar.* The men may then well have been mobilized along the lines suggested by Sandnes's interpretation of the Frostaþing law on this point. The number quoted for this Throndish army may even support the estimation he makes without actually taking the *Saga of Saint Olaf* into consideration in his discussion.

It is, in my opinion, not unlikely that a common source for *Fagrskinna* and the *Saga of Saint Olaf* has tried to make some sort of reliable estimation of the proportions of the battle based on the statute we have quoted here from the Frostaþing law. For someone in the late twelfth or early thirteenth century the paragraph in the law requiring "the arrow" to be sent as a war token through "all *fylki*" in the Frostaþing law area may have meant or implied exactly those areas quoted in the *Saga of Saint Olaf* and, with a minor adjustment, in

Fagrskinna. If so, it is easier to understand the need for the *Saga of Saint Olaf* to keep the number of men coming from *þrondheimi* [i.e., the part of Trøndelag suggested above] apart, as this may have belonged to a genuine local tradition with which a local audience of this saga may also have been familiar. The total number of the army could, on the other hand, be constructed as it were on the basis of the Frostaþing law as the saga composer and his audience in the cultural setting of archepiscopal Nidaros must have known it in the High Middle Ages. A reconstruction like this based somewhat anachronistically on an otherwise prestigious historical source would also accommodate the need for the saga to magnify the event in order to increase its symbolic value for the great tale of the Christianization of Norway. To some extent this may also apply for the *Fagrskinna.* In both these sagas the composition of the army that fought the battle of Stiklastaðir on the side of the *bœndr* was a matter that had to do first and foremost with the Frostaþing area. Of the seven political leaders or chiefs mentioned as active participants in the battle, by Snorri and the two other sagas, five belong in the Frostaþing law area. Only *Aslakr i Finney* and *Erlendr or Gerði* belonged outside the law area, coming from Rogaland and Hordaland respectively. Snorri in his *Óláfs sögur* obviously feels free to compose a huge army around these seven leaders and others, even if the common sources with *Fagrskinna* and the *Saga of Saint Olaf* are clearly visible also in his magnificently amplified version of the events that make the Christianization of Norway so conspicuous and important. Obviously both Snorri and his audience were less bothered and perhaps also less acquainted with the Throndish law of resistance in the Frostaþing law. This allowed him to form more freely the narrative that more than any other source formed posterity's perception and understanding of these events in medieval Trøndelag. It led ultimately in the nineteenth century to the choice pioneer Norwegians made of a motto for their college in the new world.

NOTES

[1]See Joseph M. Shaw, *History of Saint Olaf College, 1874–1974* (Northfield, MN, 1974), 43.

[2]See also Laurence M. Larson, ed., *The Earliest Norwegian Laws Being The Gulathing Law and The Frostathing Law* (New York, 1935), 278.

[3]Jørn Sandnes, "Slaget på Stiklestad i lys av Frostatingslovens motstandsbestemmelser" in *Kongsmenn og krossmenn. Festskrift til Grethe Authén Blom*, ed. Steinar Supphellen (Trondheim, 1992), 255–265.

[4]Bjarni Aðalbjarnarson, ed., *Heimskringla*, I–III (Reykjavík, 1939–1951).

[5]Oscar Albert Johnsen, ed., *Óláfs saga hins helga. Efter pergamethaandskrift i Uppsala Universitetsbibliotek*, Delagardieske samling nr. 8[II] (Oslo, 1922) and Bjarni Einarsson, ed., *Ágrip af Nóregs konunga sögum. Fagrskinna, Nóregs konunga tal* (Reykjavík, 1985).

[6]Sandnes, "Slaget på Stiklestad," 260.

[7]Sandnes, "Slaget på Stiklestad," 261.

Swedish Americans and the Viking Discovery of America

H. Arnold Barton

THE ONE-THOUSANDTH ANNIVERSARY in 2000 of the Viking discovery of America was celebrated with numerous commemorative events in the United States, Canada, and the Nordic countries. The subject has, however, long exercised an enormous fascination. In 1997 a full-scale bibliography of writings concerning the Vikings in Greenland and America listed some 6,400 titles in all, while not even claiming to include every possible item.[1]

Immigrants of all nationalities have always felt the need to justify their place in American society, both to others and to themselves, as well as to vindicate their emigration before their former compatriots. Characteristically they have sought to achieve status by demonstrating a long presence in America and the similarity of their homeland values to those of the dominant Anglo-American society.[2]

In both respects the Scandinavians in America have enjoyed a particularly advantageous position. Sweden was among the original colonizing powers in North America with its New Sweden colony along the Delaware River, established in 1638. The area remained under the Swedish flag only seventeen years, before being taken first by the Dutch and later by the English, and its inhabitants numbered at the time of its loss no more than a few hundred. Still, it enabled Swedish Americans at a later time to claim proudly that their people were from the beginning "colonists," rather than simply "immigrants."[3]

Since many of the New Sweden colonists were Finns—Finland

then being a part of the Swedish realm—Finnish Americans have also been able to make the same claim. Indeed, some Finnish-American historians went so far as to claim that most of the New Sweden colonists had been Finns. Norwegian and Danish Americans, too, were eager to show that their countrymen were also to be found in seventeenth-century America. In 1916 the Norwegian-American scholar John O. Evjen at least tentatively identified a number of Norwegians, Danes, and Swedes in Dutch New Amsterdam.[4]

But Scandinavians could meanwhile point to a far earlier presence in North America: the Vikings' discovery of and attempted settlement on the continent around A.D. 1000, some five hundred years before Columbus, as recorded in the medieval Icelandic sagas. The Viking voyages to the west furthermore gave stirring proof of Nordic qualities bound to appeal to the older Anglo-American groups: pride, courage, fortitude, rugged individualism, enterprise, love of freedom and adventure. The fearless Viking in the prow of a dragon ship could appear the true forebear of the western pioneer in a covered wagon.

From the time of their earliest efforts to record their own history in the later 1860s, Scandinavian Americans did not fail to make their claim of being the first Europeans on American soil. As the Swedish American O. N. Nelson declared in 1893, "The fact of it all is that Leif Erikson is the true discoverer of America, while Columbus was merely the first emigrant to America from Spain."[5]

AMERICA DISCOVERS THE VIKING DISCOVERIES

Scandinavian Americans were, however, not the first on the American side of the ocean to call attention to the Viking discovery. Anglo-American scholars had long shown an interest.[6] Already in 1773, Benjamin Franklin recalled that the "learned Swede," Pehr Kalm, who visited Pennsylvania in the mid-eighteenth century, had told him of the Scandinavian discovery of America. The real vogue appears to have begun, however, in 1820 with an account of the voyages appearing in the *Analectic Magazine* in Philadelphia, translated from an 1818 article by the Swedish philologist and antiquarian Johan Henrik Schröder.[7]

Interest in the United States was greatly stimulated with the appearance in 1837 of the Danish geographer Carl C. Rafn's *Antiqvitates Americanæ,* which provided the medieval texts concerning the Vinland voyages in the original Icelandic, with parallel Latin and Danish translations. The following year an English abstract of this work was published in New York. Rafn subsequently produced numerous writings on Vinland, mainly to prove that New England was its probable location. In 1844, the Scotsman Samuel Laing published a widely read, three-volume English translation of the *Heimskringla,* which also included the Greenland Saga.[8] Although some sober attempts were made to deal with the subject, fantasy flourished among the American enthusiasts, stimulated by alleged Scandinavian archeological finds in New England, which have long since been dismissed by scholars, and inspiring literary works by, among others, Henry Wadsworth Longfellow and John Greenleaf Whittier.[9]

Behind this early excitement one may discern American pride in the Scandinavians' close ties of blood with the Germanic Anglo-Saxons and indeed in the partial descent of Anglo-Americans from Viking settlers in the British Isles. The Vikings' descendants were, moreover, staunch Protestants, a distinct merit in Anglo-American eyes. Under such circumstances, Leif Ericson could understandably provide a more satisfactory hero than the Latin Catholic, Christopher Columbus, even though mainstream American historians long remained skeptical of claims on Leif Ericson's part.

THE ICELANDIC VINLAND SAGAS

The earliest brief mention of the Viking discovery preserved in writing comes from the German monk Adam of Bremen, around the year 1070. Over the following century there were passing references to Vinland in the Icelandic annals, suggesting that its existence was well known through oral tradition. Not until around 1190, close to two hundred years after the events related, was the first detailed account of the expeditions, the *Greenland Saga* [*Grænlendinge*], put down in writing by an anonymous Icelandic chronicler. This was followed in Iceland around 1260 by the longer and more fanciful *Erik the Red's Saga* [*Eiríks saga rauda*].

There is no need here to recapitulate in detail the history of the Viking discovery and attempted settlement in North America. Still, the two Vinland sagas, while they complement each other, differ in certain respects so that significant points in the narrative remain unclear.[10] The earlier *Greenland Saga,* for the most part a straightforward narrative, is presently accepted by scholars as the more reliable. It relates how Erik the Red, outlawed in Norway and later in Iceland for manslaughter, explored, and in 985 established a colony of Icelanders, on the west coast of Greenland. Bjarni Herjolfsson, seeking the new settlement the following year, was driven off course to two landfalls to the west that he realized could not be Greenland. The first European sighting of North America would thus appear to have taken place already in 986. Bjarni did not land but turned eastward to his intended destination.

Erik the Red's son, Leif Ericson, bought Bjarni's boat and in the year 1000 sailed westward where in succession he landed first in "Helluland," the land of the flat rocks, then in "Markland," flat and heavily forested, and finally in "Vinland," where Leif and his men built huts and spent the winter. In Vinland, they found the wild grapes from which its name derived, salmon in the rivers, lush grass, "self-sown" grain, and much milder temperatures and longer daylight in winter than that to which they were accustomed. From this tantalizing brief description, together with further details from Erik the Red's Saga, endless controversy has arisen over Vinland's exact location.

According to Erik the Red's Saga, it was Leif Ericson who both first sighted and landed in America. The two Vinland sagas meanwhile both speak of later expeditions, evidently to around 1015, in which Leif's brother Torvald, his illegitimate half-sister, Freydis, and the wealthy Icelander Thorfinn Karlsefne play leading roles. Here the details differ considerably between the two versions. It is evident, however, that the later expeditions took with them both women and livestock to establish a lasting settlement at Vinland, but that these efforts failed due to the hostility of the native inhabitants called *skrælinger* by the newcomers.

There are a few later mentions of Vinland in medieval Icelandic sources. It is, for instance, briefly referred to in the sixteenth chapter of *Olaf Tryggvasons Saga* in Snorri Sturluson's thirteenth-century *Heimskringla*. Two mentions in the Icelandic annals have in particular stirred the fantasy of later enthusiasts. In 1121 it is recorded that the recently appointed Bishop Erik of Greenland "went in search of Vinland." A later notation from 1347 speaks of a ship driven off course to Iceland from Markland, on its way back to Greenland, presumably carrying a load of timber to that treeless island.[11]

THE EVIDENCE COMES TO LIGHT

The preservation, transcriptions, and translations of the Vinland sources, from the thirteenth century to our own time, are a fascinating subject in their own right. The Icelandic manuscripts became known among continental Scandinavian scholars during the seventeenth century. In 1633 Pastor Peder Claussøn Friis brought out a Danish translation of Snorri's *Heimskringla,* which long after was widely read, especially in Norway. The first translation of the *Greenland Saga* was made by the Swedish scholar Johan Peringskiöld in 1697. Tormodus Torfæus, an Icelander in Copenhagen, brought out a Latin account of the voyages in 1705. *Erik the Red's Saga* was translated into Danish by P. E. Müller in 1817. This may in turn have inspired the Swede Johan Henrik Schröder to write the brief account in 1818 which, translated into English in the *Analectic Magazine* in Philadelphia in 1820, awakened interest in the Viking discovery in the United States. In 1837 C. C. Rafn's *Antiqvitates Americanæ* provided the Icelandic texts of both Vinland sagas, with Latin and Danish translations. In Norway, Jacob Aall, inspired by Rafn, included an abridgment of the *Greenland Saga* with his translation of the *Heimskringla* in 1838–39.[12]

To the literary evidence was finally added firm archaeological proof of the Viking presence on this continent, after the rejection of numerous earlier alleged finds. An obsidian arrowhead and the remains of chests made of larch wood that could only have come from North America were discovered in Greenland. The real breakthrough came, however, with the discovery by the Norwegian Arctic explorer Helge Ingstad and his archaeologist wife, Anne-Stine Ingstad, of an indisputable Viking site at Anse aux Meadows on the northern tip of Newfoundland in 1960. Although the Ingstads sought to prove that this was Leif Ericson's Vinland, it is now generally believed that while this was a briefly occupied Viking site, Vinland, if it were to match the descriptions given in the sagas, must have lain further south, presumably somewhere between Nova Scotia and New England.[13]

SCANDINAVIAN AMERICANS ENTER THE SCENE

The Scandinavian-American historians who took up the theme of the Viking discoveries in the later 1860s, amateurs all by later standards, thus had a well-established tradition upon which to build. It was clear enough from the sagas that the Vinland voyagers were Icelanders, most already living on Greenland. The Icelanders in North America during the later nineteenth century were, however, too few to make their voices heard in the matter. The Norwegian Americans thus "appropriated," in Odd S. Lovoll's words, the Viking discovery for themselves, making it the prime symbol of their fatherland's past glory.[14]

For this there were plausible arguments, even though Iceland at the time of the Vinland voyages had been independent of Norway. The great majority of its original settlers had come, some generations back, from western Norway or from Norwegian settlements in the British Isles. The sagas state, moreover, that Erik the Red, Leif Ericson's father, came from Norway.

The first and most influential Scandinavian American to take up the theme was the young Rasmus Bjørn Anderson, who was born in Wisconsin of Norwegian parents and who in 1868, inspired by his reading of the *Heimskringla,* began lecturing in the upper Midwest, in English, on Leif Ericson and the Viking discovery. He later wrote that this was not at the time mentioned in any American textbook and recalled that his lecture included "the most enthusiastic eulogies of the Viking age, of the *Eddas,* of the Scandinavian exploits, of the literature, music and art down to the present times . . . a most glowing tribute to both the ancient and modern Scandinavians."[15]

The earliest printed Scandinavian-American account of the Viking discoveries was evidently a brief article by the Norwegian-American editor Svein Nilsson in his *Billed-Magazin* in Madison, Wisconsin, in January 1869. It was followed late that year by an article by the Swedish-born attorney and Mexican War veteran O. E. Dreutzer, written after he had read Samuel Laing's translation of the *Heimskringla.*[16] In 1874, Rasmus B. Anderson came out with a slender volume entitled *America Not Discovered by Columbus.* Its object was not only to present a "readable and truthful narrative" of the Viking discovery, but to demonstrate that Columbus must have known of it before setting forth on his first Atlantic crossing in 1492. In particular, Anderson was convinced that Columbus had visited Iceland in 1477 and there learned of the earlier exploration.[17]

This last was a point that would repeatedly arise, particularly among Scandinavian Americans, down to the present day. In a celebrated biography of Columbus from 1828 that Anderson had read in college,

Washington Irving had taken note of a letter from the explorer in which he claimed to have "navigated one hundred leagues beyond Thule" in 1477, suggesting a visit to Iceland. Irving did not consider the possibility that Columbus might here have learned of the existence of Vinland. Nor did Jacob Aall in his abridged translation of the *Greenland Saga* in 1838. Inspired by C. C. Rafn, Aall did claim that "in every century from Leif's first discovery down to Columbus America was visited by Northmen." The Swedish author Fredrika Bremer, following a lengthy stay in Norway, nonetheless revealed how already before 1843 Aall's passing remark was interpreted there as clear evidence that Columbus had learned of the earlier Viking discovery. In America Svein Nilsson would raise this claim in *Billed-Magazin* in 1869.[18]

What is particularly relevant here, however, was Anderson's subtle but unmistakable emphasis upon the Viking discovery as a *Norwegian* accomplishment. In English usage the term "Norse" may pertain either to the ancient Scandinavians as a whole or specifically to Norway and the Norwegians. Anderson's autobiography from 1915 shows much good will toward his fellow Scandinavians, the Swedes and Danes. But *America Not Discovered by Columbus* makes clear that "Norse" for him meant "Norwegian." "The Norsemen," he wrote, were a branch of the "Teutonic race" that in early times had migrated westward and northward from Asia, finally settling in "what is now the west central part of the kingdom of Norway." Their language was "the Old Norse, which is still preserved and spoken in Iceland, and upon it are founded the modern Norse, Danish and Swedish languages." His account, he wrote, should be "of equal interest to Americans and Norsemen," and "those who first saw the sunlight beaming among the rugged, snow-capped mountains of old Norway" must feel deep pride in knowing that their own ancestors, "the intrepid Norsemen," were the first Europeans to set foot on American soil and in thus having "the claims of their native country to this honor vindicated."[19]

Rasmus B. Anderson would soon emerge as one of Norwegian America's most influential, albeit controversial, standard-bearers. He was in turn the University of Wisconsin's first professor of Scandinavian studies, American minister to Denmark, entrepreneur, and editor of the newspaper *Amerika* in Madison, Wisconsin. His book on the Norse discovery appeared in several editions, as well as in Norwegian and German translations. Beginning already in 1873, he began a campaign, together with the celebrated Norwegian violinist, Ole Bull, to erect a monument to Leif Ericson in America. This resulted in 1887 in the unveiling of a statue in Boston, the first of several raised in America since then. Of these, only that in Minot, North Dakota, near an area of Icelandic settlement, identifies Leif Ericson as an Icelander. It was above all thanks to Rasmus Bjørn Anderson that the Viking discovery would become a central Norwegian-American ethnic symbol.[20]

SWEDISH AMERICANS CLAIM THEIR SHARE

When I met him in Oslo on the millennial Leif Ericson Day, 9 October 2000, Professor Odd S. Lovoll remarked that, of course, the Norwegians made more of this matter than the Swedes. The latter, however, have been by no means willing to vacate the field. The Viking connection has been no less vital to their self-image than to that of the Norwegians. "Swedish Americans," Ulf Beijbom has written, "who ordinarily sought to avoid being singled out as 'Scandinavians' now included Leif Ericson without pangs of conscience in their Pantheon."[21]

Anderson's worthy counterpart among the Swedish Americans was Johan Alfred Enander, editor of the influential newspaper *Hemlandet* in Chicago. His goal, as he declared in a speech in 1888, was to uphold "in every sphere the honor and reputation of the Swedish name, until that name becomes a name of honor from sea to sea, comprising within it all that is great, noble, just, and true."[22]

In 1874, some five years after arriving in America and in the same year that Rasmus B. Anderson published his *America Not Discovered by Columbus,* Enander brought out the first part of his history of the United States intended for his immigrant countrymen, most of which dealt with the Vikings and their discovery of America. Enander made essentially the same points as Anderson, including the contention that Columbus had learned about the western continent in Iceland. He nonetheless went further in claiming that "the bold seafarers from the North established colonies in the land they discovered, with which Greenland and Iceland maintained contact up to the year 1347." Enander also devoted nearly a hundred pages to the sturdy virtues of the ancient Scandinavians, inspired largely by the second volume of the Swedish pastor and popular historian Anders

Magnus Strinnholm's history of Sweden from 1836, which had also given brief attention to the Viking discovery of America.[23]

Enander must have been familiar with Anderson's lecture and he may already have read his just-published account of the Viking discovery when he wrote his own, and this must surely have prompted him to challenge the latter's suggestion that it had been a purely Norwegian venture. "Certain Anglo-American authors who acknowledge that the Northmen discovered America nevertheless make a great mistake when they regard Northmen [*nordmän*] and Norwegians [*norrmän*] as synonymous," Enander wrote. "The word Northmen was during the Viking Age in the North a common name for *Swedes, Norwegians, Danes,* and *Icelanders,* therefore equivalent to the newer term *Scandinavians.*"[24]

Enander sought to assert his Swedish compatriots' claim to a share in the Viking discovery by maintaining that leaders of that enterprise were of Swedish descent, even if remotely. Both of the Icelandic Vinland sagas succinctly state that Erik the Red came from "Jaðri," or Jæren in southwestern Norway. Enander declared, however, that Erik was descended from a "mighty Viking" called Öxna Thore, whom, on the authority of the Swedish antiquarian Axel Emanuel Holmberg, he described as a "powerful inhabitant of Viken or Bohuslän (?)." There is some uncertainty whether the Viken region, around Oslo Fjord, included the northern part of Bohuslän, which in any case was an old Norwegian domain. But because it was Swedish since 1658, Enander obliquely suggested that the Swedes could also claim Erik the Red as their own, and hence his children, Leif, Torvald, and Freydis. Following Strinnholm, Enander described Thorfinn Karlsefne as "a rich and powerful descendant of the Swedish king Björn Jernsida."[25]

In 1893 the World's Columbian Exhibition was held in Chicago to commemorate Columbus's discovery of the new world. Enander reacted by publishing a somewhat revised and updated version of his account of the Viking discovery under the title, *Nordmännen i Amerika.* While it recapitulated, in the main, what he had written some twenty years before, he now widened the perimeters by maintaining that Greenland belonged to the new, rather than the old world.[26]

Enander was now fighting a war on two fronts. On the one hand, he sought to uphold the Scandinavians' rightful claim to the discovery as opposed to that of the Roman Catholic Italians and Spaniards.

On the other, he was determined to defend Sweden's stake in the enterprise, particularly in the light of the Norwegian Americans' ostentatious celebration of the Norse discovery at the Columbian Exhibition, climaxed by the arrival in Chicago of the Viking ship replica, *Vikingen,* from Norway in July 1893.[27]

Regarding the background of the discoverers, Enander now cast a wider net by emphasizing the partly Swedish origins of the Icelanders as a whole. Together with Norwegians, the settlers on the island had included "Swedish chieftains [*stormän*], from whom many of Iceland's most distinguished families traced their roots," even including the great Snorri Sturluson. Erik the Red "possibly descended from present-day Bohuslän." "Northmen" and "Norwegians," he reiterated, were not synonymous. He now recounted a tradition passed on by "the Icelandic chroniclers" of a region called "Great-Iceland" or "White Men's Land," believed to lie somewhere south of Chesapeake Bay, to which "an Icelandic chieftain, Are Marson, who was of *Swedish* origin," was driven by a storm already in 983![28]

Enander remained convinced that the Northmen had maintained a colony or colonies in North America at least up to the fourteenth century. He concluded in 1893 that "the Black Death, the Indians [*skrälingar*] and assimilation with the inhabitants of the land devastated the Northmen's colonies in Vinland as well as on Greenland."[29] There was obviously little that Enander could go on in attempting to describe a long-lived Scandinavian colony in North America, other than suppositions based upon certain finds that various enthusiasts, most notably the Harvard chemistry professor and inventor of Rumford baking powder, Eben Norton Horsford, vocally proclaimed to be of undoubted Viking origin.[30] Enander therefore prudently elaborated his vision of the Viking colony in a speech entitled "A Dream," given in Chicago in 1890.

Taking as his point of departure the laconic mention in the Icelandic annals of Greenland's Bishop Erik, who in 1121 set forth in search of Vinland, he described an imagined scene in which the bishop arrives at a thriving Viking town, to which the Newport Tower in Rhode Island still bore witness. Here, amid "large, red-painted timbered houses with turf roofs," Bishop Erik was welcomed by folk "clad in dress reminiscent of that which can still be seen in the parishes of tradition-rich Dalarna, in certain parts of beautiful Södermanland, in Norway's mountain-walled valleys and on Iceland, rich in sagas." The point is clear: The Northmen included all Scandinavians. Enander's "dream" ended with the arrival in America of the Vikings' descendants from Sweden during the nineteenth century, now armed with the weapons of peace, "to regain that part of Vinland the Good that once was their fathers' 'possession.'"[31]

In 1898 Olof Ohman, a Swedish immigrant farmer near Kensington, in Douglas County, Minnesota, an area of mixed Norwegian and Swedish settlement, unearthed an alleged runestone that created a veritable sensation. It bore a runic inscription, according to which the place was visited in 1362 by "8 Swedes and 22 Norwegians" on a journey of exploration "from Vinland westward." Although the find has since been repeatedly rejected as a forgery by experts in the field, it has had its dogged defenders down to the present day. Of special relevance here is that to accept the Kensington Stone as genuine—as many, not least Norwegian Americans, have done—would not only assert a medieval Nordic penetration far into the American heartland but would also expressly recognize a substantial number of Swedes, as well as Norwegians, as participants.[32]

Swedish America's historians by avocation would follow in J. A. Enander's footsteps at least to the 1920s. What is especially interesting here is how, in their writings, Enander's ideas became progressively simplified and categorical. Leaving aside untold numbers of ephemeral periodical articles and commemorative speeches, a couple of representatives of this school deserve attention. In 1891 the Swedish-born Lutheran pastor Axel M. LeVeau brought out in Oakland, California, a eulogy in Swedish verse on the great deeds of his countrymen in the new world. In a brief introduction he declared that it was now beyond dispute that "Northmen over a period of 350 years inhabited Massachusetts 500 years before Columbus made his discoveries." Enander had cautiously suggested that Erik the Red *might* have traced his ancestry back to Bohuslän; LeVeau did not hesitate to speak of "the widely traveled Erik the Red from Bohuslän." To add point to his presentation, LeVeau illustrated his piece with pictures of Eben Norton Horsford's alleged archaeological sites in Massachusetts.[33]

More influential in his time was Axel Fredenholm, who emigrated from Sweden in 1902 and who, following a career as a journalist with several Swedish-American newspapers, returned to Sweden in 1920. In 1922 he brought out a brief account of the Viking discovery that went well beyond J. A. Enander in its claims. Iceland, he maintained, was first discovered by the Swedish Viking Gardar, and only thereafter by the Norwegian Naddod. Around A.D. 1000, Fredenholm claimed, "a Swedish man by the name of Thorfinn Karlsefne came to Greenland. He was a descendant of Björn Järnsida, whom we know from Swedish history." Thorfinn took his wife Gudrid with him on his colonizing expedition to Vinland. There she gave birth to a son, Snorre—as recorded in the Vinland sagas. "Thus," Fredenholm declared triumphantly, "the first child born of white parents in that land [was] a Swedish child." By the thirteenth century, he also claimed—clearly with Enander's "Dream" of 1890 in mind—that the Nordic colony had developed into "what under the circumstances of that time was a remarkably well ordered society." He, too, took Eben Norton Horsford's alleged archaeological finds as unshakable evidence.[34] Later, in 1925–26, the history and achievements of the Swedes in America was commemorated with the publication of an impressive two-volume survey edited by the historian Karl Hildebrand and Axel Fredenholm. In it, Fredenholm wrote the chapter on the Viking discovery and attempted settlement of North America, which recapitulated for a wide readership the arguments of his slender volume from three years earlier.[35]

HOMELAND BACKGROUND TO RIVALRY OVER THE PAST

In broader perspective, Scandinavian rivalry in America over the Viking discovery reflected ideological conflict within Scandinavia itself during the nineteenth century. Pan-Scandinavianism [*Skandinavismen*] was a vital movement throughout the Nordic lands during the middle decades of the nineteenth century. It stressed the common descent, original language, pre-Christian religion, and culture of all the Scandinavian peoples. Scandinavianism nonetheless posed a dilemma for Norway, which as a result of the Napoleonic Wars had been separated from Denmark in 1814 after more than four centuries and reluctantly joined with Sweden in a dynastic union, albeit under its own constitution and government. Norwegian nationalists strove determinedly to create a unique Norwegian cultural profile, distinct from the Danish, as well as greater independence under the union with Sweden.

Seeking to make up for Norway's "lost centuries," the Norwegian national school of historians, best represented by Rudolf Keyser and Peter Andreas Munch at the Norwegian university in Oslo (Christiania), argued that the Norwegians descended from the purest branch of the Germanic race, which had migrated into Norway from the north, as opposed to the Swedes and Danes, who had entered the region from the east and south. More controversial yet was Keyser's and Munch's claim that the Old Norse [*norrøne*] language differed significantly from the Old Swedish and Danish, and that in it and its Icelandic variant was preserved the uniquely "Norse," or *Norwegian*, culture of the Viking Age.

For this view, Munch argued: "No proprietary right is more greatly respected among nations than that which each nation has to its historic memories. To deprive a nation of these is almost as unjust as to deprive it of a part of its territory. And such a despoliation is doubly unjust when it affects a nation like Norway which has so few historic memories that it cannot afford to lose any whatsoever, no matter how insignificant, to say nothing of the best it possesses."

Such exclusive claims to the Old Nordic heritage brought forth vigorous protests from Swedish and especially Danish scholars, for whom a common Scandinavian origin and culture was an article of faith.[36] Rasmus B. Anderson's version of the Viking discovery reflected the views of the Norwegian national romantic historians, whereas J. A. Enander and his followers held fast to the Scandinavianist creed.

SCANDINAVIAN AMERICANS AND THE VIKING HERITAGE TODAY

We may smile today at the naïve, or sly, ingenuity with which Swedish America's champions strove, not only to deny Columbus's title as first discoverer of America, but also to claim as large a share as they could for their own forebears in the actual first European discovery of the new world. To this day most Americans of Swedish descent remain firmly convinced that their ancestors had some part in the Viking discovery. Or at least that inasmuch as this was a *Scandinavian* enterprise, the Swedes, as Scandinavians, deserve their share of the credit. Popular reactions to any scholarly attempt to call any part of this tradition into question show how essential a part of their sense of identity this assumption has become. Of this Professor Erik Wahlgren of the University of California–Los Angeles, who was of Swedish descent, was sharply reminded when his criticism of the Kensington Stone in 1958 provoked a storm of indignation and anonymous letters angrily accusing him of being a traitor to his own people.[37]

More recent historical scholarship would seem in part to make the Swedish Americans' assumption somewhat less far-fetched than it might have seemed. It is now commonly accepted that a narrowly nationalist interpretation of Scandinavia during the pre-Viking and Viking periods is anachronistic. Theories of a separate Norwegian migration into the peninsula and the emergence of a distinct Norwegian culture and language by the Viking Age have long since been discredited. The Norwegian, Swedish, and Danish kingdoms were only beginning to coalesce around the year 1000 and their boundaries would long remain vague and shifting. Gardar was at least *one* of Iceland's discoverers around 860 and a certain number of Swedes, that is, persons from the regions inhabited by *Svear* and *Götar,* were indeed among Iceland's early settlers. The medieval *Landnámabók* does mention Öxna Thore and Björn Jernsida among, respectively, the forebears of Erik the Red and Thorfinn Karlsefne.[38] The saga literature gives abundant evidence of the mobility of individual Vikings or groups of Vikings throughout the Nordic lands and beyond, both eastward and westward.[39]

Thus, even though the first discoverers and early colonizers of North America *were* unquestionably Icelanders of predominantly Norwegian descent from Greenland, the discovery may rightly remain a source of pride to all Americans of Nordic origins.

NOTES

[1]Robert Bergersen, *Vinland Bibliography: Writings Relating to the Norse in Greenland and America* (Tromsø, 1997), v. There are also literally thousands of internet sites relating to the subject.

[2]On this point, see esp. Victor R. Greene, *American Immigrant Leaders, 1800–1910: Marginality and Identity* (Baltimore, 1987).

[3]The fullest study of New Sweden is still Amandus Johnson, *The Swedish Settlements on the Delaware, 1638–1664,* 2 vols. (Philadelphia, 1911), written in a strongly filiopietistic spirit. For historiographical background, see my "Clio

and Swedish America: Historians, Organizations, Publications," in *Perspectives on Swedish Immigration,* ed. Nils Hasselmo (Chicago and Duluth, 1978), 3–24, and "Historians of the Scandinavians in America," in *Scandinavians in America: Literary Life,* ed. J. R. Christianson (Decorah, IA, 1985), 42–58; Ulf Beijbom, "The Historiography of Swedish America," *Swedish Pioneer Historical Quarterly* 31 (1980), 257–285.

⁴Salomon Ilmonen, *Amerikan ensimäiset suomalaiset eli Delawaren siirokunnan historia* (Hancock, MI, 1916); E. A. Luohi, *The Delaware Finns or the First Permanent Settlements in Pennsylvania, Delaware, West New Jersey and the Eastern Part of Maryland* (New York, 1925); John O. Evjen, *Scandinavian Immigrants in New York, 1630–1674* (Minneapolis, 1916).

⁵O. N. Nelson, ed., *History of the Scandinavians and Successful Scandinavians in the United States,* 2 vols., 2d ed. (Minneapolis, 1904), 1:77.

⁶On early Anglo-American interest, see esp. Einar Haugen, *Voyages to Vinland: The First American Saga* (Chicago, 1941), 104–119; Lloyd Hustvedt, *Rasmus Bjørn Anderson, Pioneer Scholar* (Northfield, MN, 1966), 312–314; C. R. Lyle, II, "America Discovers Vinland: Scholarly Controversy in the Period 1830–1850," *Swedish Pioneer Historical Quarterly* 19 (1968), 174–193.

⁷J. H. Schröder, "On the Discovery of North America by the Scandinavians about the Year 986," *Analectic Magazine,* n.s., 2 (1820), 267–288; "Skandinavernas fordna upptäcktsresor till Nord Amerika," *Svea* 1 (1818), 197–226 (in German translation, *Entdeckungsreisen der Skandinavier nach Nordamerika in der Vorzeit* [Riga, 1821], 110–139). Cf. Hustvedt, *Rasmus Bjørn Anderson,* 312–313.

⁸C. C. Rafn, *Antiqvitates Americanæ sive Scriptores Septentrionales Rerum Ante-Columbianarum in America* (Copenhagen, 1837); Charles C. Rafn, *America Discovered in the Tenth Century,* trans. William Jackson (New York, 1838). Cf., e.g., C. C. Rafn, *Amerikas Opdagelse i den Tiende Aarhundrede efter de nordiske Oldskrifter* (Copenhagen, 1841). For other publications by Rafn, see Bergersen, *Vinland Bibliography.* See also Samuel Laing, ed. and trans., *The Heimskringla; or, Chronicle of the Kings of Norway,* 3 vols. (London, 1844), 3:344–361.

⁹See, for example, North Ludlow Beamish, *The Discovery of America in the Tenth Century* (London, 1841); B. F. DaCosta, *The Pre-Columbian Discovery by the Northmen* (New York, 1868). Cf. Hustvedt, *Rasmus Bjørn Anderson,* 313–314; Haugen, *Voyages to Vinland,* 108–113.

¹⁰Numerous translations of these sagas have come out in print. I rely here principally on Magnus Magnusson and Hermann Pálsson, trans. and ed., *The Vinland Sagas: The Norse Discovery of America* (Harmondsworth, 1965),

with Magnusson's useful introduction, 7–46. Cf. Gwyn Jones, *The Norse Atlantic Saga* (Oxford, 1986). Note also Einar Haugen's judicious attempt to interweave passages from the two sagas to produce a single, integrated narrative in *Voyages to Vinland.*

[11]Magnusson and Pálsson, *Vinland Sagas,* 28.

[12]Peder Claussøn Friis, *Snorre Sturlesøns Norske Chronica* (Copenhagen, 1633); J. F. Peringskiöld, *Heims Kringla, eller Snorre Sturlusons Nordländska Konunga Sagor,* 2 vols. (Stockholm, 1697); Tormodus Torfæus, *Historia Vinlandiæ antiqvæ* (Copenhagen, 1705), in English, *The History of Ancient Vinland,* trans. Charles G. Haberman (New York, 1891); P. E. Müller, *Sagabibliothek med Anmærkninger og indledende Afhandlinger,* I (Copenhagen, 1817); Schröder, "Skandinavernas fordna upptäcktsresor" and "On the Discovery of North America"; Rafn, *Antiqvitates Americanæ*; Jacob Aall, trans., *Snorre Sturlasons Norske Konge Sagaer,* 3 vols. (Christiania, 1838–39), 2:211–228.

[13]Helge Ingstad, *Vesterveg til Vinland. Opdagelsen av Norrøne boplasser i Amerika* (Oslo, 1965). For a full listing of Ingstad's numerous subsequent publications on the subject, see Bergersen, *Vinland Bibliography.*

[14]Odd S. Lovoll, *The Promise Fulfilled: A Portrait of Norwegian Americans Today* (Minneapolis, 1998), 250. It should be noted that during the jubilee in 2000 Iceland made impressive efforts in North America to make good its claim to the Viking discovery.

[15]*Life Story of Rasmus B. Anderson* (Madison, WI, 1915), 86.

[16]C. A. Clausen, trans. and ed., *A Chronicler of Immigrant Life: Svein Nilsson's Articles in* Billed-Magazin, *1868–1870* (Northfield, MN, 1982), 42–44; Hustvedt, *Rasmus Bjørn Anderson,* 314.

[17]Rasmus B. Anderson, *America Not Discovered by Columbus: An Historical Sketch of the Discovery of America by the Norsemen in the Tenth Century,* 3d ed. (Chicago, 1883), esp. 3, 11–16, 35, 85–92.

[18]Washington Irving, *History of the Life and Voyages of Christopher Columbus,* 3 vols. (New York, 1828), 1:44; Hustvedt, *Rasmus Bjørn Anderson,* 314; Aall, *Snorre Sturlasons Norske Konge Sagaer,* 2:218; Fredrika Bremer, *Strife and Peace; or, Scenes in Norway* (Boston, 1843), 34–36; Clausen, *Chronicler,* 43.

[19]Anderson, *America Not Discovered by Columbus,* 36–37, 49, 53–54, 57.

[20]See bibliography of Anderson's numerous writings and translations in Hustvedt, *Rasmus Bjørn Anderson,* 359–363. Cf. Einar Haugen and Camilla Cai, *Ole Bull: Norway's Romantic Musician and Cosmopolitan Patriot* (Madison, WI, 1993). On statues of Leif Ericson in the United States, see Lovoll, *The Promise Fulfilled,* 250–251.

[21]Beijbom, "Historiography of Swedish America," 269.

[22]*Valda skrifter af Joh. A. Enander* (Chicago, 1892), 1:43. (No second volume appeared.) There is no biography of Enander. See, however, Ernst Skarstedt, *Pennfäktare* (Stockholm, 1930), 54–55; H. Arnold Barton, *A Folk Divided: Homeland Swedes and Swedish Americans, 1840–1940* (Carbondale, IL, 1994), 64–67, 69–70, 115–116, 205, 216–217, 229; Dag Blanck, *Becoming Swedish-American: The Construction of an Ethnic Identity in the Augustana Synod, 1860–1917* (Uppsala, 1997), esp. 191–194, 203–209; Beijbom, "Historiography of Swedish America," 262–270.

[23]Joh. A. Enander, *Förenta Staternas Historia, utarbetad för den svenska befolkningen i Amerika*, 2 vols., 2d ed. (Chicago, 1882), 1:50, 52–148. Cf. Anders Magnus Strinnholm, *Svenska folkets historia*, 5 vols. (Stockholm, 1834–54), esp. 2:267–279.

[24]Enander, *Förenta Staternas Historia*, 1:50.

[25]Enander, *Förenta Staternas Historia*, 1:148, 164. Cf. Axel Emanuel Holmberg, *Skandinaviens hällristningar* (Stockholm, 1848), 148; Strinnholm, *Svenska Folkets Historia*, 2:273.

[26]Joh. A. Enander, *Nordmännen i Amerika* (Rock Island, IL, 1893), 5.

[27]See Odd S. Lovoll, *A Century of Urban Life: The Norwegians in Chicago before 1930* (Urbana, IL, 1988), 184–186. Cf. Magnus Andersen, *Vikingefærden. En illustreret beskrivelse af "Vikings" reise i 1893* (Kristiania, 1895).

[28]Enander, *Nordmännen i Amerika*, 13, 22.

[29]Enander, *Nordmännen i Amerika*, 33, 45–52.

[30]See, for example, Eben Norton Horsford, *Discovery of America by Northmen* (Boston, 1888); *The Landfall of Leif Erikson, A.D. 1000, and the Sites of His Houses* (Boston, 1892); and *Leif's House in Vinland* (Boston, 1893). Horsford erected, at his own expense, monuments at the alleged sites of Leif's winter lodgings in Cambridge, Mass., and of a place called Norumbega, which he presumed to be a Viking settlement. On Horsford, see Stephen Williams, *Fantastic Archaeology: The Wild Side of North American Prehistory* (Philadelphia, 1991), 206–210.

[31]Joh. A. Enander, "En dröm," in *Valda skrifter*, 1:13–18, 19, 25.

[32]The literature on the Kensington Stone is immense. Its authenticity is, for example, defended in Hjalmar Holand, *The Kensington Stone* (Ephraim, WI, 1931) and *Norse Discoveries and Explorations in America* (New York, 1940), and Robert Hall, *The Kensington Runestone, Authentic and Important* (Ithaca, NY, 1995). It is rejected in Erik Wahlgren, *The Kensington Stone: A Mystery Solved* (London, 1958); Theodore C. Blegen, *The Kensington Runestone: New Light on an Old Riddle* (St. Paul, 1968); and Williams, *Fantastic Archaeology*. On its present ethnic and local symbolic value, see Chris Susag and Peter Susag,

"Scandinavian Group Identity: The Kensington Runestone and the Ole Oppe Festival," *Swedish-American Historical Quarterly* 51 (2000), 30–51. During the later twentieth century amateur enthusiasts have claimed to find "cryptic" runic inscriptions as far afield as Oklahoma. See Alf Mongé and O. G. Landsverk, *Norse Medieval Cryptography in Runic Carvings* (Glendale, CA, 1967); O. G. Landsverk, *Ancient Norse Messages on American Stones* (Glendale, CA, 1969).

[33][Axel M. LeVeau], *Nord-bon i Amerika, eller Minnen från försvunna och närvarande sekler, 1000–1638–1892. Nordens brödrafolk i Sverige, Norge och Amerika tillegnade af Författaren* [Oakland, CA, 1891]. On LeVeau, see Skarstedt, *Pennfäktare,* 101.

[34]Axel Fredenholm, *Nordmannaspår i Amerika, eller Amerikas upptäckt av nordmännen år 1000* (Jönköping, 1922), esp. 4–5, 11–12. On Fredenholm, see Skarstedt, *Pennfäktare,* 62–63.

[35]Karl Hildebrand and Axel Fredenholm, eds., *Svenskarna i Amerika,* 2 vols. (Stockholm, 1925–26), 1:69–87. On this work as a whole, see Barton, *A Folk Divided,* 277–281.

[36]See esp. Julius Clausen, *Skandinavismen historisk fremstillet* (Copenhagen, 1900); Oscar J. Falnes, *National Romanticism in Norway* (New York, 1933), chs. 5–11; Ottar Dahl, *Norsk historieforskning* (Oslo, 1970), 36–80, esp. 57 (quote).

[37]Wahlgren, *The Kensington Stone;* Erik Wahlgren, "Reflections around a Rune Stone," *Swedish Pioneer Historical Quarterly* 19 (1968), 37–49.

[38]Rafn, *Antiqvitates Americanæ,* 89 n., 131 n.

[39]See Lucien Musset, *Les peuples scandinaves au moyen âge* (Paris, 1951), 65–66, regarding the inter-Scandinavian nature of the Viking enterprises in the west. Musset states that among the 1,002 settlers in Iceland listed in the medieval Icelandic *Landnámabók,* some thirty are identified as Swedes (65).

Letters as Links in the Chain of Migration from Hedalen, Norway to Dane County, Wisconsin, 1857–1890

Orm Øverland

METAPHORS NO LESS THAN NARRATIVE STRUCTURES have a powerful impact on our understanding of history.[1] Immigration history has a tradition of metaphors that have led us to see immigrants as "the wretched refuse of your teeming shore," as "pushed" by their demographic destiny and "pulled" by a "distant magnet," as hardy plants variously "uprooted" or "transplanted." They came in "streams" or, more threateningly, as a "flood," and they have been "melted" like scrap metal in order to become usefully Americanized. Readers will have recognized a phrase inscribed on the pedestal of a statue in New York harbor as well as references to titles of important books on immigration history.[2] The terms *push* and *pull* are so familiar that we may not be conscious of them as metaphors that make the migrating people passive troops in a mass movement beyond their own will and understanding. There is, however, a migration metaphor that envisions immigrants as decision makers, pathfinders, and pioneers, as captains rather than as foot soldiers of destiny: the chain. The military slant I may have given the often-used chain metaphor is misleading. Chain migration is about interacting individuals. There is no chain of command in chain migration. Chain migration is a process where individuals leave one community in their old homeland and resettle in one place in their new homeland where a new community is created—in a rural area, in a small town, or in a big-city tenement. No general has laid a strategy for their migration; no architect or social engineer has given them a blueprint. This is of course not news. Indeed, should one metaphor be selected to characterize the way in which migration has been perceived in the fine tradition of Norwegian-American studies which this volume celebrates in paying tribute to the remarkable achievement of Odd Lovoll, it must be the chain.

The chain is the central metaphor through which we have learned to understand Norwegian immigration. What better illustration of the chain of migration than the foundation story of the pathfinder Cleng Peerson, of the group who settled on his recommendation near Lake Erie in 1825, of the stragglers who joined them in the following years, and of their decision to have letters sent to Norway to inform would-be emigrants that they were collectively moving westward and that the future settlement of Norwegians would be in Illinois. The many immigrant routes in the years to come, from Norwegian valleys to places all over the Upper Midwest, were in similar manner the creations of immigrants who were decision makers, pathfinders, pioneers, and captains—pioneers and captains, we must remember, of either gender. In macro studies, the study of mass movements, we may lose sight of the individual men and women. In recent decades historians have demonstrated that micro studies, the detailed study of small groups of people, even single individuals, are necessary for an understanding of the migration process. Jon Gjerde's *From Peasants to Farmers,* showing how "a chain of settlements ranging from central Wisconsin westward manifests the importance of group settlement through most of the Balestrand emigration," has become a classic in the genre and a model for other studies.[3]

The experiences of many immigrants have been documented by themselves in the letters they sent home and that have been preserved—by chance or as valued family treasures. Immigrant letters can give us a deeper understanding of chain migration. In this article I will look closely at the correspondence of two generations of immigrants from the farm Li/Søre Li in Hedalen, a valley parish [*sogn*] in the township [*kommune*] of Sør-Aurdal in Valdres, Norway, who settled in the Blue Mounds area of southwestern Dane County, Wisconsin. They spelled their name "Lie" but (surely in order to retain the pronunciation) later changed the spelling to "Lee" in the United States. The first to leave was Torgrim Olsen Lie, the seventh of nine siblings, in 1857.

Their entire correspondence is not available to us. Typically, many letters sent to Anders Olsen Lie in Hedalen have been preserved, while his side of the correspondence must be deduced from what his brothers and sons wrote to him. From the years 1857 to 1867 we have only three letters. From 31 December 1869 to 7 April 1877 there are seven. From the time after the arrival of the first of Anders's four sons, Ole, in 1877, there are several letters every year. The Lie letters are in the large collection of America letters in the National Archives in Oslo and are being published in the multi-volume edition based on this collection, *Fra Amerika til Norge*.[4] The question of why some letters were taken care of and others were not is one of many that may be asked of this correspondence. But before such questions are addressed, it may be useful to take a look at the two contexts of the correspondence in Wisconsin and Norway.

Today forestry is the main source of income in Sør-Aurdal: 55% of the total area is productive forest while only 2% is farmland. *Li* means "mountain side" and the Li farms are on a steep incline facing south-west and overlooking the valley from an elevation of about 1,650 feet above sea level. In the nineteenth century there were not many alternatives to mixed farming for feeding a family, and since there was not enough arable land to sustain the growing population, the news of available land in the recently "discovered" Wisconsin was sure to awaken the interest of the more daring or perhaps the more desperate of the many who did not stand in line to inherit land in Hedalen. At the time of the 1865 census, that is, after emigration had begun, the Li farms sustained a total of 70 people, up from 32 in 1801. In 1900 the number was 59.[5] Emigration to the United States and migration to other parts of Norway cannot be said to have drained off the population. It provided necessary relief.

By 1857 the people at Li already knew where to go: the Blue Mounds area in the western part of Dane County in Wisconsin. Norwegian historian Terje Joranger has studied the chain migration processes from Reinli, the most northern of the three parishes of Sør-Aurdal, to the Blue Mounds area. In his account, regular emigration from Valdres to Wisconsin began in 1848 when two groups left Valdres, one going to Manitowoc County and the other to western Dane County. Joranger demonstrates that not only did people from Valdres tend to congregate in one area and people from Sør-Aurdal to stick together, but that people from the same parish tended to settle in the same township in Wisconsin. Most of those who came from Hedalen settled in the town of Mount Vernon, while those from Reinli and Bagn chose Springdale and Adams further east and south in the Blue Mounds Region.[6]

One of the earliest historians of Norwegian immigration was the amateur, Hjalmar Holand. What he lacks in sophisticated analysis he makes up for with his lively style and sense of character and narrative detail. This is his description of the Blue Mounds area in the early nineteenth century: "Among the characteristic features of the Wisconsin landscape are a few real mountains. Towering above the others is Blue Mounds, about 25 miles to the west of Madison. Its blue ridge rises to a height of almost two thousand feet above sea level and dominates the surrounding countryside. Dark valleys and narrow canyons furrow its ragged sides and fresh springs find their way through the layers of rock and become creeks that run off in all directions. From the mountain top you will have the widest and the most picturesque view in Wisconsin. On all sides you will see a fertile landscape with deep and forested valleys, sunny prairies and rolling ridges."[7]

Land became available in Wisconsin because the native population was forced out. It must be kept in mind that although there is little record of this in the letters sent to Norway, Indians were very much a presence all over Wisconsin in the decades of Norwegian settlement.[8] Nor were Norwegians usually the first Europeans to settle, even in the areas where they eventually predominated, as in the Blue Mounds region.[9] This in no way diminishes the initiative nor the achievements of the early immigrants from Valdres to western Dane County. First among them was Aslak Olsen Lie from Reinli, in 1848. Not only was he the organizer and leader of one of the first two groups of immigrants, but his many and lively letters were a key factor in the creation of a chain of migration between Valdres and the Blue Mounds region.[10] Our story, then, of the chain of migration between Hedalen and western Dane County begins with the arrival of Torgrim Olsen Lie in 1857, but it must be understood against the backdrop of the larger chain initiated by Aslak Lie and the fuller picture of early migrations in Wisconsin: one a voluntary migration to Wisconsin by European Americans and the other an involuntary migration through and out of Wisconsin by Native Americans.

When Torgrim decided to emigrate he was thirty-two years old. Eight years earlier he had married Marit Hermannsdatter from

Klemmetsrud, a farm not far from Li, and they had two children. Torgrim's older brother by twelve years, Anders, had in 1846 bought what remained of Li after his father, Ola Andersen, had sold the northern part in 1843. His twin sister, Olea, was married, as was his older sister, Berte Maria. Three other siblings had already died. There were also two younger brothers, the unmarried Ola, and Guttorm, who had married in 1856. It was clearly getting too crowded at Li, or "Søre Li," as their southern part of the farm was officially known— not necessarily too crowded for their comfort but certainly too crowded for their daily bread.

The letter Torgrim sent from the Pine Bluff post office dated 24 July 1857, and addressed to parents and siblings "on both sides," at Li and Klemmetsrud, may have been his first attempt at a written narrative, and it begins, as do so many immigrant letters, with words of apology for the quality of his writing, that he calls *nogle enfoldige linder* [*sic*], "some simpleminded lines." And yet his letter is concise and intelligent in its selection and organization of themes as well as its clarity of expression. He has mastered the basic rules of grammar and syntax of the Dano-Norwegian written language taught in school, even though the spelling of some words may be idiosyncratic. Torgrim's letter, the later letters by his brothers, and in particular those by his nephews speak of a literate family where reading, primarily religious, must have been an important activity. While intelligence was probably as widespread among rural immigrants as among the university students in Oslo (Christiania), mainly recruited from the genteel classes, the comparatively high level of literacy of these two generations of the Lie family places them in a minority among Norwegian emigrants of the time.[11]

The letter reminds us that this is not only in the period when immigrants crossed the Atlantic on sailing ships but at the time when most were landed in Quebec from Norwegian ships that returned to Europe, mainly to Liverpool, with lumber. They were at sea, he wrote, "seven weeks and six days" and then traveled on four trains for four days and nights from Quebec to Madison. While railway travel from Milwaukee to Madison had been possible since 1854, the line further west to Prairie du Chien on the Mississippi had been completed the year before.[12] When Torgrim and his family and the many other immigrants from Sør-Aurdal got off the train at the new depot in Black Earth it was more like a homecoming than a step into a strange land, or so it must have seemed to those who read the letter in Hedalen. Here were people from farms and crofts in Hedalen and neighboring parishes: Brager, Skinnrud, Berg, Nordby, Steinsrud, Hesjabakken, "and many others, and each received their own. Some went there and some there, God knows where they all went, I don't." Torgrim's family first stayed for a few days in the home of an immigrant from Hesjabakken while he contacted Aslak Lie, who "received us as his welcome guests" and asked them to stay with him until they became better acquainted with the place. Aslak himself came with a team of horses to help them with their possessions. Historical accounts do not seem to have exaggerated the hospitality of Aslak and Marit Lie. It was from their home that Torgrim wrote his letter.

But while the narrative of the reception in the new world must have been both heartening and reassuring for the readers at Li and Klemmetsrud, the stark account of the high price of migration may have made some question the advisability of the journey that preoccupied the minds of all: five children from Hedalen had perished at sea and four more had died after arrival. Nor was affliction of the body alone. Madness had struck one of the women on departure and they had had to make a cage for her and keep her in it for the entire voyage: "and it was a great punishment for us all." After arriving in the United States, a young unmarried woman had been so despondent that "she betrayed herself. She had gone to a creek at night and the next morning they found her dead in the water."

After his account of the dark side of the migration story, Torgrim evidently felt a need to be reassuring: "We were in a school house one Sunday and attended church service and we were both glad and satisfied by such a wise man." And he tells that he and his wife have found employment with different families, both with names he expects his readers to recognize. The family will be separated for a time, but many of their new neighbors are old neighbors, and we may assume that Marit will have her children with her. More important than the money they will get, they will be learning more of the ways of their new country, ways earlier immigrants have already adopted. The letter concludes with many greetings and messages to people back home from immigrants they have met or had letters from. An immigrant who had come a few years earlier intrudes and inserts a brief note to Klemmetsrud boasting of the better fare and higher pay available in America, in contrast to Torgrim's more sober tone. With all these messages and greetings the letter ends not in closure but in reaffirmation of a sense of home on two continents. It sets in motion a series of readings and visits in Hedalen that also will be affirmations of a real but intangible chain of thoughts, memories, obligations, longings for home, and expectations of departure, as well as the more tangible one of a new group of immigrants sure to depart from Hedalen for Blue Mounds in the spring.[13] Once the chain was established it also made possible an informal importation system where objects the immigrants needed but could not get (or perhaps did not know how to ask for) in Wisconsin were sent with members of the annual groups of immigrants. Thus Torgrim could report that the books and a spinning wheel that had been sent by Rønnaug at Sørlibakken, one of several crofts under Li, had arrived safely. Requests and the sending of thanks for objects of all kinds from Hedalen are frequent themes in the correspondence.

No letters between the first from Torgrim and a second from Guttorm Olsen Lie, dated Blue Mounds 25 July 1862, have been preserved. Since Torgrim was the first to go, his letter may have had a special status, and there are reasons why Guttorm's letter also would have had a special place in family history. Guttorm, born in 1835, left the year after Torgrim and two years after marrying Beret Andersdatter from Ingemoen, a croft in Begnadalen, the valley to the east and north of Hedalen, and one year after the birth of their first child, Maria. There are no letters to tell about their journey and arrival, nor of their first years of adjustment. In 1862 he seems well adjusted and settled.

There were, however, more important things on Guttorm's mind than his material well-being when he started his letter: "I must now in my great sadness and sorrow sit down to take my pen in my stiff and heavy hand to report to you some few simple and incomprehensible words in all brevity and simplicity and yet with a sincere and good intention. But my hand is too heavy and my tongue is too dumb."[14] We may wonder how his family reacted to these opening words. If they quickly looked further down the page they would have seen that Torgrim was dead, but the story of his death was so grotesque and told in such detail that a careful reading would have been necessary before they realized it in all its gruesomeness. He had been struck by lightning while driving home from town with a neighbor, a son of Aslak Lie, and they had both been found sitting on the seat of his wagon, "as if they had been alive except that their heads leaned back-wards." One of the two horses was also killed. His parents may have found some consolation in reflecting that Torgrim had neither lived nor died among strangers. They would also have been reassured by the Christian faith of their youngest son expressed with a piety sug-gesting that the family in Hedalen had been influenced by the lay ministry of Hans Nielsen Hauge some decades earlier.

Singing seems to have been as much a family tradition as reading, as we will see in the later career of Guttorm's nephew, Ole, as precen-tor and parochial school teacher. For Guttorm, hymns were evidently devotional texts in which he often found words of comfort for him-self as well as for others. It is impossible to say whether he knew these hymns by heart or found the appropriate stanzas for the occasion by leafing through a hymnbook, but in either case he expressed his rev-erence for these hymns by introducing his quotations with phrases like, "as the song master says" or "we must be patient and say as did the singer," ways of speech that suggest that he was as acquainted with the Book of Psalms as with the hymnbook. The hymns and the song traditions would be the same in Blue Mounds and in Hedalen. So, in seeking comfort for himself and his family at Søre Li, he quotes a hymn that would have been familiar from services in the medieval stave church in Hedalen and was probably also sung in his Wisconsin congregation. For as we may use the metaphor of the chain to speak of people migrating from one locality to congregate in another lo-cality in the United States, we may also use it to speak of how it was possible from a very early stage for immigrants to reestablish Ameri-can versions of the church and other institutions of their community in the old homeland. The chain mediated cultural and religious capi-tal, knowledge, and practice and provided immigrants with words for their feelings, thoughts, and situation. For Guttorm, knowledge me-diated through a diachronic chain reaching into a several-centuries-long Lutheran hymn tradition in Europe and through a spatial chain reaching across the ocean was at work as he sat in Blue Mounds writ-ing to parents, sisters, and brothers in Hedalen about one brother dead and buried in Wisconsin while another, Ole, was already getting ready to make the journey there from Hedalen.[15]

As if in need of distraction from his overwhelming emotions, Guttorm abruptly changes his style and gives practical information, as requested in a letter from home, about how mills function and are run "here in America." Some words about an expected poor wheat harvest lead him to reflections on the terrible Civil War as well as on the new Homestead Act, adding that the available government land "is far from here so it will cost a lot to get to where land is to be found." He concludes with congratulations to his newly married brother, Ole, advice on emigration ("I believe it would be easier for you to feed a family here than in Norway"), and some words of devotion as expressed in yet another hymn.

Ole, born in 1828, took his advice. Soon after his arrival in Primrose in 1865 or 1866, he wrote to his brother Anders, the farmer of Søre Li, that he had bought a team of oxen and was plowing with them every day. His main reason for writing, however, seems to be unfinished business in Hedalen. Just what this may have been is, as is so often the case, difficult to see from the letter since he wrote to someone who was fully informed.[16] Immigration did not necessarily mean turning your back on your affairs in the old country. Ole's good name in Hedalen was as important to him as his good name in Dane County. The chain, to remain in our chosen metaphor, did not only lead from Hedalen to Blue Mounds but was a bond between the two communities.

When Guttorm had recommended emigration for Ole, he evidently knew that Ole had more or less decided to go. When Ole wrote to his brother about emigration his tone was very different, just as Anders' situation was different from that of his landless brothers. Ole gave the standard advice found in most immigrant letters from the 1830s and to the end of the century: only those who were sure that they wanted to go should do so and, "I would not advise anyone one way or the other since I do not wish to be held responsible. But for my own part I think well of my situation here and I believe most here do the same. But there are some contrary ones who cannot stand America at all. So you will have to do as you like, but it would be nice to see you and your family here."

The next letter is from both brothers and dated Primrose, 29 May 1867, to their parents and siblings. Guttorm is first and his big news is that Olaug, their sister Olea's daughter, has arrived.[17] As in almost every immigrant letter during these early decades, Guttorm presents information on their enduring good health as "good news," which it of course was in a situation where the health of both parents was essential to the survival of the family. He also tells that he has bought land: 90 acres for $1,100—$300 down and $100 a year at 7% interest. Many letters have been lost, and it is only now that we get to know that Guttorm was wounded as a soldier in the Civil War and received a pension of $8 a month. After some remarks on the wet and cold weather that spells a bad year for barley and wheat, and some comforting words to his mother, he again expresses his faith by quoting a hymn and adding some formal but emotionally laden words of blessing: "May the grace and peace of our Father through Jesus Christ our savior, teacher, and king and through the outpouring of the Holy Ghost be with you brothers and sisters and mother, as wished by me your brother and son." For Guttorm it was as natural to write about the state of his soul as about his improving material situation.

Ole writes in a more practical and less emotional manner about theology and church organization rather than about faith. He explains that they have the same church with the same Lutheran religion as well as the same kind of Norwegian ambulatory school as in Hedalen. Indeed, the teacher is from Hedalen and their minister, John N. Fjeld, is also from Valdres. Not only are the institutions, their language, and their doctrine the same at both ends of the chain but so, too, is the local origin of the individuals who serve them. Ole, however, has other things on his mind that come before his information on church and schools: his niece's safe arrival and his satisfaction with the accounts and the money Anders has sent him. Now that he has received the money owed him in Hedalen, he is concerned that his brother has not taken any of it for himself as compensation for his trouble. As observed earlier, the chain facilitated exchanges of a spiritual and intellectual as well as a purely material nature: he sends thanks for a Bible but is unhappy that he still has not received a tool and a specially designed gun that he has requested in an earlier letter.

Olaug was the first emigrant of the second generation. She was joined by her younger half brothers, Hallstein Hallsteinsen in 1871 and Ole Hallsteinsen by 1874. More links in the family chain of migration may be a reason why more letters from after 1869 were preserved at Li. Another may be that Anders himself seems to have been thinking seriously about emigration. Although the concern with helping Olea's parents and younger half brothers to emigrate and the discussions about the advisability of emigration make for new themes in

the correspondence, Ole and Guttorm write much in the same manner and follow the patterns established in their earlier letters.

The opening sentences of Guttorm's new-year letter are formulaic. He excuses his poor but sincere writing, expresses gratitude for
good health, and complains that he has nothing to write about "that
can be of any interest to you." The harvest has been middling except
for the barley, oats, and potatoes and he gives precise measures for
the various crops on his farm, information about his livestock, and
an account of his income that concludes, "And I have consequently
found it rather difficult to pay my debts this year and pay the money
I owed as of last fall." The reason why he writes at such length about
his financial situation may be that he has had a letter from the Sør-
Aurdal poor relief commission about his sister Olea and her family.
Evidently, he has been asked to pay for their fare to the United
States.[18] This is interesting documentation of public exploitation of
the chain of migration: local authorities trying to get rid of poor
people who were a burden on their budget with the help of family in
the United States. Apparently they have offered to pay expenses to
the quay in Oslo (Christiania) and expect Guttorm to take responsibility from there. Although Guttorm asks how many family members would be included so he can figure out how much it will cost, he
makes clear that this is only *for more skyld,* literally "for fun," since he
does not have the necessary cash: "But the way the times are and
since the poor relief commission will not do more, it is impossible
even though we would very much like the whole family to come."

There were other family bonds than that to Li. Olaug had worked
for another farmer near Blue Mounds, Harald Haraldsen Stugarden,
whose mother was Olaug's father's oldest sister, and Guttorm has
heard that he was willing to pay for a ticket for Olaug's half brother,
Hallstein.[19] Olaug has been ill, but now she is well and recently married to Erik Eriksen, a shoemaker from Oslo (Christiania). They live
in Mount Vernon, only two miles from Guttorm's farm: "And I believe that he has a good income and they live well, and I also believe
that Olaug was lucky in getting a man with a trade since she doesn't
have a strong constitution. If she had married a farmer she would
have had both harder and heavier work, but now she doesn't have to
do anything more than housekeeping." Guttorm concludes his letter
in a manner we have come to expect: he brings greetings from his

brother Ole and neighbors who were also neighbors in Hedalen (including the minister John Fjeld), he begs forgiveness for his poor abilities as a writer, and he uses the words of a hymn to express his Christian faith and to comfort his aging mother.

A few days later, 10 January 1870, Guttorm wrote again, partly prompted by a letter he had just received from Hedalen, but mainly, it seems, to report that Olaug has repaid him in full for her tickets to Wisconsin. His short letter is a reminder that there was quite literal transplanting involved in the migrations from Europe. He is unhappy with the quality of oats in Wisconsin and asks for some seed-quality oats from Hedalen as well as some "gray peas." In a brief note sent in the same envelope, his daughter Maria, who emigrated as an infant, writes to her grandmother. She is attending the "English school" but "also has to study my Norwegian textbooks," and her letter is evidence that she indeed has a good command of written Norwegian. In a letter Ole wrote later that year on 29 September, he reports that his daughter is learning to read in the "Norwegian school" and that she will be attending the "English school" in the winter season. The first "American" generation appears to be bilingual and also appears to be very conscious of their Hedalen family: almost every year some of them were becoming part of their Wisconsin family.

Ole also explains that times are difficult and that he may not be able to provide the cash for tickets for his sister's sons. But he promises to do what he can. While he is convinced that his impoverished nephews would benefit from emigration, he is clearly in doubt about his brother, Anders, who has asked for advice. In the September 1870 letter he embellishes the advice he had given four years earlier: it will have to be your decision. It may be easier to get along and get ahead in Wisconsin, but he reminds his brother that immigration is no solution to life's difficulties: "trials and troubles of this world meet us here as well as there." As so many before and after him, he warns his brother that for his own sake it would probably be better to stay but that if he is more concerned with the future of his children, they should all come. But happiness does not always come with success: "If I knew that you would be happy, then I believe that it would be better for you here since I know you would have a better livelihood. But if you should not be happy and satisfied with conditions here, then it would be a difficult life even if you had a good living. So I cannot advise you one way or the other." Four years later Anders is still pondering emigration and now Guttorm gives the same advice as Ole: they will have a better income in Wisconsin, but there is no way of knowing whether they will be happy here. So he, too, explains that he cannot advise him one way or the other and that emigration must be his own decision. By this time two of Olea's sons are with them and they are getting on well.[20]

In spite of droughts or too much rain, winters too cold and summers too hot, and pests like the chinch bug, progress is steady. In 1871 Ole reports that he no longer uses oxen but has bought a team of good horses and new machinery. Expenses are high, but he gets much more work done. Prosperity has also come to Marit, Torgrim's widow, who has married a widower with two children and a quarter section of land.[21] Readers of these letters in Hedalen would have had a fairly balanced view of life in the new world: hard work was rewarded, farming had no guarantees, and emigration was not an escape from life's troubles. On 10 January 1876, Ole wrote that Harald Stugarden, Olaug's uncle who had provided money for her half brother Hallstein's ticket, had committed suicide in a mental hospital. By this time it seems that Anders had definitely decided against emigration, while his sons had plans of their own.

Dane County, however, was not the obvious destination for land-hungry immigrants in the late 1870s. As early as 1862, writing about the new Homestead Act, Guttorm had explained that there was no public land to be had where he lived. In 1874, Ole C. Johnson, a Norwegian immigrant and Civil War veteran who had been appointed Wisconsin's Commissioner of Immigration in 1871, published a little guidebook in Bergen, Norway: *Wisconsin. Et Hjem for Udvandrere* [*Wisconsin: A Home for Emigrants*] with the subtitle, "A Description of This State's Climate, Soil, Public Institutions and Progress etc." He explained that those who sought employment and who did not wish to go to the forested areas would "more easily find work in the older, settled counties," but he realized that most emigrants from Norway wanted land of their own. In his description of the possibilities offered by many of Wisconsin's counties there is no mention of Dane County. The reason for this omission is given in the sentence that introduces his survey: "In the following I will mainly describe those counties where it is easy to acquire land, where there is ample employment, and where the newcomer for these reasons may quickly create his own home."[22] Chain migration, the coming to kith and kin, is the concept that best explains why emigrants from Hedalen continued to come to Dane County in the 1870s and 1880s.

When Ole, the oldest of Anders' four sons, came to Mount Vernon in 1877 with his wife, Siri, and their infant son, he was expected. He had initially thought of going through Canada, as had his uncles, but changed his mind and landed at Castle Garden in New York on 8 July, having left Oslo 22 June, and traveled via Christiansand, Hull, Liverpool, and Queenstown. It was a tough and complicated journey by our standards, but both comfortable and fast compared to the many weeks his uncles and their families had spent on sailing ships across the North Sea and the Atlantic. Times had changed in other respects as well. In Dane County, Ole Andersen came to a settled and well-organized society far removed from the frontier conditions that his uncles, especially Torgrim and Guttorm, had had to confront. There had been changes in Hedalen as well: the letter Ole wrote 15 July demonstrates a greatly improved educational system. Not only is his letter of 2,037 words much longer than any of his uncles' but it is carefully composed, with lively narrative details, descriptions of land and sea, and with relatively correct spelling and syntax. He writes as one who enjoys it and who has had some practice.[23]

In 1857 his uncle Torgrim had described his arrival in Black Earth as a homecoming, and for Ole, twenty years later, it was even more so. Their train had come to Madison at three in the morning, but even at this hour they had soon met someone from Norway who could show them the way to "the Norwegian Hotel," where they also found someone who could drive them and their baggage to Mount Vernon, where they were welcomed by his cousin Olaug and her growing family: "and she lived very nicely and well. I had not suspected that her conditions were so wonderful." Olaug and her shoemaker husband were surely not living in a mansion, but Ole's implicit comparison is with her impoverished parents in Hedalen. They stayed with Olaug until the next day, Friday, when her half brother Hallstein followed them to Guttorm where they helped with the haying on Saturday and went to church with the Valdres pastor, John Fjeld, on Sunday, where they met more family and former neighbors—much as they would have done after a Sunday service in the stave church in Hedalen. Ole evidently began writing his letter Sunday evening, but by the time he completed it he could also describe how his uncle had brought them all their baggage, the gifts they had received from the once so impoverished Olaug and her brother Ole, and his meeting with the new husband of Marit Klemmetsrud, his uncle Torgrim's widow. There is nothing very foreign about any of this! Some months later, on 7 December, he writes of the confirmation of two of his nieces and brings news, some good, some bad, of people from Hedalen.[24] The geographical distance, too, between Wisconsin and Hedalen had been miraculously diminished since the emigration of his uncles: Ole concludes wishing his parents a merry Christmas, knowing that his letter will be with them in time to make his wish meaningful.

Ole's letters in the following years help us to understand why immigrants chose to go to a settled area such as Dane County, where land had become expensive, rather than further west where cheap land was available. For he had come to a ready-made network of family and old neighbors. This is evident when he writes on 12 January 1878 of the recent death of his little son in a whooping-cough epidemic. They had only been a few months in Mount Vernon, and yet "many people followed him to his grave and were willing to give him this last assistance. There were five teams and I cannot remember how many people." From the start he reports of a life in material comfort. To begin with he and his family had bed as well as board with his uncle Guttorm, who expected no compensation except the assistance found natural by all. The first step to independence is reported 7 April 1878, when they have begun preparing their own food. By the end of the year they were able to live by themselves, renting a farm with a house originally built by the first American from Li, Torgrim. But it is evident that Ole's heart was not in farming and he made no attempt to run the farm efficiently or to buy it. For some years he reports no more than a single cow, one or two pigs, and some chickens. There was no shortage of work in the neighborhood of Mount Vernon, Primrose, and Springdale, nor was there lack of succor for the soul. After moving to Springdale he explains that they can choose between three churches, all belonging to the Norwegian Synod, and all with excellent pastors. Carpentry is one steady source of income, but at harvest time it seems that farmers offer the best pay. For a time he is an entrepreneur, a share-owner in a grubber with his brother-in-law, Iver, who lives with them, and his cousin, Ole Børtnes. In the same letter in which he reports on this business, he also reveals that he has other aspirations. He has joined a music school in Springdale run by the precentor of the local congregation. Ole evidently had some training in music. When his brother Mikkel arrived in 1881, he found that Ole had become precentor in the Springdale congregation and was being asked to take over the position as teacher as well: "For you and for us all it was once an impossible notion that Ole should be honored with such an office, but he now stands as precentor for the Springdale congregation, called to his office by the congregation. For here it is not as in Norway, that the higher authorities appoint officers for the people. Here the people elect their officers themselves," Mikkel explained on 30 November 1881. There was certainly not much money to be gotten from either of these positions of trust, but Ole had in a short time achieved both recognition and status in his community.

Meanwhile his three younger brothers in Hedalen were thinking of emigration. Iver, the youngest, was the first to go, in 1880, and Mikkel followed the next year. Anders eventually decided to stay, and as he took responsibility for the family farm he also took responsibility for the family correspondence. The family was widespread yet close-knit. Not only did letters come to Li from family on their mother's side in Rothsay, Minnesota, but the letters from Dane County tell of a lively correspondence with family in the west as well as in Hedalen. Those from Rothsay speak of similar networks of family and former neighbors but they will not be part of this story.[25]

The question of emigration is a frequent theme in Ole's correspondence, since his brothers as well as his aunt Olea and her family were all pondering their decision. Ole's cautious advice is the same as that given by his uncles to the previous generation: do not come if you are in doubt; the decision must be yours and not my responsibility; there is no way of predicting whether you will feel at home here and those who don't are miserable regardless of their material well-being; but, if you are willing to work you will do better here than in Hedalen. For those with a larger immediate family in the Blue Mounds area than in Hedalen, the decision may not have been difficult. Only one of Anders Olsen Lie's sons, Anders Andersen Lie, stayed in Hedalen and the last to leave of Olea's sons took their parents with them, travelling with the same group as Mikkel Andersen Lie in 1881. With Olea, all surviving siblings of the first of our two generations, except the one who became the farmer of Søre Li, had come to Dane County. The journey of Mikkel and Olea and their families concludes the story of emigration from Søre Li. By the time the third Anders to be farmer of Søre Li, born in 1892, was an adult, the period of mass emigration from Norway had come to a close.

The correspondence in the following two decades, then, is not mainly about chain migration but about the effect and consequences of this kind of migration. The reception in Mount Vernon of Iver Andersen Lie, who traveled alone and without advance notice in 1880, was very much like that experienced by his brother Ole some years earlier. In Madison he discovered two "Norwegian" hotels and from there on he was among friends and family, some of whom, such as Marit Klemmetsrud, he had never met before. The next year Mikkel had very much the same experience.[26] Their responses to the situation they confronted, however, were quite different.

Iver wrote to his brother Anders 28 February 1881, demonstrating a realistic attitude to immigration: "Luckily, I was not so thoughtless as to believe that America was a paradise without any adversity and worries to offer its inhabitants. For had I had any such ideas I would long since have cursed both myself and America. But just as I was sure that I would find a more prosperous and free country, I was also sure that I would encounter the same difficulties here that are to be found the world over." A foreign language was one such difficulty, but he worked at it deliberately, both by attending school and working for "an American" "until I either will learn their language or conclude that it is impossible." In Mount Vernon there was employment and a safe home with brother Ole as well as with his uncles. In April 1882, a few months after his brother Mikkel had arrived, however, Iver traveled west, visiting relatives and friends on his way to the Mayfield and Portland area of Traill County on the North Dakota side of the Red River. Back in Dane County, he wrote on 4 December 1883: "I went west with the intention of finding free land because I thought it would be easier to get ahead that way than by settling here in the old settlements where no land is to be had except at a high price." His success was modest; he had begun making improvements on a small piece of land but had not stayed on it long enough to acquire a lease. He expected to return in the spring, but was pessimistic of being able to expand his limited holding. For several years he lived the life of a bachelor farmer in Traill County on land owned by another immigrant from Hedalen, much of the time in partnership with his cousin, Erik Børtnes. Here, too, he frequently visited and was visited by friends and family from Hedalen. We leave Iver in 1890, when he wrote on 2 February that he had bought 160 acres, a quarter section of unbroken land, for $1,500 in Traill County. His letter details what he had paid for horses and machinery as well as for a furnished home, and reports on his progress in cultivating his land. He had already harvested fifty-five acres and expected to have it all plowed by the next summer. He was $1,750 in debt, gophers were a problem, the times were not good, and many were on relief, but Iver was optimistic. By 1891, according to a letter from his brother Mikkel in Mount Vernon, he was a bachelor no more.

Mikkel and his rapidly growing family decided to stay within the Hedalen community in Springdale and Mount Vernon. His income was steady and quite satisfactory, he wrote on 23 July 1882. About nine months after his arrival in late November, he had put aside $100. By 12 February 1883, he was working on his own land! How could it apparently be easier to acquire a farm in Dane County than in Traill County? It could, of course, mainly be a difference in the personalities of the two brothers, Mikkel having greater ambitions and being more goal-directed. But this explanation would disregard one of the main reasons for chain migration, why immigrants in such large numbers preferred to come to kith and kin. For Mikkel was not alone in buying his farm. Ole was his partner and since their agreement was that Mikkel should do the farming while they both would share evenly in the crop, we may assume that the major investment in land, animals, and machinery was done by the older brother who had been there since 1877. We may also assume that the precentor and teacher of the parochial school of the Norwegian Synod congregation in Springdale would have had a good line of credit in his community. As Ole wrote on 6 February 1885, his debt was considerable and the income not sufficient to pay much on it. For some years the two brothers and their families lived on and off the same land, a kind of deal not available to Iver further west and one, moreover, that had a harmonious relationship between the two brothers as a precondition.[27] Just how long this partnership lasted is not clear from the preserved letters, but by the end of the decade Mikkel was on his own and fully responsible not only for his farm but for the debts on it as well. As for Ole, he was firmly established as carpenter and teacher, the first profession no doubt providing a better income for his family than the other.

The successes, such as they were, of the members of the family from Søre Li in the Blue Mounds area of Dane County depended on a community created by chain migration. Even the first to come, Torgrim in 1857, was not on his own but was embraced on arrival by former neighbors from Hedalen and, above all, by the pioneer of emigration from Sør-Aurdal, Aslak Olsen Lie. Perhaps the greatest success story is that of Olea, her many sons, and her daughter Olaug. In 1869 the family was a burden on the poor relief commission of Sør-Aurdal. When Mikkel came to Mount Vernon in 1882, he was impressed by the fine home of his cousin Olaug: "[S]he had everything so fine and beautiful that I had never thought she would have a home so refined and handsome in all things. They have a two-storied house, white-painted on the outside and on the inside decorated with the most beautiful wallpaper. They have all they need of food and clothes and for all this they do not owe a cent," he wrote on 18 March. By the end of the decade, several of Olaug's brothers owned farms. Their mother Olea then lived with Ole on his Mount Vernon farm and she was her son's housekeeper until he married an immigrant from Stavanger in December 1888.[28]

When we leave the Lies and the Børtneses in and around Mount Vernon in 1890, they are firmly established in an American community to which they have made important contributions. One story to be read in their letters is that of their gradual loss of interest in life in Hedalen outside of the immediate family, and their increasing preoccupation with their American lives. While they occasionally thought about and wrote to their Norwegian parents and their remaining Norwegian brother, they were always involved in the lives of their American children who knew Hedalen only through the anecdotes told by parents and relatives, most of whom were in the United States.

The America letters preserved by the generations who remained on Søre Li are a memorial to the achievements of the family's emigrants. Anyone today taking time to read their letters, however, will see that the American Lies did not write primarily to give information about the improving material aspects of their American lives.

When Guttorm O. Lie and, later, Mikkel A. Lie wrote to their former home, the condition of their souls and the souls of their family at Søre Li weighed more heavily on their minds than the condition of their farms. Mikkel's letters have far more references to the Bible than to newspapers, and his children are more important characters in his narrative than is any local or national public figure. All these letters have the main function of keeping alive the family bonds between Dane County and Hedalen. When Anders A. Lie, the farmer of Søre Li, lost his wife as she gave birth to their only daughter in 1884, when this daughter died two years later, and when his mother, Kari Mikkelsdatter, also died in 1886, the many letters from his three brothers speak of love, sharing, and support, a sense of family not disrupted by migration. Similarly, the letters from Dane County bring their messages of sorrow, not only when the older generation passes—Guttorm in 1880 and Hallstein Hallsteinsen Børtnes shortly after his arrival in 1882—but when young children in all these families end their all too short lives. The letters are human documents.[29] They form a running narrative with narrators who know nothing of what the next letter will reveal and who certainly have no thought of what a historian may make or wish to make of their narratives more than a hundred years later.[30]

From one point of view, then, these letters are of a somewhat limited use to the historian. There is so much that they cannot tell us and that can only be known through the use of quite different methods and quite different sources. That only one in each of the two generations followed in this article stayed in Hedalen is one of the more obvious pieces of information revealed by these letters, but that information is available from other sources and, moreover, says nothing about the effect of mass migration on the parish as a whole. At the other end of the chain, in Dane County, the letters alone are not a reliable source for the lives of immigrants in the second half of the nineteenth century. Census reports, records of land ownership, of births and deaths and of taxes, church records, churchyards, local newspapers—all and more must be studied for anything approximating a full picture. If the letters are left out, however, something essential will be missing from the story of immigration. What will be left out is all that was most important for the people involved: the way in which they themselves experienced the momentous act of migration.

NOTES

[1]I am grateful to Arve Brunvoll for help in identifying hymns quoted in some letters.

[2]I am not suggesting that these fine historians did not have an awareness of the individual immigrant as decision maker. My concern is with how metaphors may shape our perception and our understanding. Philip Taylor stresses the active role of the emigrant in *The Distant Magnet: European Emigration to the U.S.A.* (New York, 1971). One of his chapters is aptly titled, "Calculations and Decisions."

[3]Rudolph J. Vecoli, "From *The Uprooted* to *The Transplanted*: The Writing of American Immigration History, 1951–1989," in *From "Melting Pot" to Multiculturalism: The Evolution of Ethnic Relations in the United States and Canada,* ed. Valeria Gennaro Lerda (Rome, 1990), 25–53, is an excellent critical review of immigration history after Oscar Handlin's *The Uprooted* (1951). Jon Gjerde, *From Peasants to Farmers: The Migration from Balestrand, Norway, to the Upper Middle West* (Cambridge, England, 1985), 144. Gjerde also dicusses chain migration in *The Minds of the West: Ethnocultural Evolution in the Rural Middle West, 1830–1917* (Chapel Hill, NC, 1997), 79–131. Rudolph J. Vecoli, "The Formation of Chicago's 'Little Italies,'" *Journal of American Ethnic History* 2 (Spring 1983), is a fascinating study of chain migration to an urban area.

[4]Orm Øverland and Steinar Kjærheim, *Fra Amerika til Norge I: Norske utvandrerbrev 1838–1857* (Oslo, 1992); *Fra Amerika til Norge II: Norske utvandrerbrev 1858–1868* (Oslo, 1992); *Fra Amerika til Norge III: Norske utvandrerbrev 1869–1874* (Oslo, 1993). Four more volumes for the period up to the First World War are under preparation. Volume IV will be published in 2002. Letters included in the first three volumes will be referred to by volume and number. Letters after 1874 will be referred to by date alone. Translations are mine.

[5]Information on Sør-Aurdal is from *Aschehoug og Gyldendals Store norske leksikon* (Oslo, 1998). Information on the farms and families of Hedalen in this article is from Jon Ola Gjermundsen, *Gard og bygd i Sør-Aurdal. Bind D Hedalen og Vassfaret* (Sør-Aurdal, 1992).

[6]Terje Mikael Hasle Joranger, "Bosetningsdynamikken blant Valdris innvandrere i den øvre delen av Midt-Vesten," in *Migrasjon og tilpassing. Tid og Tanke* 3, ed. Odd S. Lovoll (1998), 111–124, and "Emigration From Reinli, Valdres, to the Upper Midwest: A Comparative Study," *Norwegian American Studies* 35 (2000), 153–196. Joranger identifies the main Hedalen settlement as Vermont (172), which surely is a slip for the intended Mount Vernon.

[7]Hjalmar Rued Holand, *De norske settlementers historie: En oversigt over den norske innvandring til og bebyggelse af Amerikas nordvesten fra Amerikas opdagelse til indianerkrigen i nordvesten* (Ephraim, WI, 1908), 184. My translation.

[8]Betty A. Bergland, "Norwegian Immigrants and 'Indianerne' in the Landtaking, 1838–1862," *Norwegian-American Studies* 35 (2000) 319–350, is the first of a projected series of studies of the relations between Norwegian immigrants and Native Americans. That the decimation and removal of the native population is a necessary part of the story of settlement is made clear in a recent account of the multi-ethnic early history of Wisconsin: Mark Wyman, *The Wisconsin Frontier* (Bloomington and Indianapolis, IN, 1998).

[9]Joranger points out that the "majority of earlier settlers" were Yankees from states further east and that there was also a substantial number of Germans there when Norwegians began to arrive. By 1880, however, 45% of the population of the town of Springdale was Norwegian. Joranger, "Emigration from Reinli," 175.

[10]Holand, *De norske*, 187. Aslak Lie, who was fifty when he arrived in Dane county, was a remarkable character and his stature and importance as leader and as artist are only gradually becoming known. An important first study of his life and work is Reidar Bakken, *Snikkaren Aslak Olsen Lie: Bygdekunstnar i Valdres og Wisconsin, 1798–1886* (Oslo, 2000). The book has an English summary and illustrations have texts in English and Norwegian.

[11]*Fra Amerika til Norge I*, No. 142. The letters that have come down to us are hardly representative of the mass of Norwegian emigrants. I would assume that a majority of those who emigrated did not write much or any at all. A close family cohesion and tradition and an interest in the written word were factors that would influence the frequency of letters. The same factors would also be decisive for the preservation of the letters through several generations in Norway. Orm Øverland, "Learning to Read Immigrant Letters: Reflections towards a Textual Theory," *Norwegian-American Essays 1996*, ed. Øyvind T. Gulliksen et al. (Oslo, 1996), 221–222.

[12]Wyman, *Wisconsin Frontier*, 182.

[13]It was quite common for several to join in writing one letter as well as to intend one letter for several recipients. International letters at this time were very expensive. In the barter economy still predominant in rural Norway, cash for postage would be a real sacrifice. In Wisconsin, Torgrim, who expected to get $17 a month in his first job, would have to work a day or so for the money he needed to pay for his first letter. The situation improved with the first international postal conference in 1863, but not until 1875, with the Universal Postal Union, did the system of international mail begin to resemble the well-run operation that we take for granted.

[14]*Fra Amerika til Norge II,* No. 89.

[15]References to hymns are frequent in immigrant letters. One of the two hymns Guttorm quotes from in this letter is a translation of a hymn by Countess Ämilie Juliane of Schwarzburg-Rudolfstadt (d. 1706) and first mediated to Norway from the German lands. Cherished by emigrants from Norway in translation, "Hvo ved, hvor nær mig er min ende," it appeared as #462 in the first of many hymnbooks compiled by Norwegian-Americans, *Psalmebog udgiven af Synoden for den norsk evangelisk lutherske kirke i Amerika* (Decorah, IA, 1874). A classic expression of the precarious, transitory character of human life, and so particularly suited to emigrants, this hymn was passed by the chain of immigrants and their descendants into the store of hymnody from Europe eventually translated into English. As "Who Knows How Near My Life's Expended," it was #579 in *The Lutheran Hymnary* (Minneapolis, 1912), a hymnbook published by the three Norwegian-American Lutheran bodies ready to unite as the Norwegian Lutheran Church of America in 1917. Guttorm's phrase about "the singer" is quoted from another letter, published in the same volume: *Fra Amerika til Norge II,* No. 152 (29 May 1867).

[16]*Fra Amerika til Norge II,* No. 129. The letter is undated but seems to have been written the spring or summer after his arrival. Gjermundsen cannot give a year for his emigration but notes that the last year his presence in Hedalen can be documented is 1865. Ole had married Gunhild Haraldsdatter from the farm Nørdre Illjanstadhaugen in 1862. She was then forty-two and gave birth to their daughter, Maria, later the same year. One of those Ole claims owe him money seems to have been his brother-in-law. In her greetings to her mother at the end of the letter, Maria resents that her youngest sister, Anne, apparently hasn't paid them for a ram and seems to suspect that she and her husband, Ole Olsen, are not taking proper care of her. Anne and Ole and their seven children emigrated in 1878.

[17]*Fra Amerika til Norge II,* No. 152. Olaug's father was Olea's first husband, Jakob Olsen Stugarden. Widowed, Olea married Hallstein Hallsteinsen and they lived on the small croft Børtnes from 1859 to 1869. Conditions there were so poor that no one tried to make a living there after they had left.

[18]*Fra Amerika til Norge III,* No. 33.

[19]Stugarden was also a farm with a high emigration rate. Only Harald's oldest brother stayed on the farm. The five other siblings all emigrated. Such close bonds to the United States may be part of the explanation why the farmer of Stugarden two generations later was the first in Hedalen to have a bicycle, a car, and a fully equipped tractor, a Fordson. The chain of migration had effects at both ends.

[20]5 November 1874. *Fra Amerika til Norge III,* No. 199.

[21]14 September 1871. *Fra Amerika til Norge III,* No. 99.

[22]Ole C. Johnson, *Wisconsin. Et hjem for udvandrere: en beskrivelse af denne stats klimat, jordbund, offentlige indretninger og frembringelser m. M.* (Bergen, 1874), 54.

[23]His brothers, when they begin to write, demonstrate the same skills and the same obvious pleasure in writing. Iver's account of his journey, dated 11 July 1880, and Mikkel's of his, dated 30 November 1881, are among the more detailed and liveliest descriptions of the emigrant journey from Norway to the Midwest available to us from this period.

[24]Although letters are preserved with greater frequency, we still have a selection only. This and other letters make references to letters that are not in the collection.

[25]Kari Mikkelsdatter was the mother of Ole, Mikkel, Anders, and Iver Lie. Her brother was Mikkel Mikkelsen Sørli, married to Ragnhild Olsdatter. Their eldest daughter, Olaug, emigrated around 1870; their son, Mikkel, in 1875; and the youngest, Kari, followed with her widowed mother in 1876. They all went to Rothsay in Wilkins County, Minnesota, where they found many other settlers from Hedalen and Valdres as well as from other parts of Norway. Their letters, too, speak of a sense of home and community in their chosen area.

[26]Iver's letter is dated 11 July 1880 and Mikkel's 30 November 1881. Mikkel had married Ingrid Andersdatter the same year he emigrated, and had they waited a week or two longer she would have received a letter (dated November 5) from her sister in Rochester, Minnesota, reporting on conditions there and explaining that they would soon probably want to go further west.

[27]One reason for this arrangement and also one for Mikkel accepting it without complaint may be Ole's declining strength, which made him unfit for heavy work, something referred to in the letters by all three brothers in these years, for instance by Ole on 2 February 1885: "[M]y health is not longer so good. But I am glad and thank God that I am as I am, for I am not so weak that I cannot work, if only the work is not heavy or hard. Moreover, I am better now than I was last year so if I may keep the health I now have, I would be happy and satisfied." Apparently he suffered from asthma.

[28]Ole Børtnes to Anders A. Lie, 2 January 1889.

[29]Also in the sense that they reveal frailty as well as nobility. All family members are not given a positive characterization and there are hints of skeletons hidden in some closets.

[30]The point that the narrators in the stories contained in such series of letters have no knowledge of the direction of their narrative has been made by Øyvind T. Gulliksen. See "Interdisciplinary Approaches in American Immigration Studies: Possibilities and Pitfalls," in the present volume.

America as Symbol in the Plays of Marcus Thrane

Terje I. Leiren

AS A POLITICAL RADICAL in Norway in the middle of the nineteenth
century, Marcus Thrane was an enthusiastic promoter of America as
the symbol of freedom for Europe's oppressed. As editor of *Arbeiderforeningernes Blad* [*Labor Associations' Newspaper*] he often recommended emigration for Norwegians who felt politically and economi-
cally trapped. America was presented as a shining example in stark
contrast to dull, lusterless, and oppressive life in Norway.[1] Eventually
taking his own advice and emigrating to the United States in 1863,
Thrane worked to project a vision of a new Norwegian American who,
by choosing to emigrate, had taken the first steps toward casting off
the cultural and class burdens of the old country. America, Thrane believed, had the power to restore and renew the sons and daughters of
Europe. Articulated in speeches and in two Norwegian-language newspapers he established in Chicago, Thrane's views of the subtle and
somewhat subversive influence of America are best presented, however, in plays written and directed between 1866 and 1880.[2] Written in
Norwegian and performed in Chicago, Thrane's plays presented his
political and cultural views, but in subtle and interesting ways they also
reflected his belief in America as a symbol of freedom and as a catalyst
in the reshaping of the lives of Norwegian immigrants. This essay will
examine aspects of Marcus Thrane's use of America to influence attitudes and action in these immigrant plays. Understanding the symbolic role of America in Norwegian immigrant culture may also offer

clues to the attitudes and adjustment taking place among the broader immigrant population in late-nineteenth-century America.

Born in Norway in 1817, Thrane grew up in a déclassé family in Oslo as the youngest of three surviving siblings. Encouraged to attend school, Thrane would later admit that he was a "dreamer." He was drawn to belles lettres, the classics, romances, tragedies, and comedies. History, he wrote, did not satisfy him.[3] Thrane quit preparatory school before taking his exams and found work as a dockside customs checker. After a year on the docks, he was given an office job and resumed his "daydreaming."[4] Dissatisfied with his situation and longing for new experiences, in 1838, at the age of twenty, he set out on a romantic journey to the continent, visiting Germany, Switzerland, and France. In Paris, he was arrested as a vagrant and, with the help of the Swedish-Norwegian consul, was eventually released and sent home to Norway where he entered the university in 1840.

In 1841, he married Josephine Buch and together they established and ran a small private school in Lillehammer. Restlessness caused him to uproot his family several times before 1848 when, while teaching at the Blue Cobalt Works [Blåfargverket] at Modum, he received news of the revolution in France. In August 1848 he became the editor of *Drammens Adresse,* a small newspaper, in which he began to criticize the static Norwegian social system and lack of political democracy. In addition, he attacked the bureaucracy and established religion. Subscriptions declined and Thrane's position with the paper was terminated.

Seeking to continue his agitation for workers' rights, in December 1848 Thrane established the first Labor Association in Norway when he convinced 160 workers to join. By May 1849 when his new newspaper, *Arbeiderforeningernes Blad,* appeared, nine more association chapters had been established and, by 1851, membership was estimated to have reached 30,000.[5] As a political agitator, Thrane advocated workers' rights and greater political participation for Norway's lower classes. His rhetoric was always crisp and occasionally revolutionary as he criticized the government for failing to live up to the promises of the 1814 Constitution. In view of Thrane's agitation and ideological views, Halvdan Koht, one of Norway's most prominent twentieth-century historians, regarded him as Norway's "first socialist."[6] Increasingly seen as a threat to the political and social system, in the summer of 1851 Thrane and several other leaders in the movement were arrested, tried, and jailed. Thrane was incarcerated until 1858 when he was released to find his organization defunct and his former supporters scattered. Some had emigrated to America.

Following the death of his wife in 1862, Thrane contemplated his own emigration from Norway. In the winter of 1863–64, Thrane and four of his children set sail for America. Arriving in New York on 2 February 1864, the family found lodging in the crowded tenement district Five Points. Thrane worked to provide for his four daughters and one son who joined the family there in 1865. Meanwhile, Thrane read extensively in order to learn as much about his new country as possible. Thrane's daughter Vasilia has noted in her memoirs that the family was surprised by the class distinctions that existed in America, especially the belief among some Americans that the lower classes possessed little, if any, culture.[7]

After two difficult years of adjustment in New York, Thrane received an offer in 1866 to move to Chicago in order to edit a newspaper. Investors and friends of Thrane hoped to establish an alternative to the existing Norwegian-American papers supporting, and supported by, the Norwegian Lutheran churches. *Marcus Thrane's Norske Amerikaner* [*Marcus Thrane's Norwegian American*] survived only four months, yet Thrane's own views of America as the land of religious and political freedom remained a central pillar of his political and cultural philosophy.[8]

By 1866, the Civil War had been brought to a successful conclusion and Norwegian immigrants, Thrane believed, needed only to take advantage of the democratic promises of the growing nation to harvest the blessings of American liberty. Thrane called on Norwegians in America to throw off the chains of old-world prejudice and superstitions. Thrane believed the influence of the Norwegian-American clergy to be especially onerous due to their rejection of intellectual and scientific enlightenment. Because of his newspaper, but also because his radical reputation from Norway had followed him to Chicago, Thrane and the ministers came into direct confrontation over Thrane's anti-clerical views. Unwilling to sustain an ongoing battle with the church and its supporters, Thrane sold his newspaper in the late summer of 1866 and turned to the theater as his means of enlightening his fellow immigrants. Thrane believed that the subtle politics of enlightenment as entertainment might influence his fellow immigrants more than direct confrontation through

Marcus Thrane (1817–1890). Archives of the Norwegian-American Historical Association (Northfield, Minnesota).

a newspaper. In October 1866 the Norwegian Theater of Chicago became the first Scandinavian-American theater, and one of the earliest ethnic theaters, in America.[9] Its repertoire included productions of plays from Scandinavia and, most notably, plays written by Thrane himself. The plays dealt with a variety of topics, including such issues as class conflict, women's rights, and religious and cultural superstition. Aiming, for the most part, at the Scandinavian immigrant audience in Chicago, Thrane demonstrated considerable humor in addition to a witty sense of irony. Political and cultural criticism was frequently subtle but, on the whole, unmistakable. If there is a general theme that runs through Thrane's plays, it is his irreverant and consistent opposition to authority, secular as well as religious. Through it all, Thrane often used America as a symbol for a better life and a new social paradigm.

For Marcus Thrane, theater and drama performed two fundamental functions: to enlighten and to entertain. Entertainment, in his view, served to sustain and confirm enlightenment. Used by Thrane as a didactic tool in his teaching in Lillehammer and in his work with the Labor associations, popular theater allowed people the needed free time to escape life's trivialities and oppressive conditions through the enjoyment of art.[10] Although the underlying conditions differed, Thrane believed that theater could fulfill the same functions for Norwegian Americans. When his attempts to establish a newspaper failed, largely due to clerical opposition, Thrane believed he could use theater as a wedge to undermine support of the Lutheran churches among Norwegian Americans. Freeing Norwegian Americans from the grip of the church was to free them from ignorance and superstition, he believed. This political justification served as the ideological underpinning for Thrane's theater. However, the artistic side of Thrane also emerged in America, thereby allowing the theater also to function as general entertainment. Using familiar settings, sometimes in Norway and sometimes in America, while often building melodramatic and comedic situations, Thrane sprinkled his plays with references to American democracy and American egalitarianism. In a broad sense, democracy and religious freedom in America symbolized humankind's opposition to political tyranny and cultural superstition.

Thrane's references to America were politically purposeful and probably also recognized by his audiences, many of whom had a shared immigrant experience. Thrane's comments on ignorance and superstition, in an unpublished manuscript of a speech he frequently gave in the 1880s, illustrate the context and background of Thrane's use of America as symbol in his plays: "Though we cannot look back [on the French Revolution] without feelings of regret, and even horror, at the revolting scenes of anarchy and bloodshed wich [*sic*] accompanied that political convulsion, yet, amid all its evils, it was productive of many important and beneficial results. It tended to undermine that system of superstition and tyranny by wich most of the European nations had been so long enslaved. It aroused millions, from among the mass of the people, to assert those rights and privileges, to wich they are entitled as rational beings, and wich had been withheld from them by the strong hand of power."[11]

In America, too, Thrane noted, there remained areas of "darkness," especially, it seems, among the supporters of the Norwegian Lutheran Church. The "strong hand of power" and the tyranny of despots included what Thrane called "the cunning artifices of priests."[12] While Thrane's speeches might contain such bombastic rhetoric, his plays were considerably more subtle, whether they criticized the clergy or social convention.

The plays performed by Thrane's Norwegian Theater in the years 1866 to 1868 served more to put questions to social standards and attitudes toward class than to take aim at the power of the clergy. In this period, several of Thrane's plays used America or American society as the standard of freedom. Thrane's belief that America could influence the personalities and change the attitudes of immigrants is apparent initially in *The Naughty Girl* of 1866.[13] Emphasizing that in America one need only do what one wishes to do, without deference to tradition or convention, *The Naughty Girl* opens with Emilie, Sophie's older sister, facing a predicament. She is unhappy because her father, Mr. Andersen, is threatened with a forced auction to repay money which is owed to Busterud, the schoolmaster. Busterud, in return, offers to drop his claim if Andersen will allow him to marry Emilie, Andersen's oldest daughter. Old-world custom, Thrane suggests, would require that an obedient daughter submit to an arranged marriage and thereby spare her father possible financial ruin. In response, the innocent Sophie, upon learning of her sister's situation, tells her sister to stamp her foot, if she must, in order to get her way. That is what she always does. "A woman," says the young Sophie, "must be cunning" in order to avoid the fate of marrying against her will. As Thrane presents it, the simple and childlike behavior of Sophie is really a façade for innocent intelligence, not unlike that of the young American republic, as she develops a scheme to convince Busterud that she, Sophie, not Emilie, is really in love with him and that they should elope. Sophie provides a sack to Busterud in which she is to be carried away but, unknown to Busterud, Sophie's real plan is to convince others that she has been kidnapped. Fearing charges of kidnapping, Busterud gives up his financial claims on Andersen, and Emilie is able to marry the man she really loves. Sophie, in the end, is revealed to be a calculating and worldly-wise thirteen-year-old, far from the apparently innocent girl she appeared to be. That Busterud, the villain of the play, is also a schoolmaster was probably not lost on Thrane's audiences. As schoolmaster, he is a representative of administrative authority and the bureaucratic elite. Consequently, the victory of Sophie and Emilie over Busterud was actually a victory of new-world intelligence and guile over tyranny and old-world conventions.

Thrane's use of America was less symbolic and much more direct in *An American Servant Girl*,[14] one of his best plays from the period of the Norwegian Theater. A one-act comedy, *An American Servant Girl* tells the story of Mr. Brun, an upper-class immigrant from Norway; his daughter, Cecilie, who finds difficulty in adjusting to the social style in America; and Dina, their Norwegian servant girl who, by contrast, finds American egalitarianism perfectly suited to her tastes. The plot of the play builds on the popular assumption that servants from the lower classes are generally ignorant and musically illiterate. Dina, however, who has learned to play the piano, does not fit the stereotype. She also presumes to be the equal of Cecilie. Such presumption may be tolerable in America, but violates social standards from the immigrants' home country of Norway. In fact, as the play unfolds, the standards of the new world clash more and more with those of the old country. It may be said that Dina, the servant, is in reality the personification of America in this play. In Scene 8, for example, she confronts the Bruns with her egalitarian views, arguing that "when we are in America, we have to be American. Habits and customs in the new world are not the habits and customs in the old world."[15]

Impudent as Dina may be in the play, she is apparently indispensable to the Brun family. When Cecilie insists to her father that he get rid of the "impudent" Dina, he replies that she must be treated kindly "or else she may pack her things and leave, just as the others have done." Dina may be impudent, Brun says, but "she doesn't steal like several others did, and she pays attention to her work."[16] In fact, it appears that in Dina Thrane has created a character who could serve as a model immigrant for members of the Norwegian-American community, someone having the ethical foundation of Norwegians while also possessing the independent and entrepreneurial spirit of Americans. Though she is called "an American servant girl," Dina is in reality an "Americanized Norwegian servant girl," something her honesty and ethical code, as Thrane presents them, tend to confirm. However, that Thrane calls her "an American servant girl" also suggests that a significant change has taken place and that Dina is not the same person she was before coming to America. Dina, perhaps like many in Thrane's audiences, found herself quite at home in America. She had shed the chains of Norwegian social conventions while retaining Norwegian ethical values.

A similar kind of change takes place in an entire family in *Seventeenth of May*,[17] a two-act song piece written and produced in 1867, where the first act is set in Norway, the second in America. The play may well be Thrane's most personal, if not his favorite. It tells the story of a Norwegian cotter, Nils Sundløkka, who wants to celebrate the anniversary of the Norwegian constitution with a day off from work. His employer, the farmer Eriksen, rejects his plea and orders him to work as usual. Nils is supported by his son, Iver, and daughter, Birthe, but Nils's wife fears for their economic security and advises that he submit. Hers is a position not unlike that of Thrane's own wife when he was actively agitating for reform in Norway in the early 1850s. When Nils persists, Eriksen takes revenge by denying his daughter Marthe's hand in marriage to Nils's son, Iver. Despondent, Iver decides to emigrate to America, where he plans to become rich and then to return to marry his Marthe. Nils, who had previously denounced emigration as a serious loss to Norway, decides to emigrate, too. In fact, like Thrane, Nils and his family are figuratively driven from Norway.

Act II finds the family in America. Nils has become a prosperous farmer in Minnesota. His wife and daughter are introduced to the audience in Act II dressed in the latest American style with their hair worn in the current fashion. Iver still misses his Marthe and is told that she has married someone else. In true melodramatic fashion, however, Marthe shows up in Minnesota after having left Norway and her family to join Iver. Also appearing is a seminary student who had proposed to Birthe in Act I, but had been turned down because he could not dance. In America he, too, had changed: "For your sake Birthe, I have become a heathen! For your sake, Birthe, I have learned to dance."[18] As Thrane presented the characters and plot in *Seventeenth of May*, America has a cleansing influence on the Sundløkka family. While they were members of the cotter class in Norway, in America the opportunity to own their own farm has propelled them to prosperity. The prescriptions of the established church and cultural convention were things of the past in Thrane's America. Ironically, but not without deliberate purpose, it is in America where Thrane suggests that the true spirit of the seventeenth of May is finally to be realized.

Although in both *An American Servant Girl* and *Seventeenth of May* the plots depend on emigration from Norway, the characters in Thrane's plays do not have to emigrate in order to be influenced by America. One such play deals with the debate about women's emancipation and gender roles in a marriage, a radical theme in the middle of the nineteenth century. *Who Grinds the Coffee?*[19] is a one-act play in which a young husband and wife argue over who should grind and make the coffee. The husband, Peter, wants his wife to get up with the sun, fire up the stove, then grind the coffee, while he sleeps. Marie, his wife, simply refuses to do so, telling Peter that if he wants coffee, he should grind it himself. Frustrated, Peter blames America for putting radical ideas into his Marie's head. Her sister has, in fact, written to his wife to tell about "how splendid it is for women in America. They don't have to get up to light the fire, they don't have to milk the cows, and they don't have to shine shoes if they don't want to. And they don't want to! They don't even want to take care of children, and all this in the name of emancipation! If it continues to be like this, God only knows what will happen to men. Damn this America."[20]

As the two argue, however, they each begin gradually to see the matter from the other's perspective, although each remains unwilling to give in. Peter notes that if he grinds the coffee, as his wife insists, he will have declared himself "in favor of women's emancipation like the Americans." Similarly, Marie refuses, saying: "Men! They

have to have their way in everything. Women are such unhappy beings, but just wait. Our time is coming. America will soon declare
women free and equal to men. Then we'll be rid of all tyrants."[21] In
the end, the couple agrees that the only rational solution is to grind
the coffee together. Thrane's conclusion, and the moral of the story,
is that a marriage should be seen as a partnership with responsibilities shared equally between husband and wife. For Peter and Marie,
the influence of America brought about a new relationship between
them as they were able to break down the stereotypical roles of old-
world society. In this deceptively modest little play, Thrane antici-
pates a later "Who makes the coffee?" debate by more than a century.

Misunderstanding, greed, honesty, love, loyalty, and faithfulness
are all themes broached in Thrane's plays. In the popular style of the
day, he often also added music, sometimes original and sometimes
plagiarized from well-known contemporary sources. Perhaps the
most important of Thrane's musical comedies which incorporated
an immigration theme and the clash between the old and new cultures was *Holden,* written in 1880.[22]

Holden tells the story of the Bernt and Oline Muus divorce scandal.
Bernt Julius Muus was one of the leaders of Norwegian Lutheranism
in the United States and principal founder of St. Olaf College. In
1880 it was charged that he had mistreated his wife for years. Muus
claimed ownership of a $4,000 inheritance his wife received when her
father died in Norway. In doing so he cited a husband's right to de-
cide for the family and the obligation of a wife to remain obedient to
her husband. The Muus affair scandalized the Norwegian-American
community and provided additional fodder for Thrane's anti-clerical
writings. He borrowed liberally from the newspaper accounts of the
trial, put his particular slant on events, added recognizable melodies
to his own lyrics, and produced one of his best satirical plays. In addition to his criticism of the clergy and their conservative old-world
views, Thrane also commented on the cause of women's rights in
Holden, in much the same manner as he had in *Who Grinds the Coffee?*
Two hugely successful productions of *Holden* were presented at the
Aurora Turner Hall in Chicago in 1880. Sprinkled liberally with the
borrowed music of Gilbert and Sullivan's *H.M.S. Pinafore,* the play was
a great success. Press reports told of enthusiastic audiences echoing
shouts of "Author!" as Thrane was brought to the stage amid thunder-
ous applause at the conclusion of the performances.[23]

While *Holden* and several other of Thrane's plays received popular

praise and critical acclaim from the Norwegian-American press, at-
tendance at most of Thrane's plays appears to have been sporadic. In
spite of his humor and intellectual strength, Thrane was always considered to be an outsider, an agitator, and a non-believer by most
Norwegian immigrants in America. His opponents, especially the
Norwegian-American clergy, had early succeeded in identifying him
as anti-Christian, while other conservative Norwegian-American leaders marginalized him or avoided him. That he retained his humor
and personal balance was probably a credit to his family, his own
strong philosophical beliefs, and the loyalty of his close friends. After
1884, when he retired from active work, he developed a somewhat
reclusive grumpiness. His faith and optimism in the future began to
fade as he faced his own mortality. A return to Norway for a visit in
1882–83 had resulted, not in the joyous return of a prodigal son, but
in general hostility from Norwegian authorities and ridicule from
the conservative press. In 1887, his friend August Spies was executed
for his part in the Haymarket Square bombing a year earlier, an exe-
cution that Thrane considered a travesty of justice.

Like many other creative spirits, Thrane was a bundle of contradictions. He was political through and through, but he frequently
showed his sensitive, artistic side. He remained a rabble-rouser and a
gadfly, even while enjoying life as a doting grandfather. In an unper-
formed play finished around 1884, *The Assassins,* set in Germany in
1876, one of Thranc's characters reflects on America, perhaps in
much the same way as Thrane himself did. "America," the playwright
wrote, "is neither a republic, a monarchy, an aristocracy, a democracy, an anarchy, nor a mobocracy, it is a 'rascalocracy.'" Harkening
back to one of his first impressions upon arriving in New York in
1864, Thrane noted that in America "everything is for sale." In spite
of this, he also wrote about the richness and the potential of the
American continent: "In America, nature is abundant and overflow-
ing. . . . If there were a government which even somewhat worked
hand in hand with the richness of nature, America would be such a
paradise."[24] To the end of his life, Thrane recognized America's
problems, but he also saw its vast potential. In this, he shared the vision of millions of contemporary immigrants. Through his speeches,
newspaper articles, and especially his plays, Marcus Thrane has left a
unique and important record of one man's personal relationship
with his adopted country.

NOTES

[1]See Terje I. Leiren, *Marcus Thrane: A Norwegian Radical in America* (Northfield, 1987), and Marcus Thrane, "Om kreditlov," *Arbeiderforeningernes Blad,* 29 June 1850.

[2]Thrane's changing views of America are discussed in Terje I. Leiren, "Lost Utopia: The Changing Image of America in the Writings of Marcus Thrane," *Scandinavian Studies* 60 (1988), 465–479. See also Thrane's notebook, "Alt," Ms. 4° 1733, Marcus Thrane Papers, Nasjonalbiblioteket (hereafter cited as *NB*), Oslo. Most of Thrane's plays, letters, and notebooks are located in the National Archives in Oslo. The manuscript of one play, *Dannelse fremfor alt,* is located in the University Library at the University of Bergen.

[3]Marcus Thrane, "Autobiographical Reminiscences," translated by Vasilia Thrane Struck in a 1917 manuscript in Marcus Thrane Papers, *NB,* Oslo.

[4]Thrane, "Autobiographical Reminiscences."

[5]See *Marcus Thrane's Norske Amerikaner,* 13 July 1866; Oddvar Bjørklund, *Marcus Thrane: sosialistleder i et u-land* (Oslo, 1970); Tore Pryser, *Klassebevegelse eller folkebevegelse: En sosialhistorisk undersøkelse av thranittene i Ullensaker* (Oslo, 1977).

[6]Halvdan Koht, "Sosialismen til Marcus Thrane," in *Det tyvende aarhundrede,* August, 1912.

[7]Vasilia Struck, "Marcus Thrane," manuscript in Marcus Thrane Papers, *NB,* Oslo.

[8]See Terje I. Leiren, "The Reemergence of a Misunderstood Radical: Marcus Thrane's Norske Amerikaner," in *Scandinavians and Other Immigrants in Urban America,* ed. Odd S. Lovoll (Northfield, MN, 1985).

[9]For an overview of the ethnic theater in America see Maxine Schwartz Seller, "Introduction," in *Ethnic Theatre in the United States,* ed. Maxine Schwartz Seller (Westport, CT, 1983), 3–17.

[10]Marcus Thrane, "Folketheater," *Arbeiderforeningernes Blad,* 23 March 1850.

[11]Marcus Thrane, "Ignorance and Superstition." Handwritten manuscript, Ms. 4° 1774, Marcus Thrane Papers, *NB,* Oslo.

[12]Thrane, "Ignorance and Superstition."

[13]Marcus Thrane, *Det uskikkelige pigebarn,* Ms. 4° 1770, Marcus Thrane Papers, *NB,* Oslo.

[14]Marcus Thrane, *En amerikansk tjenestepige,* Ms. 4° 1768, Marcus Thrane Papers, *NB,* Oslo.

[15]Thrane, *En amerikansk tjenestepige.*

[16]Thrane, *En amerikansk tjenestepige.*

[17]There exists no known manuscript for this play. It is, however, mentioned several times in Thrane's notebook, "Alt," and it received extensive reviews in two Norwegian-language papers, *Emigranten* and *Skandinaven,* when it was first performed in Chicago in May, 1867.

[18]Review of *Syttende mai,* in *Emigranten,* 25 May 1867.

[19]Marcus Thrane, *Who Grinds the Coffee?* Ms. 8° 309, Marcus Thrane Papers, *NB,* Oslo.

[20]Thrane, *Who Grinds the Coffee?*

[21]Thrane, *Who Grinds the Coffee?*

[22]Marcus Thrane, *Holden,* Ms. 4° 1758, Marcus Thrane Papers, *NB,* Oslo.

[23]Review of *Holden,* June, 1880, clipping in Marcus Thrane Papers. A biography of Bernt Julius Muus, with a comprehensive discussion of the divorce scandal, is: Joseph M. Shaw, *Bernt Julius Muus: Founder of St. Olaf College* (Northfield, MN, 1999), 257–306.

[24]Thrane, *Attentaterne,* Ms. 4° 1767, Marcus Thrane Papers, *NB,* Oslo.

Traveling on His Trade: Martin Tranmæl's Stay in the United States and the Radicalizing of the Norwegian Labor Movement

Jorunn Bjørgum

AT THE CONGRESS of the Norwegian Labor Party in 1918, the party leadership was taken over by self-styled revolutionaries of the radical left wing. The leaders of this radical wing were the close friends and political partners Martin Tranmæl (1879–1967) and Kyrre Grepp (1879–1922), who were installed as chairman and general secretary of the party respectively. At the same time the Labor Party adopted a new political platform, endorsing revolutionary mass action rather than parliamentary activity as its primary political strategy.

This takeover of the party and the new revolutionary political platform was the result of a radicalizing process within the Norwegian labor movement that had lasted almost a decade. In the year 1919, the Norwegian Labor Party even joined the new Communist International, the Comintern. The Norwegian group was one of the very few old European social democratic parties to do so, and this event is still considered exceptional in European history. This membership in the Comintern, however, lasted only a few years. After a devastating internal struggle, the party seceded from the International in 1923. This resulted in a split, and the splinter minority formed a new party, the Communist Party of Norway. Comintern membership thus amounted to little more than an episode in the history of the Norwegian Labor Party. The process of radicalizing forming the background of the episode, nevertheless, had a lasting impact on the party. Until well into the 1960s the Norwegian Labor Party had an image of being, at least in certain respects, more radical than other social democratic parties in Europe. This was the case throughout the 1920s and 1930s and well into the postwar years, that is, into the period when the Labor Party dominated Norwegian politics and was, in fact, in almost continuous charge of the government from 1935 till 1965.

Why was this so? How did the Norwegian Labor Party acquire this radical image and political profile? How can the radicalizing of the party in the beginning of the twentieth century be explained? This has been a much discussed question in Norwegian historiography, and is the basic theme under consideration here. Along the way I will look at the relevant historiography and the role of Martin Tranmæl. In this connection, I shall also discuss in a more detailed way the impact on Tranmæl of his American experiences. As we shall see, Tranmæl stayed in the United States for several years at the beginning of his career, from 1900 to 1905, with only one short interruption. What aspects of his political philosophy he might have picked up during these years is one of the questions I will discuss. A central point, of course, will be the influence on Tranmæl of the "Wobblies," taking part, as he did, as an observer at the founding congress of the Industrial Workers of the World (IWW), in Chicago in June 1905. This study thus reflects the interest of Odd Sverre Lovoll in transatlantic connections between Norway and the United States. It is also a venture in directing scholarly attention to a theme that deserves much more attention in studies of immigration: the role of returnees in the history of the nations from which they departed and to which they returned.

The obvious point of departure for considering the historiographical tradition is a classic article by the historian Edvard Bull (1881–1932), published in 1922.[1] Bull himself had been active within the radical wing of the Labor Party before 1918, and after the split in 1923 he was co-chairman of the party until his premature death in 1932. He wrote his now famous article to apprise fellow historians of the unique Norwegian development of Norwegian socialism. Here Bull inquires into why left socialism was so much stronger in Norway than in neighboring Sweden and Denmark. For Bull the symbol of this strength was the takeover of the Labor Party by the radical wing in 1918. Edvard Bull came up with a highly complex answer involving economic, social, and political factors as well as topographical ones. Only his main points follow here.

The so-called "Bull thesis" combines economic and social factors to argue that the Norwegian working class differed from that of the other two Scandinavian countries due to the special history of industrial development in Norway. Specifically, Bull pointed to the establishment, after Norwegian independence in 1905, of a huge new electrochemical and electrometallurgical industry based on hydroelectric power. This development created a new sector in the Norwegian working class, a group consisting mostly of unskilled workers directly recruited from rural areas. These former agricultural workers did not, Bull argued, inherit the traditions of the older portion of the working class. According to Bull, their background made these newly recruited workers more open to revolutionary ideas than the older segment of the working class. The consequent reshaping of the working class in Norway, Bull concluded, also resulted in a remodeling of the labor movement as a whole. In terms of party politics this meant that the radical wing of the labor movement gained support from an ever growing group of the members of the Labor Party until the balance of power shifted decisively at the party congress of 1918.

According to Bull, special features of Norwegian politics made these developments possible in the Norwegian Labor Party. It was possible, for example, for the Norwegian Labor Party to keep a more radical political profile than its Scandinavian counterparts because it was not necessary for the Norwegian party to form any sort of alliance with the Liberal Party in order to obtain a parliamentarian political system or universal suffrage. These things had already been established in Norway, as they had not been in Sweden and Denmark. Bull also pointed to some aspects of political development in Norway related to World War I. Finally he pointed to a personal factor: Martin Tranmæl's excellent leadership of the radical wing and his extraordinary power as an organizer.[2]

Who, then, was Martin Tranmæl? He was born to a farming family in Trøndelag in 1879. He developed a keen interest in politics in his childhood home, witnessing numerous discussions on the tumultuous political life of Norway in the 1880s and early 1890s. This was in the aftermath of the Norwegian constitutional democratic "revolution" of 1884, which established a parliamentarian political system, and in the era of the dawning national struggle with Sweden in the 1890s that resulted in Norway's secession from its union with this neighboring country in 1905. As a youth Martin Tranmæl was a bookworm, devouring every book, especially on history, in the small local library. He might have become a teacher, like so many gifted youths from the countryside in this period. Instead he was declassed, or proletarianized, through a kind of personal earthquake. His father had to leave the farm as a consequence of his alcoholism, something which turned Martin Tranmæl into a teetotaler for the rest of his life and thus also contributed to the strong anti-alcohol tradition in the Norwegian labor movement throughout the remainder of the century. After this "earthquake," Tranmæl turned for an occupation to housepainting and he soon ended up in the expanding city of Trondheim as a worker in the building industry. There he joined the local trade union and thus also the Norwegian Labor Party, because of the so-called collective membership of most of the unions in the party. The party had been founded in 1887 as a general workers' union, but by the turn of the century it was developing into a "normal" parliamentarian party. Its first representatives were elected to the Storting, the Norwegian parliament, in 1903.

Although working for his living as a painter in the building industry, Martin Tranmæl soon turned to journalism, as well. Together with some other party members, in 1899 he founded the first socialist newspaper in Trondheim, *Ny Tid* [*New Time*]. Tranmæl edited as well as wrote for the paper and in writing started what was later to become his main profession in life, journalism.

Before that career got under way, however, Martin Tranmæl went to America, where his first stay lasted from March 1900 to March 1902. In order to learn the language, he spent almost a year in West Superior, Wisconsin with his two elder brothers who had immigrated several years earlier and taken up farming. Then he traveled west through Minnesota, North Dakota, and Montana to San Francisco, California and then finally to Los Angeles. He earned his living along the way as a painter in the building industry and joined his American union, the International Brotherhood of Painters. After a visit to Norway to take part in the elections of 1903 as a political agitator, Tranmæl went back to America for another couple of years until the end of 1905, resuming his traveling activity, but again spending most of this time in Los Angeles.

While staying in America, Tranmæl wrote numerous letters to *Ny Tid,* describing his journey and the places he visited, commenting upon political events in the United States, and describing and editorializing on many of the harsh labor conflicts taking place during these years. In numerous articles he told his Norwegian audience about the history of the American labor movement, ranging through topics as diverse as early efforts to organize workers in the first part of the nineteenth century, contacts with Marx's First International, the Knights of Labor, and the story of the national federations of the 1860s uniting into the American Federation of Labor (AFL) in 1881 under its well-known president, Samuel Gompers (1850–1924). Tranmæl also described the development of the American socialist party and the split between Daniel De Leon (1852–1914) and Eugene V. Debs (1855–1926). Martin Tranmæl himself joined the Debs branch on the West Coast and in his letters to *Ny Tid* he always referred to it as "our" party, thus reflecting an international socialist setting.

Through his membership in the American Socialist Party Martin Tranmæl learned at least three important lessons. The most important, perhaps, came from attending an evening school organized by the party. He studied Marxism, national economics, and sociology, paying special attention to Marx's theory of exploitation, with which he was preoccupied throughout the rest of his life. For a European to go to America to learn about Marxism may seem odd, but to Martin Tranmæl this schooling in America was fundamental to his later thinking.

More indirectly, Tranmæl also acquired something else to take back to Norway from this experience: the idea of such evening schools. When he returned to Norway, he started almost immediately to organize similar courses for the workers and members of the labor movement in Trondheim. He would continue this activity for years to come. After his faction had conquered the leadership of the Labor Party in 1918, the party itself started educational activity on a scale unheard of until then. Others, of course, evinced the same interest in such activity, but Tranmæl himself contributed considerably to the effort. This is certainly in part an outcome of his American adventures. This sort of schooling has been an important element in the cultural tradition of the Norwegian labor movement ever since. The example of the American Socialist Party, among other factors, played a definite role in this development.

Another practice of the American Socialist Party that Martin Tranmæl brought with him back to Norway was the habit of holding outdoor, informal meetings at which the speaker invited the audience to make critical comments or to pose questions. This was a way of agitating that Tranmæl copied very often throughout his period in opposition. He paid particular attention to what he had learned about getting in contact with the audience by inviting questions and establishing a dialogue. He often made a point of his having learned this practice in America.

The second important element of Tranmæl's American education was his contact with the Industrial Workers of the World, the so-called "Wobblies." Tranmæl was present as an observer at the founding congress of IWW and he described the event in his letters from America to *Ny Tid*. He often referred to this in later articles and he drew on the experience in numerous speeches or lectures in workers' associations all over Norway, Sweden, and Denmark.

In presenting the IWW to his *Ny Tid* audience, Tranmæl made a point of the revolutionary and modern character of the new movement. He regarded the modern aspect as especially important. Tranmæl specifically emphasized the IWW's being class-based and built on the common interests of all workers regardless of trade or occupation. As the IWW slogan put it: one big union for all workers. Tranmæl further underlined the organization's focus on the class struggle by comparing the IWW, positively from his point of view, with the American Federation of Labor (AFL), which he criticized for being too cooperative and positive towards the capitalists. Finally, he praised the IWW for having a political, specifically an anticapitalist or socialist purpose, as an ultimate goal: "the emancipation of the workers through the conquering of the means of production." That was the goal of the IWW, according to Tranmæl, and he even reckoned with the possibility of the new organization being a sign of unification in the American socialist movement. He justified this hope with reference to the performances of both Debs and De Leon at the founding meeting, both of whom he described as having giving "brilliant speeches."

Tranmæl did not give any quotations from the opening speech of William Dudley ("Big Bill") Haywood (1869–1918) to his *Ny Tid* audience, but he must have appreciated and agreed with Haywood, who said: "We are here to confederate the workers of this country into a working class movement that shall have for its purpose the emancipation of the working class from the slave bondage of capitalism. . . . The aims and objects of this organization should be to put the working class in the possession of the economic power, the means of life, in control of the machinery of production and distribution, without regard to capitalist mastery. . . . [T]his organization will be formed, based and founded on the class struggle, having in view no compromise and no surrender, and but one object and one purpose and that is to bring the workers of this country into the possession of the full value of the product of their toil."[3] Martin Tranmæl would certainly have agreed with these words.

From a more strictly organizational point of view, Tranmæl pointed toward and regarded as positive the IWW's lack of high membership fees, and its consequent capacity to include all kinds of workers, and its organizational division into industrial departments with local branches instead of into trades or crafts and such national unions. Tranmæl concluded that the IWW was certainly the most modern and consistent [*mest rettlinjede*] movement within the economic sphere. That was why, he continued, its principles and methods were of international importance. It was broad enough, he stated, to include all workers, but too consistent [*rettlinjet*] to contain reactionary and compromising elements. Tranmæl's conclusion was very optimistic indeed: "The most interesting aspect of the movement, though, is the great interest and the enthusiasm driving the effort; the old conservative labor leaders Gompers and Mitchell have declared war on the new ones—that is a clear token of their being on the right track. The year 1905 will stand out as a most remarkable year in the history of the trade union movement. From America the new principles will most certainly become victorious throughout Europe."[4]

The third lesson that Martin Tranmæl brought with him back home from the United States was a new understanding of the development of capitalism as seen through the many harsh labor conflicts of these years. Tranmæl told his *Ny Tid* readers about several strikes during his stay in the United States, paying special attention to a protracted miners' strike in Colorado. He was intensely preoccupied with the brutal methods employed by the capitalists and with the way in which they were supported by the public authorities with military as well as with police forces. He described with great feeling the disruption of meetings, deportations, various provocations, and episodes of harassment against the strikers and their families, some of them clearly unlawful.

Tranmæl's conclusion was clear. This was a system that should not be tolerated, that ought to be finished off in order to be replaced by a socialist one. His anticapitalist position and socialist convictions were thus strongly fortified by his experiences in America. His observations of these labor conflicts functioned as a kind of proof in practice, as he saw it, of the Marxist theories that he had learned at the evening school of the Socialist Party in Los Angeles. A special aspect of this conclusion is worth noticing, however. Having seen the willingness of public authorities to support the capitalists, Tranmæl was further confirmed in his belief that it was necessary for the laboring classes to seize and to control political power. The primacy of politics was, ever after, deeply embodied in his political credo. Thus, when IWW from about 1908 turned to syndicalism proper and away from politics, Tranmæl did not follow, but rather advocated the opposite course of action.

In addition to the more general lessons drawn from observation of labor conflicts in the United States at this time, Tranmæl also paid keen attention to the way in which these workers' organizations, especially the Western Federation of Miners led by Big Bill Haywood, conducted their struggles. He was very much interested in the means used by the strikers. He was particularly impressed with the extensive use of sympathy strikes, boycott or blockade, and cooperation, all elements that later found their way into his own political message back home in Norway.

When he returned from America in December 1905, Tranmæl immediately got a job as a full-time journalist for *Ny Tid*, quitting his trade as a painter and taking up his life's work in journalism. He also immediately involved himself in the politics of the labor movement. He was sent as a representative to the national congress of the Labor Party in 1906 and he was also elected a member of the party's national board, a position he held continually into the 1960s. At the local level he took part in establishing in Trondheim a branch of the Social Democratic Youth Federation, i.e., the Labor Party's youth organization founded on a national level two years earlier. (Recall that Martin Tranmæl was still not more than twenty-six years old in 1905.) For several years to come, this local youth association was to be an organizational base for Tranmæl. From this base he provoked a debate in the labor movement about its ends and means and from this position he initiated and took his great part in building the radical wing, the radical opposition within the movement. From this position he took the lead in organizing the group that took over the leadership of the Norwegian Labor Party in 1918.

The real beginning of this radicalization process occurred in November 1911, when Tranmæl launched a program for reforming, or as he preferred to say, for revolutionizing the Norwegian labor movement. Before turning to this history, however, one more comment on Tranmæl's American experiences is in order.

His tramping around in the United States may, from one point of view, be seen as an instance of the centuries-old habit of European journeymen "to travel on their trade," to translate literally the Norwegian phrase *"å vandre på sitt fag."* It was the custom of these itinerants to travel from country to country earning their living by working in their craft or trade and at the same time learning new methods in their crafts, as well as languages and traits from other societies' traditions and cultures. As is well known, revolutions and fashions, among other things, have been spread through Europe by wandering journeymen through the ages. In 1914 this saga ended and the tradition associated with it died when World War I caused borders to be closed. Martin Tranmæl's travels to and within the United States may be considered a late instance of this tradition. What is more, he continued this practice after he had returned to Norway. During several years he took a couple of months off from *Ny Tid* and traveled around Europe, again earning his living as a house painter and working with other traveling journeymen. In addition to Sweden and Denmark, where he also took up political agitation, he also traveled in Germany, Austria, Italy, France, the Low Countries, and England. In the United States he had learned English and now he acquired a passable knowledge of German, the international language of the European labor movement up to World War II. Along the way, Tranmæl studied politics as well as local labor movements all over Europe, visiting parliaments as well as local branches of the social democratic parties. For example, he followed some of the debates on reformism in the German party. He also learned about the living and working conditions of the laboring classes in different countries and, as he had in the United States earlier, he studied several labor conflicts. Thus, both his years in the United States and these travels in Europe may be seen as an important part of the political education of a rising political leader.

In November 1911 a meeting of the new local association organized by Tranmæl in Trondheim adopted a statement written by him. It contained the first version of his program for reforming or, as he liked to say, revolutionizing the Norwegian labor movement. The so-called "Trondhjem Resolution" states: "The meeting declares, that the trade union situation now demands that the organizational efforts be put on a more revolutionary ground than before. The meeting, accordingly, points to the following as a natural program: A. 1. The written binding wage agreements should be abolished. 2. The insurance system should be discontinued. B. As means of struggle should, first and foremost, be used: 1. Strikes. 2. Sympathy strikes. 3. Boycott. 4. Obstruction. 5. Sabotage. 6. Cooperation. C. The organizational structure should be changed thus: 1. The national federation should be transformed to the central organ, to the common denominator [fællesnævneren]. 2. This should be divided into sections according to the big industries—industrial unions, that is. 3. Local associations should be established to take over, among other things, the local agitation. They also should be given influence over the stipulation of working conditions."[5]

Tranmæl's program had a double objective. One goal was to change the division of labor within the labor movement. The other was to restructure the trade union movement accordingly. Following the prevailing thinking of the time, the socialist strategy of the labor movement was in charge of the parliamentarian social democratic party, in Norway called the Norwegian Labor Party. The ultimate socialist goal was to socialize the means of production, that is, to establish a system where the means of production would be politically controlled. Preferably this would be a system where the working class, said to be the majority of the people, would through its representatives possess political power. According to the common thinking within the international socialist movement, this socialist goal ought to be reached through the ballot, that is, through existing, more or less parliamentarian, political systems. The trade unions, on their part, were assigned the task of supporting the party and also, of course, the task of assisting the members in obtaining the best possible wages and working conditions through negotiations with the employers.

Tranmæl, however, proposed to change this division of labor between the Labor Party and the trade union movement. In his opinion it would never be possible to socialize the means of production through the existing political system, through parliament. Instead he wanted to put this objective on the agenda of the trade union movement in its capacity of being the organization directly attached to the sphere of production, as well as in its capacity of being the most class-based organization of the labor movement. The strategy was revolutionary mass action, as the slogan ran, and the argument was that mass action must be organized by the organization where the masses were to be found, that is, by the trade union movement. This would be the vital nerve [*livsnerven*] of the labor movement, as Martin Tranmæl put it. Accordingly, he also wanted the presumably reformed or revolutionized trade union federation rather than the Labor Party to take over the leading role in the labor movement. The party, in his opinion, had degenerated into a "hyper-parliamentarian" institution without the capacity to lead the masses in action.

The other aspect of Tranmæl's program was to restructure the trade union movement to fit it for its new strategic task, for taking on a revolutionary goal. In his opinion the trade union movement needed, on the one hand, to change its organizational pattern, and on the other it needed to change its politics. From the organizational perspective, Tranmæl wanted a stronger and more centralized national federation, in accordance with the IWW's concept of "one big union." He also wanted this federation to be based on a combined system of industrial divisions and local class-based associations regardless of the members' trades or crafts. Where trade union politics were concerned, Tranmæl primarily wanted the trade unions to be able to act on the spur of the moment and immediately when opportunities were promising, without being bound by earlier agreements or hindered by timidity on the part of the leaders. "Direct action," was the slogan. Furthermore, he wanted a more aggressive policy generally. He also held that new means of struggle should be taken into use. In addition to strikes, he mentioned sympathy strikes, boycotts and blockades, obstruction, cooperation, and sabotage, all means of struggle that he had learned about in the United States.

In 1911, when he launched his program, Martin Tranmæl had, through his extensive travels, also been influenced by French and Swedish syndicalism as well as by the New Unionism in England under the leadership of Tom Mann (1856–1941). Nevertheless, I maintain that his main source of inspiration was from the United States through the IWW. This is clear from his insistence that working-class control over the means of production belonged on the agenda of the trade union movement. The IWW had done this, and the words of Big Bill Haywood at the founding congress are apposite: "The aims and objects of this organization should be to put the working class in possession of the economic power, the means of life, in control of the machinery of production and distribution, without regard to capitalist mastery."[6] Although Tranmæl had added the concept of revolutionary mass action, he borrowed the basic idea of this being the main task for the trade union movement from Haywood and the IWW. This was also the case with several elements of Tranmæl's suggestions for a change of the organizational structure of the trade unions, in particular the idea of one large, class-based union with divisions along industrial lines. The struggle of the Wobblies had also impressed on him the importance of means such as sympathy strikes, blockades and boycotts, obstruction, sabotage, and cooperation.

When the Trondhjem Resolution containing Tranmæl's program was adopted it did not at first receive much attention. Only when the editor of the Labor Party's chief organ, the Oslo-based *Social-Demokraten* [*The Social Democrat*] used the resolution to make a frontal attack on Tranmæl did it become widely known. Tranmæl thus got the chance to discuss it at a whole series of meetings, both in Trondheim and in Oslo, with the president of the Trade Union Federation, Ole Lian, as well as with other top leaders of the Norwegian labor movement. At one of these meetings Tranmæl uttered his ever after famous words about dynamite in the boreholes as a means to deter potential strikebreakers from going into a mine during a strike.[7] This, of course, turned him into a famous person almost overnight.

All of this launched Tranmæl's program with a flying start. The established leaders of the labor movement had hoped that the members would be appalled by his message once they could explain its dangers. The opposite occurred. Martin Tranmæl proved himself a charismatic and convincing speaker. He soon, indeed, came to be known as one of the best speakers in Norwegian history and was compared favorably to the oratorical giant Bjørnstjerne Bjørnson, to whom Tranmæl had listened in his youth. Tranmæl's practice of inviting objections and critical questions from the audience, a method he had learned in the United States, had a positive effect as well. After the first series of meetings, he took to the road, bringing the message to local unions and labor associations all over southern and central Norway. Publicity beforehand made people curious and caused them to flock to his meetings. His convincing appearances did the rest. Soon he had acquired a considerable number of supporters and thus had laid the foundation for building an organized opposition within the Norwegian labor movement.

Tranmæl's campaign was organized and probably paid for by the Youth Federation, of which he was a member. Its local in Trondheim was, in fact, his home base until 1918. This national youth federation gradually developed under the leadership of Kyrre Grepp into an organized opposition within the Labor Party. From 1912 on Grepp was Tranmæl's political partner and close friend and in the same year became a member of the central committee of the Labor Party. While the Youth Federation was a very important organizational platform for the conquest of the leadership of the Labor Party in 1918, it was not the only one. Another was Tranmæl's paper *Ny Tid*. Early in 1913 Tranmæl was offered the position of chief editor of *Ny Tid* after a very close vote in the local labor organization owning the paper. The decision was clearly political, the majority taking Tranmæl's side in the internal struggle that had been developing in the Norwegian labor movement ever since the Trondhjem Resolution.

With Martin Tranmæl in charge of *Ny Tid*, the left wing of the Labor Party got a new organizational platform, which was to be of immense importance to the radicalizing process. At a time without other media than papers, magazines, and popular meetings, the control of a newspaper was invaluable, indeed, for broadcasting a political message. Tranmæl of course seized the opportunity and once installed as editor he initiated several debates in the paper's columns on the ends and means of the labor movement. Through his editorials his influence on public opinion within the movement grew steadily.

Another aspect of this development is worth noticing as well. Other left-wingers followed suit in several other local newspapers belonging to the labor movement, so much so that in the crucial year 1918 almost all the editors and a great many journalists in the labor press supported the opposition's taking over the leadership of the party. From another perspective, the labor press over the years developed into a veritable stronghold of the left wing. This is not too surprising, perhaps, since journalists constituted the intellectual strata of the movement.[8] The strongest, most important stronghold was *Ny Tid,* under the leadership of Tranmæl. This created a sort of double power system within the labor movement. There was one intellectual center in the top leadership in Oslo and another in the editorial offices of *Ny Tid* in Trondheim.

In connection with the national congress of the Trade Union Federation in 1913, Tranmæl systematically outlined his opinions on most topics to be discussed at the congress and through the columns of *Ny Tid* he also prepared for concerted action at the meeting. When he himself was prevented from being a representative at the congress by certain leaders through bureaucratic means, he covered the event as a journalist for his paper. Thus, he was both able to take part in the opposition's discussions before the meetings and immediately, or at least the next day, to give his opinions on what was going on and how events were to be understood.

Tranmæl followed up the 1913 congress by launching in *Ny Tid* a plan for organizing an opposition. This was a plan for establishing a national organized oppositional section within the trade union movement. An invitation to all local trade unions in the country was published in *Ny Tid.* Through the local labor association in Trondheim that he had initiated in 1910 and where he had launched the *Trondhjem Resolution* in 1911, Tranmæl now took a great part in organizing an oppositional convention in Trondheim. It met between Christmas and New Year's Eve, 1913, and founded the Norwegian Trade Union Opposition as a formal organization within the Trade Union Federation, with its own board, chairman, and secretary.

The political platform of this oppositional organization was a revised version of the *Trondhjem Resolution.* Its opening paragraph stated: "Because the trade union movement is the vital nerve [*livsnerven*] of the labor movement, the task of which is to transform the societal conditions, the natural consequence must be that this objective is given a prominent position in the economic or trade union activity—thus, that one not only strive for the improvement of the workers' conditions within the capitalist state, but that one struggle for shattering that state and for introducing a socialist system of society."[9] Thus the trade union opposition chose as its goal the establishment of a socialist strategy as the main purpose of the trade union movement. The intended consequence of the program was to restructure the organizational pattern and the politics of the trade union movement accordingly.

From the very beginning this organized trade union opposition worked together with the Youth Federation. Several members, like Tranmæl himself, belonged to both organizations. At the same time the trade union opposition in itself may be said to have been part of the party opposition consistent with the system of most of the unions' collective membership in the party. This double basis of a labor movement opposition, including both a closely connected trade union and a youth movement, was a unique phenomenon compared with labor opposition in Sweden and Denmark as well as in most other European countries at the time. This is the most important factor in explaining the phenomenon of the organized opposition or left wing taking over the old social democratic party, the Norwegian Labor Party, in 1918.

There were opposition movements within labor parties in other European social democracies as well, but the Norwegian case was the only one where the opposition in the end got the upper hand. Again, Norway's was the only labor movement where the trade union opposition worked so closely together with the pure party opposition and was so integrated in a joint oppositional undertaking. This meant that the left wing or the opposition in the Norwegian labor movement had a broader social and organizational basis than elsewhere. Thus, it had broader support from the working class proper than was the case with most other social democratic oppositions. We may again ask how this came about.

One way of understanding this is to return to the thesis of Edvard Bull and to his emphasis on the transformation of the Norwegian working class in the wake of the industrial surge connected to the huge new electrochemical and electrometallurgical industry built around 1905. When Tranmæl started his campaign for transforming or revolutionizing the labor movement, his message was most eagerly received by the newly proletarianized workers attached to these new industries. That may be explained, in its turn, by various factors, but the most important was that Tranmæl's trade union program, partially imported from the United States, was very well suited to the life and working conditions of workers at the new plants and in their newly established societies.

Thus was created the exceptionally solid basis of the left wing in the Norwegian labor movement. This, both socially and organizationally, was a fundamental premise for the left wing's further growth and growing influence. The new elements of the working class flocking to Tranmæl's banner never constituted a majority, however, either in the working class or in the labor movement. The support of the left wing by these new workers, although fundamental, is not an adequate or sufficient explanation for the great shift in 1918. To explain this several other factors must be taken into consideration as well. Most importantly, we must explain how the oppositional minority in the labor movement finally turned itself into a majority.

This process was deeply connected to the consequences of the outbreak of World War I in 1914. Norway was a neutral during the war, although sometimes called a "neutral ally." In spite of Norway's neutrality, the consequences of the war were hard felt by its people. Since the Middle Ages, Norway has been completely dependent upon import of food. The necessary importing of food was very much hindered by the war, and the result was both a serious lack of food for a large part of the population and a sharp rise in food prices. Some people profited from the situation, social differences deepened, and class antagonisms were sharpened.

How would the workers react to this development? And how would the labor movement act towards the employers as well as towards the political authorities? In all its nakedness, this was the pending question shaping the debate and setting the terms of the struggle within the labor movement. In this debate the left wing's appeal for direct action and revolutionary mass action got a new life, while the established leaders of the labor movement gradually appeared to be less able to cope with the situation. They were unwilling to employ the radical means proposed by the left wing, means which seemed appropriate to more and more people. Finally reaction turned inwards and into a rebellion against their own labor movement leaders.

Throughout 1916 and 1917, a dialectical political process developed where a growing number of the members of the labor movement lost faith in their old leaders and turned to the opposition, to the left wing. More and more members were radicalized. This radicalizing was further stimulated by the news of the Russian Revolution and of tendencies to social upheavals in other European countries throughout 1917 and in the beginning of 1918. The radicalizing of

Norwegian workers in 1917 was intensified by a pending threat of hunger. When the United States had entered the war, it began to restrict Norway's importation of food, although earlier America had defended the rights of neutrals. An agreement on the matter between Norway and the United States was not reached until spring 1918, one week after the congress of the Labor Party where the crucial shift took place. When the established leaders of the labor movement seemed to hesitate and not really to grasp the seriousness of the situation, the left wing acted convincingly, mobilizing people and appearing sufficiently trustworthy to gain the support of more and more members. Then the shift came.

After the left wing had taken over the Norwegian Labor Party and installed Kyrre Grepp as the new chairman and Martin Tranmæl as the new general secretary, it did not manage to stage a revolution in Norway. During a nationwide general strike in 1921, Tranmæl and his companions did their utmost to rouse people to expand the strike to the political level, but little came of this. The revolutionary moment in Europe in the wake of the end of the war had passed, only to be replaced by economic crisis and political reaction, in Norway as elsewhere.

On the other hand, Tranmæl and Grepp and the other leaders of the old left wing acted in a sufficiently moderate way to consolidate their power in the Labor Party. Grepp died in 1922, but Tranmæl continued to be the real leader of the party throughout the interwar years. After a new split in 1923, when a new opposition established Norway's Communist Party, Tranmæl installed two new protégés from the old left wing as formal party leaders, one as chairman and the other as general secretary, while he himself continued to direct the politics and the development of the party from his position as editor of the party's chief organ *Social-Demokraten*.

One of the new protégés, Einar Gerhardsen (1897–1987), was one of the resistance leaders during the German occupation of Norway in 1940–1945 and barely survived as a prisoner in a German concentration camp. In 1945 Gerhardsen took over as prime minister in Norway and he was in power almost continuously until 1965, all the while with his close companion and mentor, Martin Tranmæl, as a grey eminence and as a member of the central committee of the Labor Party.

That Einar Gerhardsen and the Labor Party rose to this dominant position as a result of the success of the left wing in conquering the

Labor Party in 1918 must to a great extent be attributed to the special character of this faction, consisting as it did not only of a party opposition proper, but also of an organized trade union opposition. The main architect of this opposition was Martin Tranmæl who, in creating this force in Norwegian politics, drew heavily on his experiences as an itinerant laborer in the United States.

NOTES

[1]Edvard Bull's article was originally published as "Die Entwicklung der Arbeiterbewegung in den drei skandinavischen Ländern 1914–1920," *Archive für die Geschichte des Sozialismus und der Arbeiterbewegung* 10 (1922), 329–361. It appeared later in Norwegian as *Arbeiderbevægelsens stilling i de tre nordiske land 1914–1920* (Trondheim, 1922).

[2]Jorunn Bjørgum, *Martin Tranmæl og radikaliseringen av norsk arbeiderbevegelse 1906–1918* (Oslo, 1998).

[3]Quoted in Melvyn Dubofsky, *We Shall Be All. A History of the Industrial Workers of the World* (Chicago, 1969), 81.

[4]*Ny Tid,* 27 December 1905.

[5]*Ny Tid,* 14 December 1911. Also published as a pamphlet by the Local Labor Association in Trondheim, December 1911; reprinted in *Tidsskrift for arbeiderbevegelsens historie* 1 (1976), 214–221.

[6]Quoted in Melvyn Dubofsky, *We Shall Be All,* 81.

[7]*Social-Demokraten,* 5 January 1912, here cited from Per Horntvedt, "'Dynamitpatronene i borehullene' og de borgerlige avisers reaksjoner på Tranmæls tale" (M.A. thesis, University of Oslo, 1971).

[8]Bull also pointed out as one part of his explanation of the special Norwegian development that the fact that this invasion of the labor press by left-wingers was possible at all was one factor in differences between Norway, on the one hand, and Sweden and Denmark, on the other. According to Bull, this had to do with a decentralized tradition in Norway in general as well as in the Norwegian labor movement in particular. This decentralized tradition Bull explained partly with reference to topography and partly with reference to the difficulty of communicating in Norway, which left all central authorities, including those within the labor movement, less able to interfere in local situations.

[9]See note 5 above.

The Story of the Bergsten Brothers in Canada: Ethnic Barriers, Unfavorable Sex Ratios, and the Creation of Male Households

Sune Åkerman

EMIGRATION RESEARCH in the Nordic countries concentrated for a long time on measuring and mapping the dramatic movement of millions of people who migrated across the ocean. When this research began, historians knew only some basic facts about the structure of migrant groups. With new research tools and perspectives they can now move forward and analyze in greater depth the dramatic development of the transatlantic migration. This reorientation of emigration research is quite consonant with the overall inclination of contemporary historians to reorient the discipline to its original humanistic sources. In northern Europe a new scholarly network encompassing the universities of Archangelsk, Tromsö, Uleåborg, and Umeå seems to be well suited to take on such a challenge.

One of the key questions within social science research has been the intriguing relation between individuals and the larger groups to which they belong. In this article I would like to combine knowledge acquired in the 1970s with an autobiographical point of view where the emigration process will be seen through the eyes of individuals.

In the archives of the Institute of Emigrants in Växjö in south central Sweden, in a region typical of those from which there was a heavy emigration, there is a mass of material from the period of the great emigration. Pictures, photos, diaries, autobiographies, letters, and other materials abound in this very rich archive. Among the autobiographical texts given to the institute there is a manuscript by

Vilhelm Bergsten. It was given to the institute in 1992, some years after his death. Here I want to use his autobiographical account to test the hypothesis that individuals of the lower classes may under certain circumstances provide valuable insider's information about the mechanisms of mass emigration.

Bergsten was the son of a small farmer living not far from the city of Eskilstuna just south of Stockholm. His education included the ordinary compulsory course of six years typical for most emigrants. In addition he received some basic, primarily practical, training at an agricultural school. He left this school with low marks, and very disappointed because of a conflict with one of the teachers. He had difficulty finding work suited to his training and eventually decided to emigrate to Canada where he lived in Manitoba, Saskatchewan, Alberta, and finally the Northwest Territories. He first earned his living as a farmhand and as a lumberjack. Later he claimed a homestead in Valleyview in the foothills of the Rocky Mountains northwest of Edmonton, Alberta. Here he settled for a time together with his younger brother Dan, managing along the way to put up buildings, to cultivate a few acres, to buy cattle and horses, and to participate in a local society dominated by Swedish immigrants. Finally Vilhelm Bergsten joined an Irish friend who had decided to try his luck in the gold fields of the Northwest Territories. For several years Vilhelm hung on under these tough circumstances, without making much money, before returning to Sweden after eleven dramatic years in Canada. His brother Dan also returned home. Unlike Vilhelm, however, Dan returned to their farmstead in Valleyview and remained there for the rest of his life.

Vilhelm brought only a few dollars back to Sweden, but he also returned home with something much more valuable, experiences and impressions from the new world. His mastery of the English language turned out to be of great value to him. As a farmhand he had acquired English by reading one of the big Chicago newspapers subscribed to by his employer. The years 1926 to 1937 must have been the most important and dramatic in Vilhelm Bergsten's whole life. In old age he sat down to tell about his time in Canada and he did so vividly and in great detail. Since his experiences in the prairie provinces were typical of the situation of laboring men in Canada, he provides a social perspective "from below." His capacity for observation, his intelligence, and his skill in writing, however, were far above the average for an uneducated immigrant from Scandinavia. In this he was unlike the many illiterate immigrants who arrived in the United States and Canada from Europe.

Our research program dealing with demographic development, the relations between governments, and religious and ethnic conditions in Scandinavia can easily be used as a starting point for an analysis of Vilhelm Bergsten's autobiographical notes. Bergsten often makes remarks about the central government in Ottawa and its handling of natural resources, law and justice, immigration policies, educational questions, culture, transport, etc. The involvement of Canada in World War I is treated rather negatively, from a pacifistic point of view, but does not reveal the pro-German attitude otherwise typical of Swedish-Americans. The passivity of the government in face of the Great Depression in 1929–33 is likewise strongly criticized, although Bergsten recognizes some measures taken to help the most poverty-stricken.

Bergsten considered an unrestricted immigration policy in the midst of a serious economic crisis really stupid and thought that it revealed a cynical attitude toward Canada's citizenry. Ottawa's handling of the land question, on the other hand, receives much praise. This is not at all surprising if we consider the fact that the Bergsten brothers along with tens of thousands of other land-hungry immigrants received homesteads for free from the government as a part of its effort to develop the vast almost uninhabited parts of western Canada. It is quite evident that Bergsten's generally low esteem for the central government of Canada was colored by his resistance to the politically dominant ethnic group, the English.

It is a recognized fact that people's religious affiliations and their needs have been of utmost importance among immigrants in North America. Therefore we have to ask how a person like Bergsten reacted to religious life in Canada. Emigrants from Scandinavia in the twentieth century typically belonged to a more urban, industrial group of people than the first generations that left Europe in the nineteenth century. Bergsten himself typifies this later wave when he reveals an almost atheistic attitude in religious matters. Nevertheless he was raised in pious circumstances in Sweden by a mother who was a strong believer and who often complained about her son's antireligious views. Bergsten, however, was forced to accept the important role that religion had come to play in immigrant society. Therefore he participated actively in the building of a church in Valleyview and he seems generally to have been more involved in the church life of the Canadian settlement than he ever had been in Sweden.

Although the official history produced by the Augustana Synod is silent on the matter, Bergsten tells us about the tension between the Swedish Mission Church and the Augustana Synod in their settlement. This friction seems to have delayed the building of a church. Bergsten also complains about some people "who did not care about the institutions that a society needs," a matter that delayed the construction work even more. When the timber intended for the church building had been cut, it was stored in the open air for such a long time that it was almost destroyed. Thus "donated work" seems not to have been of the highest priority, at least in this instance. For a long time services had to be held in the school building, itself also a product of collectively donated work.

Generally speaking, Bergsten did not hesitate to air his negative opinions about greedy and uneducated clergy who lived contrary to the Christian message. He even passes on rumors about the Swedish parish pastor who was said to have been a professional poker player in his earlier life! Another Lutheran pastor also working in the Valleyview district was punished for sexual involvement with children, something that Bergsten reports about with satisfaction. Nevertheless Bergsten could also acknowledge the practical side of church life and its social implications for the settlers. He quite often complains about the dominance of materialistic matters in the crude life of the immigrants. From his point of view religious worship at least acted as a brake on the obsession with all the material pursuits that occupied people in their hard daily life. One gets the feeling, however, that Bergsten found both the building of a field for sporting events, in which he was most active, and his involvement in amateur theatrical work at least as valuable and presumably more stimulating than church life.

THE ETHNIC LANDSCAPE

In the milieu where Bergsten was brought up in Södermanland, and especially in the countryside, in the beginning of the twentieth century there were very few opportunities for Swedes ever to meet persons from other cultures and continents. The movement overseas meant a most dramatic change in this respect. On the emigrant steamers destined for North American ports one could encounter thousands of people most of whom belonged to nations other than one's own, people of strange habits who spoke unknown languages. Even during the crossing, Bergsten realized that he had entered a multiethnic period of his life. He makes quite a few comments about the appearance, habits, and behavior of other nationalities onboard, including not least those of emigrants from eastern Europe.

When Vilhelm Bergsten and his brother Dan had settled down in Valleyview in Alberta they lived in a Scandinavian colony with Norwegians and Swedes and also people of some other nationalities. This did not mean, however, that they were ethnically isolated. On the contrary, they encountered people from all corners of the world almost every day. Their farm happened to be situated on the road between High Prairie and Valleyview, just beside a river-crossing with a lot of traffic. Here they actually made some money when they used their horses to help drivers of automobiles that had gotten stuck on the steep banks of the river.

Among the ethnic groups that Bergsten described and commented upon in his manuscript are Norwegians, Icelanders, Old Swedes, Hungarians, Irish, Russians, Scots, French, Welsh, Germans, Black people, different tribes of Native Americans, Chinese, Finns, English, Italians, Swiss, Jews, Danes, Dutch, Austrians, Poles, and Czechs. This is quite a long list, but it does not exclude the possibility that Bergsten had met with people of other nationalities he did not bother to mention and characterize. This must certainly have been the case with his brother Dan, who lived long periods of time among hoboes and people of the most mixed background in his search for jobs in railway construction, logging camps, and other places.

Striking in Bergsten's text is the fact that the author almost never talks about "Americans" or "Canadians." He seems to have had a strong sensibility to the ethnic background of most people in this immigrant society. The other side of this coin was a sudden awareness of his own Swedishness. Presumably this is typical of the immigrant situation. Now and then he describes his Swedishness, often by contrasting it to what he thinks of other nationalities. Here the real point of reference was the English, the "charter members," as it were, of the Canadian society. Bergsten found them pretentious and prone to overrating their own capacity in comparison to all other immigrant

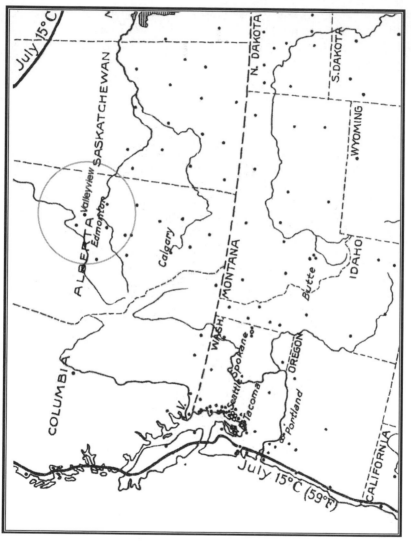

This map shows the location of Valleyview in relation to other Swedish communities in the western provinces of Canada in 1921. Adapted from Helge Nelson, The Swedes and Swedish Settlements in North America, 2 vols. (Lund, 1943), 2:#4.

groups. He reports with great amusement about a soccer match between the Scandinavians and the English in Valleyview, where the individual skills of the latter could not stand up to the good organization and system of the Norwegian and Swedish players. It is easy to see, however, that this story betrays an inferiority complex that must have been typical for most uneducated immigrants in Canada, who were initially handicapped by their poor knowledge of the English language.

A MENTAL MAP

It may be possible to discern concentric circles of ethnic identity plotted in relation to the Swedish group. Scandinavians form the inmost circle, while a second includes the Germans, the Dutch, the Finns, etc. A third circle takes in Greeks, Italians, Russians, and so on, while an outer circle contains Blacks, the Chinese, and others. Individual attitudes like those we find in Bergsten's manuscript can be compared with the rate of intermarriage with different ethnic groups. From just one single immigrant we learn, among other things, the importance of specific experiences that are in turn related to basic collective attitudes and values. We may also be able to register changes in the attitudes over time, as well as creation or dissolution of prejudices. In the case of Bergsten, his appreciation of the Irish seems to have been higher than we would expect from the Scandinavians, and we can also see that he changed his mind regarding Native Americans from a rather negative to a most benevolent outlook. Here, however, we must bear in mind the long gestation period before he prepared his manuscript. Much had happened in the world and to Bergsten between the 1930s and the 1980s!

When Bergsten describes other nationalities than his own he very seldom differentiates between, for example, north and south Italians or between Germans from Bavaria or Hamburg. He also seems to be unaware of the differences between Ukrainians and Russians. When it comes to his own Swedish compatriots, however, he always labels them according to the region of their birth and the dialect of Swedish they used. Thus it is possible to talk about two levels of ethnic awareness. Bergsten breaks down the Swedish-speaking immigrants into the following groups: Värmlanders, Norrbothnians, Härjedalians, Norrlanders, Jämtlanders, Vestrobothnians, Dalecarlians,

Södermanlanders (from his own home province), Scanians, Stockholmians, Hallanders, Upplanders, Smålanders, Ostrogothians, Vestrogothians, Medelpadians, Old Swedes (from the Ukraine), Ostrobothnians (from Finland), and other Swedish Finns. Although Bergsten creates a hierarchy of place for other nationalities, he does not do so for former inhabitants of the Swedish provinces. He tends to describe immigrants from the remote northern part of Sweden as positively as people from the Lake Mälaren region where he himself had been brought up. He seems, in fact, to have admired some of the tough northerners for their ability to cope with the hard climate and wilderness of western Canada. The most unpleasant person he ever met in Canada, on the other hand, was a foreman on a railway construction job from the province of Ostrogothia, close to Bergsten's home in Sweden. There was also a bragging womanizer from Dalecarlia. This indicates that he was able to make a clear distinction between nation and personality.

Only when he comments upon the United States and Americans does he tend to make some crude generalizations of a rather negative nature. He had, however, no firsthand experience of the country south of the border other than that gained during a short stay in New York just before he returned to Sweden in 1937. Some of the settlers in Valleyview were Swedish-Americans who had migrated from the Midwest and who could tell about the conditions in the United States. As mentioned above, Bergsten also read American newspapers quite regularly. He found the American capitalistic system disgusting, a waste of both human and natural resources that tended in his view to create criminality on all levels in society. Never, he writes, would I consider marrying an American woman. They are too spoiled!

THREE DIFFICULT HANDICAPS

It is quite obvious that the ethnic awareness and attitudes so openly disclosed in the case of Bergsten generated problems for the immigrants. They created both real and mental barriers for recently arrived "greenhorns" in search of marriage partners. If Bergsten felt alienated in relation to women of American "old stock," they would in turn never have accepted him as a partner. Most likely he and his brother Dan expected to find Swedish or Scandinavian girls to share their lives with when they made their homestead claims. They knew from home how impossible it was to farm without a woman taking her part. They had, however, chosen to live in an area where there was a tremendous shortage of females of marriageable age. The Valleyview district could be labeled "Land of the Bachelors," as could most similar areas in the countryside or wilderness of Canada in the interwar period. From the point of view of a male in search of a mate, lumber camps, railway work, or threshing gangs were even worse. Females were almost altogether absent in such places. Most laboring men dreaming of a farmstead had to dwell in such surroundings for quite a long time to earn some money and simply to survive. This was clearly the case with the Bergsten brothers even long after they had settled in Valleyview. The need for ready cash often forced them out to work quite far away from their new home. As mentioned above, Vilhelm Bergsten even tried desperately to improve his economic situation as a gold miner in the distant Northwest Territories.

Ethnic barriers, a shortage of females, and poor economic conditions combined with language barriers added up to a most frustrating situation for all these bachelors in areas where immigrants had settled. Even if the gender ratio had been different, the ethnocentrism of most nationalities as well as the religious barriers would have prevented the marriage market from operating smoothly. Had ethnocentrism been removed, there would still have been the extremely poor economic conditions that most immigrants had to cope with for many years. What kind of life could these men possibly offer a woman?

BUILDING A HOME WITHOUT WOMEN AND CHILDREN

When the Bergsten brothers made their claim in the Valleyview district, they intended to cultivate their own land, build their own houses, buy their own cattle, and have their own separate economies. Soon, however, they realized that it would be wiser to cooperate in all matters and to create a sibling household. To learn how they managed to do this is a most fascinating story. I presume that many such stories could be told if we had access to empirical evidence. Vilhelm Bergsten's autobiography gives us at least one excellent opportunity to examine this process.

This text records year by year, often month by month, and sometimes even week by week what happened on the homestead in the foothills of the Rocky Mountains. It covers practical details involved

in making the claim after choosing the site of two farmsteads, culti-
vating the soil, buying horses and cattle, building houses and barns,
making their own furniture, etc. Even more interestingly, it gives us
inside information on the mental side of life in this tough environment with its long and extremely hard winters.

Compared to other social and demographic information used by
historians, an autobiography can tell us directly about things we
otherwise can only guess about. Here we can learn how and why the
Bergsten brothers emigrated and how they got information about
opportunities for employment while they were moving across the
continent to their final destination in Alberta. Vilhelm Bergsten, or
"Bill," as he was called in Canada, tells us also about the hardships
they met as farmhands and lumberjacks, how they experienced the
North American labor market in general, with its demand for work
intensity. (Studies of work intensity at home in Sweden at the turn of
the century had, in fact, led analysts to conclude that Swedish labor-
ers worked more slowly and less energetically than their counterparts
in North America.) We get to know the Scandinavian social network
that helped the two brothers to find their claim in Valleyview. We
learn how excited they were over the beautiful scenery with the red
willow bushes, the small river close to their place with its clear water,
its steep banks, the forest and the open fields in this area so similar to
the countryside they knew back home. They soon realized that there
were plenty of fish in the river as well as game to hunt in the forest.
Vilhelm also tells us about the strange and solemn feeling of preparing the soil for its first harvest ever. It was a case of "soil wrong side
up," as a Native American remarked to Vilhelm.

In this context the familial arrangements of the Bergsten brothers
demand our interest most of all. As intimated above, the chances of
finding a girl of marriageable age who was not already engaged were
extremely slight. Again and again Vilhelm returns to the fact that
women were few and far between and observes that the poor bachelors lived a hard and frustrated life. He points out that their eating
habits and drinking behavior created severe health problems. Lone-
liness and homesickness were the twin children born in this situation. Isolation and disappointment could easily end up in mental illness, as Bergsten wisely observes.

A comment on the physical appearance of these brothers is in
order. According to Vilhelm, his brother Dan was almost a giant.
Even if this description of Dan is exaggerated, it is quite clear that he

was very tall, big, and strong. Compared to his brother, Vilhelm was small, but known as clever. On the surface this pair may remind us of characters from John Steinbeck's *Of Mice and Men,* but this comparison would be quite misleading since Dan also had a good head on his shoulders. Dan had, indeed, vacated a position as assistant shop-keeper in a very big hardware store in Eskilstuna to accompany his older brother overseas. Dan had a tender relationship to their mother, to whom he wrote often and regularly. Vilhelm used these letters many years later in preparing his autobiography. Dan also took care of house and animals more than his older brother did. He loved to cultivate vegetables and he was the one who most often prepared their food. More often than Vilhelm, Dan stayed home and improved buildings, making repairs and caring for the animals. He did all of this, for example, during Vilhelm's long stay in the goldmines of the Northwest Territory. When really hard work was needed, however, Dan left Valleyview to take on the challenge of improving the household economy of the two brothers. It seems a bit odd, especially in the context of the interwar period, to think of this giant of a man baking a nice "three-layer cake" for the Christmas table and preparing other traditional Swedish dishes almost as easily as he could carry home a heavy burden on his shoulders from far away High Prairie or impress employers and others with his exceptional strength.

It is evident that this "sibling household" was to the advantage of our brothers. They could build something for the future by combining their talents and planning their approach to the labor market. It was of course practical to work together on more advanced tasks like moving their barn, a task made necessary by the encroachment of road building on their land. It must be stressed, however, that they also had good neighbors who helped each other out quite often. In old age Vilhelm remarked in a somewhat nostalgic mood that life in Valleyview was hard but very satisfactory from a social point of view. People cared for others out there, he recalled.

Not all families managed as well. Vilhelm noticed that he and Dan got along quite easily, unlike certain other bachelors and brothers in the vicinity. This was a prerequisite for a sibling household. There were, of course, some tensions between the Bergsten brothers, often caused by the fact that Vilhelm refused to cook. Milking their few cows could also cause trouble. This was something always left to women back in Scandinavia, and much to their surprise Vilhelm and Dan realised that American women never had to milk. In general, however, the Bergsten brothers seem to have managed quite well together. Vilhelm, as a matter of fact, admired his younger brother not only for his strength but also for his caring attitude towards others and for his intelligence.

SWEDISH BACHELOR FARMERS IN CANADA

In this article an autobiography has been used to shed light upon the effects of the uneven sex ratio of certain areas of Canada in the interwar period of the twentieth century. This is the tale of two Swedish boys of marriageable age who entered a society where women were hardly to be found. The story of the Bergsten brothers in Canada in 1926–1937 tells us about frustrations and hardships as well as achievements and happiness in building a farmstead from scratch in the wilderness. The solution turned out to be a male "sibling household," which has been presented from various aspects in the framework of our accumulated knowledge of the mass emigration from the Scandinavian countries.

REFERENCES

References for this article include, in addition to the Bergsten manuscript in the archives of Emigrant Institute in Växjö, the following: Kenneth O. Bjork, "Scandinavian Migration to the Prairie Provinces 1893–1914," *Norwegian-American Studies* 26 (1974); J. Dahlie, "Writing Ethnic History: The Generation Series and the Limits of Pluralism," *Canadian Review of Studies in Nationalism* (Fall 1983); Lars Ljungmark, "Swedes in Winnipeg up to the 1940s: Inter-Ethnic Relations," in *Swedish Life in American Cities,* ed. Dag Blanck and Harald Runblom (Uppsala, 1991); Lars Ljungmark, "The Northern Neighbor: Winnipeg, the Swedish Service Station in the 'Last Best West' 1890–1950," in *Swedes in the Twin Cities—Immigrant Life and Minnesota's Urban Frontier,* ed. Philip J. Anderson and Dag Blanck (Saint Paul, 2001); Lars Ljungmark and Sune Åkerman, "Swedes in Canada," in *Meddelanden från Landsarkivet i Härnösand* (Härnösand, 1998); Nelson Helge, *The Swedes and Swedish Settlements in North America,* 2 vols. (Lund, 1943); Harald Runblom, "The Swedes in Canada: A Study of Low Ethnic Consciousness," *Swedish-American Historical Quarterly* 33 (1982).

American, Norwegian, or North Norwegian? Dilemmas of Identity for Immigrants from Northern Norway in the United States, 1900–1930

Einar Niemi

THIS ARTICLE IS ON FIRST-GENERATION north Norwegians in the upper Midwest and their approaches to culture and ethnicity, as mirrored on the individual level and in their organizational life. Dilemmas of regional identity are, of course, a familiar field of study for the distinguished scholar honored by the present volume of essays, Odd Sverre Lovoll. In numerous studies he has documented that Norwegian immigrants organized along ethnic and cultural lines. Not least of these is his recent groundbreaking work, *The Promise Fulfilled*, a splendid example of thematic focus and perspective.[1] Lovoll's authorship began with a close examination of regional identity of Norwegian-American immigrants. I refer, of course, to his *A Folk Epic: The* Bygdelag *in America*.[2] In the present article I will examine different attitudes and positions toward the north Norwegian immigrant community, as represented by the group centred on Nordlandslaget, the Nordland regional association in the United States. I will focus in particular on three central figures. I draw heavily here on Lovoll's studies, both with regard to empirical findings and interpretive perspectives. In spite of his warnings against such practice, however, I rely in some measure on fiction as historical evidence, with the obvious dangers implied. I hope that this little study will thus represent a modest contribution to one of Odd Lovoll's early fields of interest, the regional and local dimensions of home country memories.

REPRESENTATIVE FIGURES

Ole E. Rølvaag (1876–1931) was, of course, a key figure in Norwegian-American culture. He was also, however, a northerner. His literary works demonstrate, as many critics have noted, that his north Norwegian background was of enormous significance for him, not only as raw material for literature, but also as the basis of his identity. Rølvaag was one of those who took the initiative to organize Nordlandslaget, the "regional association" or Norwegian *bygdelag* for his home region. He sat on its board for many years, was chairman for a time, and was on the editorial board of the society's quarterly journal, *Nord-Norge* [*North Norway*]. In a number of other contexts, he also participated as a northerner. He belonged, for example, to a small, select, private circle of northern Norwegians who for many years came together for fishing trips, dinners, debates, and celebrations at which "We can sound off to one another, and we can laugh, and we can play cards," as another member of the circle, the attorney John Heitmann (1871–1965), put it in a letter to Rølvaag.[3]

Apart from Rølvaag, this inner circle consisted of Heitmann, who was also born on Dønna, and the poet Julius B. Baumann (1871–1923), born in Kiby, near Vadsø in Finnmark, but whose family originally came from Helgeland.[4] Since Heitmann lived in Duluth and Baumann in nearby Carlton, they would often meet in the Duluth home of the generous and well-to-do Heitmann. As a result, they were often called the "Duluth Circle." Although less well remembered than Rølvaag and Baumann, Heitmann was a poet of some standing, an essayist, and a feared and admired debater who liked to appear in newspapers and magazines under a variety of pseudonyms, the best known of which was "Bjarne Blehr." Baumann and Heitmann, perhaps more than literary historians have realized, acted as Rølvaag's literary advisers. They were his confessors and "brothers" from "the fairytale kingdom back home" [*æventyrriget der hjemme*].[5]

Another member of the group, but just beyond the inner circle, was the newspaper editor Jørgen J. Fuhr of Duluth (1877–1930), born in Lenvik, Troms, with a background that smacked of the fairy tales. He lived a life reminiscent of Ibsen's Per Gynt, Falkberget's Bør Børson, or Hamsun's August. By 1917 Fuhr had established himself as a press baron in the upper Midwest and he had great plans for both newspapers and colonization projects in Canada. He married

Anna Dahl (1891–1959), a registered nurse who was born in Meløy, Nordland. She had come to the United States on a Red Cross exchange program in 1918 and stayed. She came in contact with the Nordlandslaget group early on and was already a close friend of Rølvaag and of Baumann when she met Fuhr. She was for a time editor of the society's journal and contributed fine fiction and essays. When her husband died, she took over his press empire and became the first "press queen" in the Midwest.[6] Also in this circle, but somewhat farther out, we find Waldemar Ager (1869–1941), who lived in Eau Claire, Wisconsin. Born in Fredrikstad, he was married to a woman from northern Norway, Gurolle Blesten of Tromsø.[7]

Several of the central figures in the movement advocating the retention of Norwegian identity in America were thus northerners, while several of the standard bearers for southern Norwegian background, like Ager, were also closely connected with the Nordlandslaget group. The northerners thus backed two horses, a national Norwegian one and a regional north Norwegian one. They also managed for the most part to cope with the dual identity this entailed, although not without certain complications that we shall examine.

North Norwegian mobilization and organization in the United States, especially in the upper Midwest, raises questions. How did the northerners organize? How did they handle issues of integration? What kind of identity did they create for themselves? What kind of contacts did they have with the northern region back home? To the extent that they felt, or wanted to feel, Norwegian, were they also northerners? A study of this small circle of influential persons we have identified may shed further light on central issues concerning the first generation's encounter with America, although there are certainly risks that they may not be adequately representative.

In the period under investigation, attitudes among northerners ranged from an expressed will to total integration on American premises to radical ethnic mobilization. In general it seems that the northerners had a pronounced need to root their identity in north Norwegian regionalism. But there was a certain ambivalence: many of them were concerned both to claim Norwegian national identity and eagerly to accept their transplantation into American society. There were, indeed, clashes of loyalties among them. The north Norwegian enclaves they established were, however, more important to them than the Norwegian ones as therapeutic aids in the period under investigation, offering refuge and security. Ethnicity as such appears not only as something created to further certain aims, but also as an emanation of something essential, something that had its origins in more existential needs.

However, the north Norwegians expressed their identity selectively. The identity they constructed in the United States did not embrace all immigrant groups from northern Norway. Some groups, as we shall see, were excluded. Moreover, it must be added that the persons selected for this study represent the cultural leadership, an elite that is hardly representative of rank-and-file north Norwegians, a feature also observed in other studies.[8] Nevertheless, they each reflect attitudes and emotions found widely among the first generation of north Norwegians in America.

NORDLÆNDINGENES FORENING AND NORDLANDSLAGET

From the outset, there was contact between Nordlandslaget, the largest north Norwegian regional organization in America, and Nordlændingenes Forening [Association of North Norwegians] in Oslo. Nordlændingenes Forening, founded in 1862, was the oldest *bygdelag* in the Norwegian capital. A great many well-known north Norwegian artists, politicians, and civil servants belonged to the elite of the association, including the composer Ole Olsen (1850–1927); Ole Tobias Olsen (1830–1924), who was, among other things, known as the "father of the Nordland railway"; Sivert Andreas Nielsen (1823–1904), who sat in the Storting [Parliament] almost continously from 1859–1900, who eventually became President of the Storting, and who by reason of his political commitment to northern Norway was known to political colleagues as the "Trumpet of the North," after the epic poem of Petter Dass; and Anton Christian Bang (1840–1913), professor at the University of Oslo and bishop of Oslo, 1896–1912.[9] When Nordlandslaget was founded in the United States, there were direct contacts with the *bygdelag* in Oslo.

Nordlandslaget was the fifth Norwegian *bygdelag* organized in the United States. It was founded in January 1909, after preparatory meetings in 1908. Nordlandslaget thus belongs to the small group of pioneering associations. When the *bygdelag* movement was at its height in the 1920s, there were almost fifty associations. Central to the general motivation of the *bygdelag* was the defense of local and folk culture, as opposed to urban and high culture. The annual conventions were particularly important for this purpose.[10]

In the summer of 1908, Bishop Bang visited the United States to unveil a statue of Henrik Wergeland donated by Nordmandsforbundet [Norsemen's Federation] to Det Norske Selskap i Amerika [The Norwegian Society of America]. In Minneapolis, he met a number of emigrant northerners privately. On a rowing trip on Lake Minnetonka, he proposed a north Norwegian *bygdelag* in the United States, drawing analogies with the history of Nordlændingenes Forening. By this time, there were estimated to be about 40,000 immigrants of north Norwegian origin in the United States.[11]

In the bylaws of Nordlandslaget, the regionalist dimension was clearly stated: "The aim of this association will be to work among people from northern Norway, to strive for the preservation of their traditions." From the beginning, there was an emphasis on measures that might benefit northern Norway. A "foundation fund" was set up and several collections were made for specific projects. Until well after World War II, money was collected for such projects as nursing homes, voluntary nursing associations, and schools in the region. The largest projects prior to about 1920 were the "tuberculosis campaign," which supported preventive measures in northern Norway; the "school campaign," which planned large-scale investment in various secondary schools in northern Norway; and the "lifeboat campaign." The last-mentioned project was also the most successful. A lifeboat was commissioned from Collin Archer in Larvik, and in 1911 the boat, *Nordland,* went into operation in Lofoten. It had cost 13,000 Norwegian *kroner.* The history of the boat was to be both glorious and dramatic. It operated in the seas around the Lofoten Islands until World War II.[12]

The archives of Nordlandslaget contain extensive correspondence between people on the board of Nordlændingenes Forening and central figures in Nordlandslaget. A pronounced feature of this correspondence is common commitment to northern Norway. A number of specific projects and ideas are discussed, but ideological issues connected with more fundamental regionalist questions are also aired. What we see here is a strong mobilization on behalf of a region described as previously neglected, exploited, and unjustly treated, but one that had great potential for the future. This mobilization occurred in the diaspora communities in Oslo and in the United States long before equivalent moves took place in northern Norway itself. However, the mobilization harbored certain ambivalences.

It was in part backward-looking, quasi-romantic, and rooted in various key myths derived from the idea of a glorious past, in which different versions of "homemaking myths" are recognized. Here it is instructive to consider our findings in light of the notions of "constructive" or "instrumental" projects in theories of nationalism.[13] This is expressed, for instance, in a large number of historical articles and essays in *Nord-Norge,* in which the age of the sagas in northern Norway receives particular attention, that is, the "age of liberty" under the Earls of Haalogaland, which was marked by flourishing trade and resistance to the kings of Norway. Tore Hund is in particular depicted as a north Norwegian liberator.[14] In fact, it is in *Nord-Norge* that we find the first signs of attempts to offer integrated interpretations of early north Norwegian history, in spite of the fact that many of the contributions are marred by amateurism and eccentricity.[15]

At the same time as it looked to the past, this mobilization was future-oriented, rooted in notions of modernization that focused precisely on the great unrealized potential of the region, materially and otherwise. Here we can compare our findings with the notion of "constructive" or "instrumental" projects in theories of nationalism. The idea of northern Norway emerging from the recesses of memory, in Hamsun's words, appearing *"bak de hundrede mile"* [from hundreds of miles away] and moving toward a new golden age, was strong among the emigrants, as Baumann puts it in his great poem "*Haalogaland*":[16]

> A fleet of shining white sails
> sweeps forth across the gleaming sea—
> the bridegroom is coming,
> the northerner is coming!
> Sail after sail and prow after prow
> sail in row upon row to the harbour.
> The groom is coming,
> the northerner is coming.
>
> My glorious, beautiful Haalogaland,
> you waited centuries for the man of the North,

now I give you my mind and heart.
I write your name by the flames of the Northern Lights,
swear allegiance to you and embrace you
and light our altar candle.

NAMING NORTH NORWAY

But there was a tension here, expressed symbolically in terms of the geographical distinction between *Haalogaland,* the old medieval name of a part of the region, and *North Norway,* the new, invented designation. Ambivalence on this matter was present throughout the entire history of Nordlandslaget, and it can be clearly seen in the society's journal. However, it is clear that, for the key figures on both sides of the Atlantic during the pioneering days of regionalism, in the decade up to about 1914, notions of modernization were strong, as was the idea of northern Norway as a single region. We see this in the "invention" of the name "Nord-Norge." For documentation of this "invention," we must turn to the correspondence between northerners in Oslo and the Midwest.

Nordlandslaget chose *Nord-Norge* as the title of its journal beginning with the third issue, of December 1914. The first two issues, of spring and summer 1913, were simply called *Nordlandslaget.* From autumn 1914 onward, *Nord-Norge* appeared regularly, eventually as a quarterly publication, right up to the late 1970s, bound in hard covers. Since about 1980, it has been published as a rather unpretentious newsletter. *Nord-Norge* was probably, both qualitatively and quantitatively, the foremost of all *bygdelag* publications in the United States and the most long-lived. It also became a forum for a number of north Norwegian authors living in Norway who had not yet established a regional readership in their own country. Among the subscribers we find many inhabitants of northern Norway and members of the north Norwegian community in Oslo.

Nord-Norge became one of the very first manifestations of the concept of northern Norway, indicating a qualitatively new departure in regionalism. Until this point there had been no real collective name for the region. Expressions like *det nordlige Norge* [the north of Norway] were used. Likewise, the ecclesiastical designation *Tromsø stift* [Diocese of Tromsø] tended to be used, alongside *Nordlandene* [the northern counties] and *Nordlandene og Finnmarken* [the northern counties and Finnmark] as well as the historical name *Haalogaland,* even though the historical Haalogaland did not include Finnmark. The name was an issue for the north Norwegian communities in Oslo and the Midwest, and it became the subject of some debate. In correspondence beginning in 1916 after the issue had actually been resolved, between Ole Olsen of the board of Nordlændingenes Forening and the editor of *Nord-Norge,* Julius Baumann, the story unfolds of how the name emerged. Ole Olsen replies to Baumann's enquiry: "Who created that word? Well, bless me, but it was Sivert Nielsen and I. We were sitting one evening in 1894 in Nordlands Forening, which in those days had premises in the Hotel Royal on Jernbanetorvet. We happened to touch upon that clumsy phrase 'Nordland and Finnmark': 'What if we called it Nord-Norge,' said Sivert Nielsen, 'and then spread the word?' We did, and it was a pleasure to see them take the bait."[17]

In the same correspondence, Olsen and Baumann, both from Finnmark, also discuss intraregional differences within northern Norway. Baumann writes that it was not always easy to identify oneself as from Finnmark in Nordlandslaget. He and other Finnmarkers, called *taraskolpene,* a derogatory nickname for people living in the fjords of Finnmark, often felt that they were no more than a mere "echo" of the "compact majority" of northerners.[18] Ole Olsen responds on the basis of his own experience: "There is somehow rather a difference in rank between a *'Nordlænding'* (either a native of Nordland County or a northerner in a general sense) and a *'Finnmarking'.* . . . You see, the *Nordlænding* is in a sense the grander of the two, he takes all praise and accolades in his ample embrace,—and that's been the custom from blessed Petter Dass onwards, the *Finnmarking* is, so to speak, shunted way out onto the periphery, where as a rule he must be content to play a tolerated second fiddle and is seldom allowed over onto the same side as the first violins. Now, both of us being *Finnmarkinger,* we can, therefore, at least among ourselves, cast aside the fig leaf of shame. What I want to say is: all the honor and praise that I have received so much of in my long life—it has all been given to me as a *Nordlænding*—if I have remarked that I am from Hammerfest, then people have given me to believe that that's a cut from the same cloth. Such things can be profoundly vexing."[19] This was to provoke a debate in Nordlandslaget about changing the name of the association in line with the change in the name of the journal. However, it was decided to retain the original name, largely out of respect for the history of the association.

NORDLANDSBAAT OR VIKING SHIP?

How did northerners respond to the movement for Norwegian identity in the United States and what was their position in that movement? Here we will limit ourselves to a look at some examples from the great celebrations of the centenary of the sailing of the *Restauration* in 1825. The centenary celebrations in 1925 were the greatest collective mobilization in the history of the *bygdelag*. The main responsibility for the jubilee was shouldered by the *bygdelag* associations. The main celebration in 1925 occurred over three days in June in the Twin Cities of Minneapolis/St. Paul. President Calvin Coolidge himself took part. It aroused great enthusiasm when in his speech the president stated that Leif Ericson ought to be acknowledged as the true discoverer of America.[20]

During the celebrations, every participating *bygdelag* was to have a whole day to celebrate the event in its own way, while on the other days were to be shared events. Nordlandslaget immediately decided to give its celebration a distinctively north Norwegian profile. A full year in advance, at the annual convention, it was decided to bring objects from northern Norway that might underscore the special nature of north Norwegian culture. The merchant Hans Meyer of Mo, Nordland County, who had long been a subscriber to *Nord-Norge* as well as a contributor of literary items, was asked whether he might be willing to organize a collection of objects that the association might purchase. Meyer immediately offered to donate a fully-equipped *nordlandsbaat* [Nordland boat] of a type called *færing* [four-oared boat] and arrange for free transport to Minneapolis. In a letter to the society, he thought that the boat and its gear ought to be the beginning of a collection for a north-Norwegian museum in America. This idea had previously been aired in *Nord-Norge*.

The boat, fully equipped and rigged, was exhibited at the Minnesota State Fairgrounds, where a full-size copy of *Restaurationen* was also exhibited. There was enormous interest in the exhibition, but according to *Nord-Norge,* there was little doubt that the *nordlandsbaat,* "this rare visitor from Nordland," was by far the main attraction. Hundreds of northerners gathered around the boat, discussing "how well it handled in high winds." The *bygdelag* convention arranged by Nordlandslaget at the same time attracted approximately 1,000 northerners.[21]

Nothing came of the idea of a north-Norwegian-American museum. *Nordlandslaget* instead chose to support the Norwegian-American museum in Decorah, Iowa, work on which had begun in 1877 at Luther College in Decorah. Nordlandslaget donated the *færing* to the museum. It can still be seen there together with another boat that also celebrates north Norwegian seafaring traditions, a little sailing boat in which the Haram brothers of Balsfjord sailed across the Atlantic in 1933 for the Chicago World's Fair. Just twenty-five feet long, this was the smallest boat that until then had crossed between the old world and the new world.

On the whole, seafaring traditions and coastal culture were awarded pride of place in the celebration of north Norwegian identity. This was evident two years later after the centennial celebrations at Nordlandslaget's annual convention in Duluth, Minnesota, the largest port on Lake Superior and the largest inland port in the world. The association had maintained close contact with the north-Norwegian sea captain Kristian Folgerø of Sandnessjøen, Nordland, who planned to sail the Atlantic in a *nordlandsbaat.* The boat was a *fembøring,* an example of the largest type of *nordlandsbaat,* with five or six pairs of oars. Built in Rana, it was called the *Leif Eriksson.* The rest of the crew of four was also from northern Norway. In the spring of 1927, Folgerø completed the Atlantic crossing, following the route taken by Leif Ericson. The boat arrived in Duluth during the north Norwegian convention, and it was reported that tens of thousands were there to greet it, including 1,000 north Norwegians. The mood was particularly buoyant among the northerners, who felt that "once more old Nordland has been honored."[22]

While the boat was intended to celebrate the sailing culture of the north, to the American public it was a Viking ship. And the northerners were flattered. No doubt many had no objection to being identified as the descendants of Vikings. On its way into Duluth, the boat was decorated like a Viking ship, with a dragon's head and shields along the sides. The *nordlandsbaat* had never been equipped in such fashion.

Later it was placed in Lake Shore Park, Duluth, which was promptly re-named Leif Ericsson Park. The boat remains there to the present.

Symbols and rhetoric are another aspect of identity. The most ob-vious symbols and rhetoric among north Norwegians in the United States were intimately associated with the roots of their identity in the sea and coastal culture. For Norwegian-American communities generally, the most typical symbols were and still are the Vikings, in-dependent farmers [*odelsbønder*], folk costumes, the Hardanger fiddle, and rose painting. For northerners, however, the clearly dominant symbol was the *nordlandsbaat*. Soon after its establishment, it was de-cided that the symbol of Nordlandslaget would be a *nordlandsbaat* with its sails set, or more precisely, the most traditional and most legendary of all north Norwegian boats, the *fembøring*. The logo was designed by a member of the association, based on a painting by artist Thorolf Holmboe, who was born in Vefsn, Nordland. This logo adorned the cover of *Nord-Norge* from issue No. 3 onward. The covers of the first two issues featured a picture of a bearded fisherman with an enormous cod in his right hand. The *fembøring* also appeared on the society's letterhead and all other material produced by it, includ-ing its banner. *Nord-Norge* printed a large number of stories and ar-ticles about the *nordlandsbaat*. A particularly central theme was the long sea voyage from Helgeland to Lofoten, then on to Finnmark, and even as far as the Murmansk coast, Kola peninsula, Russia, for sea-sonal fishing. For many, the boat came to represent in their memo-ries virtually the whole of life back home. One local association affiliated to Nordlandslaget was even called *Fembøringen* (Seattle, Washington); others had names like *Nordlyset* [Northern Lights], *Midnatsol* [Midnight Sun], *Nordkap* [North Cape] and *Nordlands Minde* [Nordland Memorial].

Food, especially food consumed at special occasions, was also closely associated with the northern celebration of the sea and coastal roots. For the banquets held at Nordlandslaget conventions, there had to be fresh fish, preferably the old "Sunday fish," halibut. Whenever Heitmann wanted to get the busy Rølvaag to visit him in Duluth, fish was the surest bait which with to lure him there. Anna Dahl Fuhr did likewise, promising salt herring and potatoes, halibut and cod, as well as rhubarb wine and cloudberry compote, all typical of north Nor-wegian cuisine.[23] Baumann liked to visit Rølvaag, provided he could make serious inroads into his store of lutefisk![24]

Cover of a number of Nord-Norge *issued in honor of Julius B. Baumann and displaying the emblematic Norland fishing boat, the* fembøring. *Archives of the Norwegian-American Historical Association (Northfield, Minnesota).*

RHETORIC AND METAPHOR

Rhetoric likewise is filled with phrases and metaphors taken from fishing and coastal life. A central term is *høvedsmann*, the old title of the skipper of a fishing boat. For northerners, the chairman of Nordlandslaget at the time was never anything but *høvedsmannen*. In American terminology, there was only one appropriate term, *president*, which indeed was, and is, the official American title of Nordlandslaget's chair. Other terms invested with strong symbolic values were the names of seabirds. Anna Dahl's sketch *"Maakene"* ["The Seagulls"] in *Nord-Norge* was a classic that had a great appeal to north Norwegian immigrants. She had managed to paint a symbolic image of emigrant northerners as seagulls, *længselens fugler* [the birds of desire] who may be encountered "wherever sea swells between the countries of the world."[25]

In both letters and *Nord-Norge*, we find rich material for the study of the rhetoric and metaphors used by northerners in the United States. It is so conspicuous that it must have been consciously developed as an identity marker. Here there is space only for a few samples from more extensive texts. In the last letter Ole Rølvaag wrote to his brother Peder, who was still living in Rølvaag on Dønna, he describes, among other things, the illness that would ultimately take his life. But he is now optimistic, after having been rather ill for some time: "I have once more been very poorly; this time I came rather close to the land of eternity, but in the nick of time, an offshore breeze blew up and soon I had open sea before me once again. Now I lie here treading water."[26] A further example is taken from an account of a journey to a *bygdelag* convention; there are, incidentally, many such accounts, both in the letters and in the columns of *Nord-Norge*. The voyage described here, by an ordinary member of the society, to the convention in Bemidji in northern Minnesota was by automobile, but it is an excellent reflection of both north Norwegian language and fishing terminology: "We slipped our moorings early Saturday morning, had a fair wind for a while, and we'd almost started thinking that this here wasn't going to be much of a voyage, but then in the dusk a storm began brewing, and before we could say Jack Robinson, we were in the middle of furious seaspray, . . . , we both thought it was the *draug* [a headless man believed to appear to those about to drown] up to his old tricks, and no sooner had we thought of him, than we both got so fearful for our lives, we could hardly breathe, and since we were carrying no great ballast, we had to go with the wind with three reefs in the sail. And so it went for ages in heavy seas. Then all of a sudden the wind turned, and we had to start tacking, and you can imagine us sailing, catching the spray, indeed not just catching it, it was lashing in over boat and crew alike, and we were sailing so hard that the bolts leapt out of their holes and the sea washed in like a torrent. . . . But Ola Dahl, he knew what to do; he took off one of his boots—and bailed like a madman, for the anchor was gone overboard and was lying a long way off. . . ."27

It is hardly surprising that the key song at all events organized by northerners at the time was Elias Blix's "*Aa, eg veit meg eit land*" ["Oh, I know a country"], which was early adopted as the "northerners' national anthem." Blix had, in fact, been a member of Nordlænd-ingenes Forening in Oslo. He had also been Professor at the University of Oslo, as well as Minister of Church Affairs. It is probably less well known that it was a north Norwegian emigrant who set the lyrics to music, namely, Johan Gregor, born 1868 in the parish of Mo, who went to the United States in 1888. He was a teacher of religion, a clerk, and a watchmaker, who ended up as a farmer in North Dakota. Other well-known songs which Gregor set to music include Blix's "*Gud signe vårt dyre fedreland*" ["God bless our dear fatherland"] and Bjørnstjerne Bjørnson's poem to Welhaven, "*Lyt nu, du ludende sanger*" ["Listen now, you great singer"].

Apart from "*Aa, eg veit meg eit land*," one literary text more than any other became the rallying cry of the northerners, namely the long piece Julius Baumann wrote for the Nordlandslag convention of 1920, *Hilsen til nordlændingene ved stevnet* [*Greetings to north Norwegians in convention gathered*]. It would be read aloud and quoted at conventions until well after World War II and was reprinted again and again. It is full of strongly evocative rhetorical terms and phrases. Written in his local dialect, a few stanzas must serve as samples of the whole.28

> Now we remember the whale as he lay beating,
> when dolphins and porpoises and orcas proud
> raced leaping out to sea;
> while the crab flapped wildly in the shallows,
> while tunny and porbeagle and Greenland shark calmly
> slipped into the huge deep.

And halibut and wolffish and haddock and pollack
and cusk and rosefish and ling and cod—
and capelin and sprat and herring—
we took them with hook, line and seine,
with handline and troll, if, our luck was in with
the wind—in calm and stormy waters.

Now you remember the birds on the isles and skerries
and the wings and eggs and down and feathers
and the screech and racket and calls.
Now you remember the ospreys and falcon and divers
and skuas and gulls and kittiwakes so grand,
and fulmars sitting in the boat.

Within Nordlandslaget, people wanted to celebrate not only the distinctiveness of their cultural background, but also the northern mentality and ways. This is a matter of genuine autostereotypes, of the kind often found in minority and immigrant communities. Julius Baumann's attempts to capture the scene and mood at one of the association's early conventions may serve as an example of autostereotype. This convention differed from those he had experienced elsewhere, for northerners had their own ways. Particularly remarkable were their "rapidity of gait and movement, their quick speech and colorful manner of talking, their sharp and fleeting glances, their sudden and unexpected change of facial expression, and their cheery and bold greetings."[29]

ATTITUDES TOWARD IDENTITY

What, then, was the identity of the north Norwegians like in this period? And not least: What did they *wish* their identity to be? Obviously, the first question is more difficult to answer than the second, although the latter is by no means easy. There is no doubt that there is, unsurprisingly, a discrepancy between identity and expressed attitudes. The difference is, of course, due to many factors, not least of which are individual experience and personality. I will illustrate this by returning to the three figures who formed the inner core of the "Duluth Circle": Baumann, Rølvaag, and Heitmann. Baumann was probably the one who struggled most with a "divided heart." Both his correspondence and his writings indicate as much. On the one hand, he wished to show that he had integrated, that he was a loyal American. This is expressed particularly during and after World War I, in both his poetry and his editorship of *Nord-Norge*. In the journal, he published a series called *Nordlandsgutter i verdenskrigen* [Nordland Boys in the World War], about north Norwegian immigrants who fought in the war as American soldiers.[30] In his poetry, we find a great deal about the efforts of Norwegians on behalf of their new fatherland. They are idealized as heroes in the long epic poem "*Pioneren*" ["The Pioneer"].[31]

> When the Civil War brought blood and fire,
> I joined up behind the banner of the North.
> At Murfreesboro we bravely stood,
> in Chickamauga we fought man to man—
> there our brave Colonel Heg met his fate.

Baumann wished so dearly to settle into life in America. As he puts it in the final stanza of "*Pioneren*":

> And here, my friend, in this beloved place,
> where I have drunk the cups of sorrow and of joy,
> here I wish to find peace in my grave
> at last, as the evening sun dips
> and gilds the gleaming water with her rays.

On the other hand, no Norwegian-American writer wrote as much about his yearning for northern Norway as Baumann. This is probably also a major reason why he came to be such a well-loved poet and why he was read so widely. While in "*Pioneren*" he wanted to find "peace in [his] grave" in his new homeland, in "*Barndomshjemmet*" ["My Childhood Home"] he dreamed of being buried in the old country:

> So, Mother, squeeze your child
> lovingly to your breast.
> Where I can rest secure
> from the wild din of the world;
> there I will find peace and calm
> in the snug shelter of Mother Earth.

This yearning never gave him peace, as he admits in "*Mindernes skute*" ["The Ship of Memory"]:

> A ship comes every Christmas from the North
> with the dearest cargo that can be taken on board.
> Well do I know both her masts and her hull,
> for she sails so often on voyages to the west.

This sense of longing and loss was to remained unresolved because Baumann never managed to visit the old country, although he often made plans to do so. During the lengthy illness that ended with his death, he was still, in letters to Rølvaag, expressing the hope that he might realize his greatest dream of all, that of "striking out" for Norway, ideally in the early spring, "since I have to go to the far north of the country."[32]

Baumann was in fact torn between the positions of Rølvaag and Heitmann, whose stances represented the extremes of the cultural debate within the group. Baumann's attitudes were ambivalent, sometimes unclear, but they also changed depending on with whom he had most contact at any given moment. Heitmann probably gives a fairly apt assessment of Baumann in a letter to Rølvaag: "Yet you must know that he is a man of moods, vibrating at every touch like a violin—only finer and more sensitive than the most finely tuned violin."[33]

Rølvaag's position as the most determined defender of the "ancestral heritage" in the cultural struggles resulted for a time in virtual anti-Americanism. America stood for materialism, a cold society, and a lack of cultural life. Immigrant cultures, especially the western and northern European ones, would actually save America. By preserving their "ancestral heritage," the immigrants would thus save their own souls and futures as well as the United States. North Norwegian culture was, for Rølvaag, an integral part of the "ancestral heritage," but also an important added dimension, not least on the personal level. In his capacity as a college professor and in his own home, perhaps because he was married to a woman whose family was from southeastern Norway, he always spoke a standard Norwegian. At all gatherings of northerners, on the other hand, he used an unadorned Helgeland dialect all his life.

In long exchanges of letters and in public debates Heitmann usually preferred to use a pseudonym. We may assume that in private gatherings, Rølvaag's and Heitmann's different attitudes clashed. Heitmann dismissed Rølvaag's strong emphasis on the uniqueness of the Norwegian people, and he also had his doubts about the bitterness Rølvaag often displayed in debate. Heitmann wished Rølvaag would be more conciliatory.[34] This was not an age of decline in American culture and immigrant cultures were not acutely threatened, Heitmann maintained against Rølvaag.[35]

A possible explanation for the extremity of what Einar Haugen called Rølvaag's ethnic imperative may be the fact that it took a long time for him to gain recognition as an author.[36] Rølvaag had to struggle very hard, and he was long in financial straits. It was only after the American publication of *Giants in the Earth* that recognition and money finally came his way. The thought of an ageing father back home in Nordland who had not forgiven him his "betrayal" of the fishing life haunted him all his adult years. It was all "part of the emigrant tragedy."[37] As a college professor, Rølvaag felt only partly successful. To be sure, he was very much liked as a teacher, but he never really had a proper academic career. He never proved himself as a scholar. His visits to Norway, on the other hand, gave him inspiration and respite, and he received recognition there before he did in the United States. Rølvaag, in other words, dearly wished to be a Norwegian. But his personal need to be a northerner, at least from time to time, was a pressing one. However, when he had finally gained recognition, he became more and more of an American.[38]

Heitmann wished to exemplify the "melting pot." Time after time he held up the United States as a promising country for people of ambition and determination. Unlike Rølvaag, Heitmann thought the old world, Norway included, was suffering from numerous "diseases" and defects. It was not Norway that had given him his opportunities in life. It was in America that he had found and realized his potential. It was in America that he had created for himself a profession he could be proud of and a future. The people of the old and new worlds may have been alike, but their environment had shaped them differently and given them different opportunities. In the cultural debates about the "ancestral heritage" that raged around 1920, Heitmann clearly favored the "melting pot," but he nonetheless thought such views need not lead to the loss of personal identity, even though the original Norwegian culture would no doubt inevitably be lost in time.[39]

However, when he appeared as a northerner, Heitmann also dis-

played elements of the "divided heart." He frequently visited northern Norway in summer and it was northern Norway he missed and
sought refuge in, not Norway. For him, Norway remained associated
with, for instance, royalism, for which he felt nothing but contempt,
although he had even personally met the Crown Prince![40] No one
could describe the summer evenings of his visits back home to
Dønna as he could, in letters, stories, and poems: the cod-fishing and
midnight feasts of fresh cod, the view from Dønnesfjellet, the company of neighbors, the spiritual pick-me-up that it all gave him.
Heitmann had a wide network of contacts with north Norwegians,
both at home and in the United States, probably greater than that of
either Baumann or Rølvaag. He also to a great extent cultivated the
friendship of ordinary people, especially north Norwegian fishing
families around Lake Superior. It is probably correct to say that
Heitmann no longer wished to be Norwegian, but instead wanted to
be American. He was, in fact, both American and north Norwegian.

These three biographical examples illustrate the ambivalence that
first-generation immigrants must often have felt in their relationship
to the host country and their old homeland, as well as to the region
from which they originally came. Emigration had probably most
often occurred as a result of a calculated choice. The will to build a
new life in the new country was, of course, there. The transition was
not, however, without strong emotional challenges. Assimilation
could be painful without this necessarily implying defeat. One con-
crete expression of this was the simple fact that around twenty-five
percent of Norwegian emigrants migrated back home. The great
transatlantic exodus, involving tens of thousands of northern Norwegians, thus expresses a phenomenon closely linked to modernity.
The ambivalence seen in northern Norwegian immigrants' search
for identity in the new world is, therefore, no surprise. As Zigmunt
Bauman has shown, ambivalence is probably the most significant aspect of modern human experience.[41]

MINORITIES WITHIN A MINORITY

Let us finally ask the question of who the organized north Norwegian
immigrants were and how representative they were of immigrants
from the region. First and foremost they were north Norwegians in
the literal sense of the word, that is, they originated in North Norway.

If we examine Nordlandslaget's membership registers and the members of the board throughout the survey period, we find that people from Nordland, and Helgeland in particular, dominated in terms of numbers. We must draw the same conclusion from an examination of qualitative facts, such as careers and public offices. There were, of course, exceptions. If we once again examine the geographical spread of Nordlandslaget's members, only a handful of members up to approximately 1930 were from Finnmark. On the board we do, indeed, find a few, including two from Finnmark as chairmen, Baumann in 1922–1924, who died before the end of his last period as chairman, and the pharmacist P. Bernhart (1928–1929), born in Vadsø, whose business was based in Sioux Falls, South Dakota. These two were, of course, not representative of most immigrants from Finnmark, Bernhart because of his strong social and economic position, and Baumann because of his position as a poet and perhaps also because of kinship and family connections with Helgeland. Baumann's mother was born on Dønna, his father in Rana, and they moved to Finnmark just before their son was born.

Perhaps more remarkable is the total absence among members of Nordlandslaget of people from northern Norway of non-Norwegian ethnic background. For this period, it is not possible to identify a single Sami or Kven [Norwegian of Finnish descent] among the members. To be sure, not many Samis had emigrated, but there were some. Kvens, on the other hand, had experienced considerable emigration, and had also settled in large numbers in the Midwest, Nordlandslaget's heartland.[42] With very few exceptions, we find the same absence in other contexts.[43]

Nord-Norge would eventually print a lot of material about the Sami: articles, travelogues, surveys of cultural history, and literary pieces. Not surprisingly, this material bears the hallmarks of exoticism, paternalistic attitudes, and to some extent also social Darwinism and racist thinking. The derogatory and discriminatory attitudes to which these two groups had been subject from Norwegians back home were thus expressed in the new world as well.[44] Even an author like Baumann, who could write very sympathetically of Sami, could display prejudices and stereotypes, as in a stanza in the abovementioned poem *Hilsen til nordlændingen ved stevnet:*[45]

> And the reindeer and Lapps and the Skolps and people,
> and deerskins and koftes and belts and daggers,

and Lapp witches and yodling and yoiking;
and farm dogs and lynx and lasso and tents,
and tendons and deerskin-boots, skulls and right
down to drinking and smoking.

Nord-Norge also occasionally published jokes and stories in which Samis were shown in a negative light. There is hardly any mention of Kvens at all. This shows that notions like "northern Norway" and "northerner" were in fact selective and exclusive notions for the organized north Norwegian immigrant community. Some people fell through the net. They remained anonymous, as they had also largely been anonymous in the old world. We cannot discuss here the issues raised by this fact, such as the question of what kinds of networks and organizations these people developed. But in the perspective taken in this brief study, the American expression "lost generation" comes to mind when we think of the fate of these ethnic groups in the new world in this period. They were minorities within the minority.

NOTES

[1] Odd S. Lovoll, *The Promise Fulfilled: A Portrait of Norwegian Americans Today*, rev. ed. (Minneapolis, 1999). See also his *The Promise of America: A History of the Norwegian-American People* (Minneapolis, 1984); *A Century of Urban Life: The Norwegians in Chicago before 1930* (Champaign, IL, 1988).

[2] Odd S. Lovoll, *A Folk Epic: The* Bygdelag *in America* (Boston, 1975).

[3] Letter of 7 December 1929, in Rølvaag Papers, the Norwegian-American Historical Association Archives, Northfield, Minnesota. On Heitmann, see Orm Øverland, *The Western Home: A Literary History of Norwegian America* (Northfield, MN, 1996), 206–207.

[4] On Baumann, see Øverland, *The Western Home*, 181–182, 206, 230–234; Einar Niemi, "Amerikafeber. Om utvandringen fra Vadsø og om vadsøværinger i USA," in *Varanger. Årbok 1996* (Vadsø, 1996), 57–82.

[5] I have searched the extensive collections of letters left by Rølvaag, Heitmann, and Baumann deposited at the NAHA Archives at St. Olaf College. To give some impression of the extent of this material, it contains 169 letters from Heitmann to Rølvaag alone, many of them over 20 pages long.

[6]Einar Niemi, "Anna Dahl Fuhr—Meløyjenta som ble avisdronning i Amerika," in *Årbok for Meløy historielag 1994* (Bodø, 1994), 12–25.

[7]Einar Haugen, *Immigrant Idealist: A Literary Biography of Waldemar Ager, Norwegian American* (Northfield, MN, 1989). See also, Øverland, *The Western Home*, 324–345.

[8]See, for example, Dag Blanck, *Becoming Swedish-American* (Uppsala, 1997), 28–29; Ulf Beijbom, *Svenskamerikanskt. Människor och förhållanden i Svensk-Amerika* (Växjö, 1990), 146–155.

[9]On the history of the association, see Nils A. Ytreberg, *Vær hilset! Nordlændingenes Forening 1862–1962* (Oslo, 1962); Einar Niemi, "Regionalism in the North: The Creation of 'North Norway,'" in *Acta Borealia* (Tromsø, 1993), 33–45.

[10]The major work on the *bygdelag* movement in the United States is Lovoll, *A Folk Epic*.

[11]*Nordlandslaget av Amerika og Kanada. 75 aars jubileum 1909–1984* (1984), 46–47.

[12]*Nordlandslaget*, 53–56.

[13]On such myths, see Orm Øverland, *Immigrant Minds, Immigrant Identities: Making the United States Home, 1870–1930* (Urbana and Chicago, 2000), 1–21.

[14]Håvard Dahl Bratrein and Einar Niemi, "Inn i riket. Politisk og økonomisk integrasjon gjennom tusen år," in *Det gjenstridige landet*, vol. 1 of *Nordnorsk kulturhistorie*, ed. E.-A. Drivenes, M. A. Hauan, and H. A. Wold (Oslo, 1994), esp. 158–159.

[15]One keen contributor of historical material was Berner Loftfield, born in Mo, Nordland, in 1861, who moved to the United States around 1890. He was eventually employed in the Minnesota state "grain department" in Minneapolis. He was a "great defender of Norwegianness" and an "exceedingly good public speaker" (*Nord-Norge* 52 [1929], 19). As early as 1901, he published (privately) a richly illustrated tome entitled *Norge*. In a long series of issues of *Nord-Norge*, especially in the first half of the 1920s, he discussed various topics of north Norwegian history and offered daring interpretations. His writings tended to result in lively debates, with some contributions from authors in northern Norway, for example, Johan Beronka of Vadsø (author of *Vadsø Bys historie*, of 1933) and A. B. Wessel of Sør-Varanger (author and publisher of a number of works of local history in Finnmark).

[16]   En flaate av skinnende hvite seil
        svinger sig henover havets speil—
        brudgommen kommer,

nordlændingen kommer!
Seil efter seil og stavn efter stavn
stevner i rækker og rad mot havn.
Brudgommen kommer,
nordlændingen kommer!

Mit herlige, fagre Haalogaland,
som ventet i sekler paa Nordens mand,
nu gir jeg dig sind og hjerte.
Jeg skriver i flammer av nordlys dit navn,
sverger dig troskap og tar dig i favn
og tænder vor alterkjerte.
All translations mine.

[17]Letter from Ole Olsen 22 February 1916, in Julius Baumann Papers, NAHA Archives.

[18]Letter from Baumann to Olsen 28 March 1916.

[19]Letter from Olsen to Baumann 15 May 1916.

[20]Odd S. Lovoll, *Det løfterike landet. Historien om norsk-amerikanerne* (Oslo, 1983), 190–191; Øverland, *The Western Home,* 207–208.

[21]On the centenary celebrations and Nordlandslaget, see *Nordlandslaget av Amerika og Kanada*; and *Nord-Norge* 37 (1925), 2–12, 20–28.

[22]*Nord-Norge* 45 (1927), 9–11; *Nordlandslaget av Amerika og Kanada,* 76.

[23]Letter from Anna Dahl Fuhr to Ole Rølvaag, 18 April 1926, in Ole Rølvaag Papers.

[24]Letter from Baumann to Rølvaag, undated, probably early 1923, in Rølvaag Papers.

[25]Anna Dahl, "*Maakene,*" in *Nord-Norge* 20 (1920), 2–3.

[26]Letter dated 23 September 1931, in Rølvaag Papers.

[27]"Vi kasta løs tidlig paa lørdags morran, hadde bra bør utover en stund, og vi begyndte næsten at tænke paa at det her vart ikke stor seiladsen, men saa i graalysninga begyndte det aa brygge op til storm, og før vi vidste ord av det var vi oppe i et forrykende sjørokk, . . . , vi trodde begge det var draugen som var ute med strekene sine, og naar vi begyndte at tænke paa draugen, saa blev vi saa livende redde at det næsten tok pusten fra os, og da vi ikke hadde større ballast maatte vi lense unna med tre klør neaat. Og slik gik det da en lang tid over braat og brand. Saa med en gang snur vinden sig, og vi maa til aa krysse, og dere kan tro vi seilte, sjødrev stod indover, ja ikke bare stod indover men slog indover baade baat og mandskap, og vi seilte saa fryktelig at nu[g]la sprat ut tur med høle saa sjøen stod ind som en foss. . . . Men

han Ola Dahl, han visste raad; han tok av sig ein av sjystøvlan—auste som besat, for ankeret hadde gaat overbord og laa og fløit langt bort paa. . . ." (*Nord-Norge* 88 [1923] 2).

> [28]   No minnes vi kvalen naar hajn laag aa braut,
> naar sprengar aa nisa aa staurvant saa kaut
> seg stupa omkap utpaa have;
> naar krabben hajn baska i sjøskaarpa vildt,
> me stjørja aa haabrajn aa haakjærring stilt
> glei unner di store i kave.
>
> Aa kveita aa steinbit aa hysa aa sei
> aa brosma aa auer aa longa aa skrei—
> aa laada aa bresling aa silla—
> di tok vi paa kveitva, me lina aa not,
> me juksaan aa daarga, om, me heil imot
> va vijn—i storm som i stilla.
>
> No minnest du fuglan paa haalma aa skjær
> aa vengan aa æggan aa duna aa fjær
> aa skrike aa alon aa laaten.
> No minnest du feskørn aa spejnfalk aa lom
> aa jaabon aa maasen aa krykja saa grom,
> aa havhest som sæt seg i baaten.

[29]Odd Lovoll, cited in the introduction to *Nordlandslaget av Amerika og Kanada,* 1.

[30]In several issues of *Nord-Norge* from 1918 onwards.

[31]On Colonel Heg and north Norwegian participation in the American Civil War, see Waldemar Ager, *Colonel Heg and His Boys,* trans. Della Kittleson Catuna and Clarence A. Clausen (Northfield, MN, 2000). Baumann's first collection of poetry, *Digte,* was published in 1909; the prize-winning collection, *Fra Viddern. Nye Digte,* came out in 1915; and finally *Samlede Digte* was published in 1924, the year after his death.

[32]Undated letter from Baumann to Rølvaag, but clearly written in late winter 1923, in Rølvaag Papers.

[33]Letter dated 5 December 1922, in Rølvaag papers.

[34]Letter 20 December 1922.

[35]Letter "Wednesday evening," December 1922.

[36]Einar Haugen, *Ole Edvart Rølvaag* (Boston, 1983) 24.

[37]Theodore Jorgensen and Nora O. Solum, *Ole Edvart Rølvaag: A Biography* (New York, 1939), 342.

[38]Note the self-explanatory subtitle of Gudrun H. Gvåle's Rølvaag biography, *O. E. Rølvaag: Nordmann og amerikaner* (Oslo, 1963). Øverland claims that Rølvaag primarily "speaks as a Norwegian American, not as a Norwegian" (*The Western Home*, 205).

[39]These debates are in the literature usually referred to as the "S debate" and the "Bjarne Blehr debate" after the to-the-point contributions signed "S" and "Bjarne Blehr," especially in Fuhr's paper *Duluth Skandinav*. Both at the time and in the literary histories there has been some speculation as to who was hiding behind these signatures. Having examined the correspondence in the NAHA Archives, it is quite obvious that "Bjarne Blehr" was Heitmann, and there is a strong probability that he was also the man behind "S." Rølvaag in particular was attacked in the contributions signed by these correspondents. See Jorgensen and Solum, *Ole Edvart Rølvaag*, 304–306; Gvåle, *O. E. Rølvaag*, 256; Øverland, *The Western Home*, 206–207.

[40]Letter to Rølvaag, 22 September 1925, in Rølvaag Papers.

[41]Zigmunt Bauman, *Modernity and Ambivalence* (Cambridge, 1995).

[42]Einar Niemi, "Emigration from Northern Norway: A Frontier Phenomenon? Some Perspectives and Hypotheses," in *Norwegian-American Essays 1996*, ed. Ø. T. Gulliksen et al. (Oslo, 1996), 127–156; Einar Niemi, "From Northern Scandinavia to the United States. Ethnicity and Migration, the Sami and the Arctic Finns," in *Migration och Mångfald. Essäer om kulturkontakt och minoritetsfrågor*, ed. Dag Blanck et al. (Uppsala, 1999), 155–170.

[43]One exception was the Sami Nils Paul Xavier: see Einar Niemi, "Nils Paul Xavier: Sami Teacher and Pastor on the American Frontier," in *Norwegian-American Studies* 34 (1995), 245–270. See also Ørnulv Vorren, *Samer, rein og gull i Alaska. Emigrasjon av samer til Alaska* (Karasjok, 1989); English edition: *Saami, Reindeer, and Gold in Alaska. The Emigration of Saami from Norway to Alaska* (Prospect Heights, IL, 1994); Kenneth O. Bjork, "Reindeer, gold, and scandal," in *Norwegian-American Studies* 30 (1985), 130–195.

[44]For a monograph on such attitudes and Norwegian minority policies towards Samis and Kvens, see Knut Einar Eriksen and Einar Niemi, *Den finske fare. Sikkerhetsproblemer og minoritetspolitikk i nord 1860–1940* (Oslo/Bergen/Tromsø, 1981.)

[45]   Aa reinan aa skaaltan aa skaalpan aa folk,
      aa pæsken aa kofta aa bejlte aa dolk,
      aa ganfinn aa jodling aa jøiking;
      aa buhujn aa gaupa aa lasso aa tejlt,
      aa sena aa komaga, skalla aa hejlt
      nerover te drekking aa røiking.

Reading Norwegian-American Cookbooks:
A Case Study

Deborah L. Miller

WHAT CAN WE LEARN about Norwegian America from the cookbooks its women have produced? I suggest here that aspects of both Norwegian-American ethnicity and Norwegian-American adaptation to the larger American culture can be illuminated by studying these books, which include recipes these women contributed, selected, organized, and published for their congregations. More than women's journals and letters, recipes are formulaic and communal, but like journals and letters, they reflect personal experience and personal history, demonstrating what one scholar has called "the community cookbook emphasis on personal testimony—the image of real women behind each dish."[1]

FROM COOKING TO COOKBOOKS

Food was coin of the realm in many Norwegian-American enterprises during the first half of the twentieth century and beyond. The *bygde-lag*, organizations of people from the same rural Norwegian districts, made regional foods a hallmark of their reunions, as Odd Lovoll makes clear in his pioneering study of this network of associations. The Valdres Samband led the way, instituting a *gjestebø*, or feast of traditional dishes, in 1902.[2] Ladies Aids in rural and urban Lutheran churches often prepared lunch for *bygdelag* gatherings, and this was often an important part of these meetings. These women planned and executed food sales of many other kinds as well, featuring both Norwegian and American foods. *Lutefisk* dinners, ice-cream socials, and chicken dinners were all popular church fundraisers in the 1920s and 1930s. By that time in many congregations, Ladies Aids had raised funds to build church basements and equip them with kitchens. This allowed Aid meetings to move from members' homes to new communal facilities and eased the task of preparing fundraising dinners.[3] Norwegian Americans also used food to raise funds for other ethnic organizations and causes. To give just two examples, supporters of St. Paul's Lyngblomsten Home for the elderly staffed dining halls at county and state fairs in the 1910s, 1920s, and 1930s. In the 1950s, the Norse Centennial Daughters in St. Paul gave *torsk* [codfish] dinners on Leif Ericson Day to raise funds for a Leif Ericson statue on the State Capitol grounds.[4]

How did Norwegian-American women move from cooking for their families and organizations to publishing cookbooks of their own and their fellow church members' recipes? Church suppers, bake sales, and dining halls at county fairs provided some of the experience needed to produce cookbooks in many congregations. Norwegian-American charitable cookbooks can thus be viewed in the context of making and selling food to audiences small and large. Putting on a fundraising dinner involves considerable work: deciding what will attract paying customers, reckoning ingredients and quantities, buying supplies as cheaply as possible, doing the cooking and serving, and cleaning up afterward. All of this involves organizational as well as culinary skills. Publishing a cookbook requires additional competences. This effort calls not only for creativity, diplomacy, and organizational talent inside the congregation but also for negotiations with publishers or printers, selling advertisements, promotion, and selling the finished cookbooks. These were newly acquired skills for many Ladies Aid members.

Norwegian Americans published several types of cookbooks during the twentieth century, ranging from commercial to personal. The greatest number were compiled by church women's groups and other organizations.[5] One characteristic that distinguishes charitable from commercial cookbooks is that books produced by voluntary organizations must include recipes from as many contributors as possible. This is why such books often include several recipes for the same dish. Because each book reflects all the women who donated

recipes, each such charitable cookbook may be thought of as a constructed portrait of its community. Publishing a cookbook is, by defi-
nition, a public act and a cookbook is thus a public text.[6] Publication
takes an activity associated with women's domestic work and presents
it to a larger public. As one scholar of cookbooks has said, charitable
cookbooks "formalized the informal exchange of recipes among
women. They moved the culinary expertise of women from private
interpersonal transactions into a coordinated collective enterprise,
whereby accumulated kitchen wisdom sustained large community
organizations."[7]

The ubiquitous charitable cookbooks were not, of course, invented
by Norwegian immigrants. They borrowed the form from American
neighbors. Fundraising cookbooks began to be published in the
United States around the time of the Civil War, and until well into
the twentieth century most of them came from Protestant church
women's groups. As the nineteenth century went on, Methodists,
Presbyterians, and Episcopalians in the Upper Midwest began to
publish and sell books of their recipes to help support their congregations. Fundraising by cookbook was also undertaken by women's
groups other than those of churches to raise money for causes like
the Grand Army of the Republic, the Eastern Star, the Young Men's
Christian Association, and the Young Women's Christian Association.
As Janice Longone has pointed out, "Fundraising cookbooks improve the quality of community life with the funds they generate and
they provide as well a record of regional culinary cultures."[8] Anne
Bower elaborates on this idea, noting that the books "raise money
for the religious, educational, historical, and professional institutions
of society, but also provide a space in which women assert their
own values."[9] Producing an organizational cookbook was indeed a
very American thing to do, and from the beginning most recipes,
even in the Norwegian-American organizational cookbooks, were for
"American" food, whatever that was thought to be at a given time
and place.

Another important type of cookbook for Norwegian Americans
contains only Norwegian or Scandinavian recipes, adapted for American ingredients and measurements. These are usually the product of
one or two authors, or of a business. Julia Peterson Tufford began
publishing what became a very popular small book of the first kind in
Minneapolis in 1940. Her *Scandinavian Recipes including the Smörgåsbord*

reached its twenty-first printing in 1964, when it sold for $1.00. An early and widely used book of the second kind, originating from a commercial concern, was published by the Mohn Printing Company of Northfield, Minnesota, in 1924. This company, a Norwegian-American business, offered its cookbook to the Ladies Aid of St. John's Lutheran Church in Northfield to sell as a fundraiser, with their name on the title page. The women accepted the offer and sold a number of the books. The next year, 1925, a slightly modified version appeared as the official cookbook of the commemoration of the centennial of the beginning of mass emigration from Norway to the United States.

In recent years another type of Norwegian-American cookbook has appeared: the family reunion cookbook, often compiled to honor a special cook in the family. These books are usually privately published and are rarely sold or distributed to other than family members. Elisabeth Olness Emerson of Minneapolis was kind enough to provide a copy of the one she and her mother assembled in 1994, called *Family Recipes and Stories*. The reach of this book was extended with the participation of a cousin in Norway, who contributed recipes from the farm where Elisabeth's mother was born and raised. The intention behind books like this is well stated by Emerson in her introduction: "As changes within the family create absences and distances, traditions can help close those gaps and bring us closer. Foods passed down from generation to generation give a sense of home and person and roots." A brief genealogy and a set of family photos round out the book, which includes American favorites like zucchini bread and cherry Jell-O as well as Norwegian foods like *flatbrød* and *rommegrøt*, variants of a dry, crisp, wafer-like bread and a sour cream porridge familiar throughout Norway.[10]

CHARITABLE COOKBOOKS

Among twentieth-century Norwegian-American food and recipe books, charitable cookbooks compiled by Ladies Aids and other women's organizations play an important role. As texts, what did these books include? Throughout the century such publications usually contained many, and sometimes all, of the following elements: a drawing or photo of the church; one or more poems, sometimes humorous; table prayers in Norwegian or English or both; a brief history of the congregation or the Ladies Aid; thanks and acknowledg-ments to the cookbook committee or the entire organization, whose members are sometimes listed by name. Such a book often had an in-formal table of contents, but until the 1970s it rarely had an index. Bible verses related to food or other quotations often opened each section. Many times the books contained advertisements from the businesses of their community. The heart of each book was the recipes, with their contributors' names attached.

Sometimes the recipes included several that the committee had solicited from famous women, usually wives of contemporary state and national political figures. A 1940 cookbook from a rural Min-nesota congregation featured recipes from the wives of the Presi-dent of the United States and the Governor of Minnesota. Eleanor Roosevelt sent a brief note of good wishes with a recipe for kedgeree, a fish and rice dish. Esther Stassen also sent a note with her recipe for Dream Cakes. The owner of the copy I studied wrote in the margin of the latter recipe, "No good—too sweet!"[11] Some cookbooks re-flected cultural values, ethnic and otherwise, or added humor by including mock recipes, for such things as Happy Husband or Elephant Stew. If the cookbooks were assembled by the women themselves with the aid of a local printer, they seemed to reflect their creators' values and intentions more faithfully than those sent to community cookbook publishers elsewhere who had developed a standard structure and design into which the recipes were slotted. Ladies Aid cookbook committees of all denominations were more likely to take the latter, easier route to production as the twentieth century went on.

An early Norwegian-American cookbook issued to raise funds is the *Phi Kappa Phi Cook Book*, published by a student group at St. Olaf College in Northfield. The second edition, published in 1908, was dedicated to the daughters of the United Norwegian Lutheran Church of America. Its preface states the reason for the publication: the idea that college girls do not know much or care much for cook-ing. "This . . . is not the case among the girls of our own institution and we hope a few years of college life will never counteract the good influences or training along these lines which they have received in their good Norwegian homes," say the compilers. Therefore, they continue, "In order to keep up this interest among our college girls, we the girls of St. Olaf College have undertaken the publication of this book."[12] The proceeds went to help furnish the first girls' dormitory at the college. Another early example of a cookbook compiled by young women is reported in a history of Our Saviour's Lutheran Church in Minneapolis as appearing shortly after 1900. Pastor and Mrs. J. W. Preus noticed that the use of Norwegian in the Ladies Aid there hindered many second-generation young women from joining, since they spoke only English. In 1907 English-speaking women of the congregation organized an English Ladies Guild, fifteen members of which produced a cookbook in 1911 that raised several hundred dollars.[13]

THE WOMEN OF *MINDEKIRKEN* AND THEIR COOKBOOKS

Specific examples of Norwegian-American church cookbooks suggest what can be learned from the study of these community sources. The first two cookbooks published by the Norwegian Lutheran Memorial Church of Minneapolis, Minnesota in 1942 and 1950 will provide data for a case study. *Den norsk lutherske Mindekirken* was not, to be sure, a typical Norwegian Lutheran church. It was founded by people who wanted a church that would continue to use the Norwegian language at a time, the early 1920s, when many other Lutheran churches in Minnesota were abandoning Norwegian for English as the language of congregational life. Nevertheless, this congregation was emblematic of the Minneapolis Norwegian-American community in particular ways. The cookbooks produced by the *Mindekirken* Ladies Aid grew out of their considerable experience in using food to raise funds for their church at *fløtegrøt* [sweet cream porridge] suppers, *lutefisk* [dried cod soaked in lye, rinsed, and then boiled or baked] dinners, running a *rømmegrøt* [sour cream porridge] booth at the 1925 Norwegian immigration centennial celebration at the state fairgrounds, serving *bygdelag* banquets, and preparing lunches for Norwegian language school participants.[14]

Scholars of earlier community cookbooks report that "[t]he usual community cookbook involved a small committee of women who determined the selections with an eye to representing the membership and its cuisine, variety, and quality. Local cuisine was usually portrayed with a combination of pride in tradition and au courant sophistication," with a statement introducing the book to the effect that: The compilers have tried to collect the best recipes, old and new. "In addition to being representative, recipes had to be trust-worthy, and thus a claim of reliability appeared in almost every . . . cookbook." "In a limited community everyone's specialties were well known, having been tasted at church suppers or during the course of home entertaining. . . ." The donors "undoubtedly submitted only those recipes good enough to be acknowledged publicly."[15] The *Mindekirken* cookbooks considered here provide specific examples of the ways in which Norwegian-American cookbooks exemplified some of these generalizations drawn by students of other American church cookbooks.

Often the women who produce a cookbook will explicitly tell readers what they are about, as the young women from St. Olaf did in 1908. The 1942 *Mindekirken* cookbook, titled *Cook Book of Tested Recipes,* proclaims its purpose in a preface that also identifies the range of recipes included and their origins. "What we have aimed to do," the editors say, "is to make a cookbook of selected and tested recipes that are both reliable and deliciously different. Many of our members have for many years served as cooks in wealthy homes in Minneapolis, and others have cooked in private homes where economy was an essential factor."[16] Having addressed the social and economic range of their recipes, the compilers move on to ethnic matters: "We have also included many Scandinavian delicacies so popular with our American public." This sentence demonstrates that the Ladies Aid knew well the emblematic role that *Mindekirken* and its culinary traditions played in the Twin Cities, and it frames the in-clusion of old-country recipes as a favor to Americans, rather than as a way to pass immigrant recipes on to American-born Norwegians. The illuminating preface is matched at the back of the book by an impassioned exhortation in Norwegian, in clear contrast to the English used almost everywhere else in the book. It invites readers to join the church by appealing to nostalgic memories of attending church in Norway, beginning: "Listen! The bells are calling. The melodies of the hymns, old, dear, familiar, rise up to praise God." It concludes: "The ancestors' church customs, the ancestors' language—come, come, come!"[17] Not many Lutheran cookbooks recruited new members for the congregation so directly. The contrasting use of English and Norwegian suggests that these women hoped to reach a larger audience than their own Norwegian-speaking congregation with their recipes, but realized that language would restrict actual membership in the congregation.

One question that needs more investigation is how the women decided to categorize the recipes they or their mothers had brought from Norway. Some cookbooks had a section called "Norwegian Recipes," "Scandinavian Recipes," or "Foreign Recipes." Other times such recipes were scattered throughout the book, and thus placed together with the other recipes for cookies or fish or meat according to the appropriate category. Approaching the cookbooks produced by the women of *Mindekirken,* I hypothesized that earlier cookbooks would have the Norwegian recipes throughout all sections, and that later books would separate them into a category by themselves. The *Mindekirken* books did not, in fact, follow this pattern. The 1942 book has a section called "Scandinavian Delicacies" at the back, but there are also a number of Scandinavian recipes in other sections. (The chapter giving recipes for soups, for example, includes Norwegian Sweet Soup, Swedish Fruit Soup, *Fiske Suppe* [Fish Soup], and *Trondhjem Suppe* [Trondheim Soup]). By calling this section "Scandinavian" in 1942, the compilers accommodated recipes and perhaps hoped for readers from Swedish- and Danish-American circles. They solicited recipes from members of other Twin Cities Scandinavian-American churches and women in other places, possibly relatives or former members of *Mindekirken* who had moved away. Each recipe contributed by someone who was not a church member included either a church name, like Immanuel or Zion (Swedish), or a town name, like Mound, Minnesota, Fargo, North Dakota, or Sioux City, Iowa. In the 1950 cookbook all of those identifiers were gone, but they must have been important for the women who assembled the first cookbook.[18]

Other categories in the 1942 cookbook included Salads, Meat and Fish, Poultry and Game, Luncheon Dishes (by far the largest category, perhaps reflecting an interest in having a variety of dishes to serve at Ladies Aid luncheons, or possibly women's patterns of sociability), Pies and Pastries, Desserts, Pickles and Preserves, Bread and Rolls, Cookies and Doughnuts, and Cakes. Many women contributed both American and Norwegian recipes, but almost all are in English, even in the "Scandinavian Delicacies" section. The exceptions are several recipes donated by three women, Mrs. Dagny Leifson, Mrs. Marie Haugen, and a Mrs. Johanesen, for dishes such as *Julekake med Bakepulver* [Christmas cake with baking powder], *Sørlands Vafler* [waffles in the style of Sørland], *Potetssmultringer* [potato doughnuts], *Kokosmakroner* [coconut macaroons], and *Surkaal* [sauerkraut].

This 96-page book includes advertisements from local Norwegian-American businesses such as Wold's Furniture Store on Washington Avenue South, Augsburg Publishing House, Christ Brodahl's Home Bakery on Cedar Avenue, and Anfin Odland's grocery not far from the church on Twelfth Avenue South. The wives of Brodahl and Odland were, indeed, members of the *Mindekirken* Ladies Aid and contributors of recipes to the congregation's cookbook. Scholars have emphasized the importance of advertisements in community cookbooks, one pointing out that "in these pages, the mostly male business community is bound together with women's recipes, all in the context of a powerfully sanctioned institution," in this case a Norwegian-American Lutheran congregation. In soliciting enterprises dominated by males for financial support, women's organizations also "commodified their own domestic processes and products, selling the recipes and then feeding the profits back into the . . . church."[19]

In 1950, after the 1942 book had been out of print for some years, the Ladies Aid published what it called a revised and expanded edition, correcting errors and adding new recipes. The much shorter foreword thanks those who contributed recipes and adds in its acknowledgments some idea of what it takes to produce such a cookbook, noting "those who have done the work of compiling, arranging, and typing; also the committee for advertising and the selling committee." The 1950 cookbook producers credit by name the general chairman, the wife of Consul General Thorgeir Siqveland, and the chairmen and members of all the committees. The 1950 edition thus brings these representative women a bit more forward into the public eye as individuals than had been thought appropriate in 1942. The page in the Norwegian language devoted to recruiting new members for the church is moved forward in the book but cast in more subtle terms, listing the church's address, the pastor, the times of Sunday services, and concluding with an echo of the 1942 exhortation: "The ancestors' faith, the ancestors' language, the ancestors' church customs, everything festively Norwegian—Welcome!"[20]

Categories of recipes are arranged quite differently in the 1950 book. Most notably there is no separate section for Scandinavian recipes. Two recipes for *fløtegrøt,* given here as a "sour cream pudding," appeared in this book; there had been none in 1942 in spite of the many *fløtegrøt* suppers the Ladies Aid gave, year in and year out, as fundraisers. By the same token, the 1950 book included a recipe for *lutefisk,* which did not appear in the 1942 book, again in spite of the many *lutefisk* dinners given by the Ladies Aid. None of the recipes in 1950 were given in Norwegian, and none of the women were identified by church or town, even though the recipes of some nonmembers from the earlier edition were used in the second edition as well.

Both cookbooks used the same cover design, with a small picture of a *stabbur,* or traditional storehouse, plus two goats, a cow with a bell around its neck, and a man and a woman in costume holding containers of food. Both used Norwegian colors of red and blue. The 1950 publication replaced the stapled, paper-covered book of 1942 with a spiral-bound volume encased in plastic covers. This book was designed to open flat, for easier use in the kitchen.

Who bought and used these cookbooks? Other women in the congregation certainly, but to be successful fundraisers the cookbooks had to be marketed beyond that group. The minutes of the Ladies Aid make clear how that happened in the case of the 1950 cookbook. Urged on by Mrs. Siqveland, the women not only sold advertisements to include in the cookbook. They bought space in Norwegian publications to promote it, especially in the months leading up to Christmas. In the 1951 annual report, Mrs. Siqveland was credited with being "the driving force in cookbook sales," by selling hundreds of them. She took the books with her to Aid meetings at other churches, to *bygdelag* gatherings, even on vacation to the west coast, announced the minutes. By 1952 the minutes tell a tale of sales not only within the local and national Norwegian communities, using expected means of marketing like a table at Norway Day in Minnehaha Park, but beyond as well into the larger Minneapolis community. Powers Department Store invited the Ladies Aid to display its cookbook in a store window display with a Norwegian theme, and at the April meeting of the Aid, Pastor Elias Rasmussen himself announced that 350 cookbooks were sold during the two weeks the window had been on display.[21]

CookBook

OF TESTED RECIPES

PUBLISHED BY THE LADIES AID SOCIETY OF
THE NORWEGIAN LUTHERAN MEMORIAL CHURCH

Cover of Mindekirken *cookbook of 1942. Courtesy of Deborah L. Miller*

INDIVIDUAL PORTRAITS AND A GROUP PICTURE

Reading the minutes of the Ladies Aid from the years when the cookbooks were produced casts further light on contributors and workers. The minutes include an evolving list of members and their addresses as well as their roles as officers or skilled workers in the many activities of the Aid. They include Mrs. Sverre Dalland, secretary for many years, who may have been chosen for her beautiful, legible handwriting and her ability to distill the essentials of a meeting into a page in the minute book, and Mrs. P. O. Peterson, often the leader of cooking teams for *lutefisk* dinners. With their names and addresses, sometimes in conjunction with the names of their husbands, we can identify these women in other sources, including Minneapolis city directories. From the occupations listed in the directories we get an inkling of how that most elusive American category, class, may have played a role in the Aid and in the larger congregation. For example, one frequent contributor of recipes to the 1942 book is Karen Wang, listed as a maid to a member of Minneapolis's social elite, Mrs. Dorothy Atkinson, at 2400 Blaisdell Avenue. Husbands included a city policeman, a Dayton's salesman, and a painter. Several of these women were married to owners of small businesses, including grocery stores, bakeries, and florist shops.[22]

The recipes themselves can add detail to our sense of individual women. Mrs. P. O. Peterson, for example, contributed many recipes, including Veal Birds, Dumplings, Very Good Luncheon Dish, Meat Stuffed Cabbage Rolls, Peach Jam, Ice Water Pickles, Christmas Bread, and Chocolate Chip Cookies. Hers are also some of the briefest recipes, which often give just a list of ingredients, with a quantity for each. Her recipe for *Sprutbakkelse* [pressed cookies], in the "Scandinavian Delicacies" section, reads as follows: 1 cup sugar, 1 cup butter, 3 egg yolks, 2 1/2 cups flour.[23] Cookbook purchasers who did not know how to combine the ingredients or what to do with them once they were mixed would find no assistance from Mrs. Peterson. The fact that the women who assembled the cookbook did not add instructions indicates that they were writing and publishing for their peers, women who already had the skills and experience to make *Sprutbakkelse,* but who might try Mrs. Peterson's recipe to see if they and their families preferred it. Studies of community cookbooks elsewhere have shown that their recipes often assume considerable expertise and experience on the part of readers. They reflect a situation in which girls and young women learned to cook from watching and helping their older female relatives or cooks with whom they worked in domestic service. As one scholar has noted, "experienced recipe writers have acquired a language of collective competence that . . . attests to these cooks' confidence that they are members in good standing of a collective culture."[24] Contributors to *Mindekirken*'s cookbooks whose recipes include editorial comments like "Delicious!" or even informative ones like "Serves 8" probably had more experience with American recipe forms from commercial cookbooks. They may also be younger cooks who include what they would like to see in other recipes. A close reading of the recipes themselves as a whole brings a group portrait of these women into focus. Such a reading supports the contention that charitable cookbooks are constructed portraits of their community.

The minutes of the Ladies Aids illustrate the effect of cookbooks as commercial projects on these groups. Once the work of producing the 1950 cookbook was done and the very different work of promotion and sales began, the minutes began to include more numbers: how many cookbooks still "on hand," with the English phrase noticeable in the Norwegian of Mrs. Dalland's reports; the amount of money brought in from that month's sales; and the total in the cookbook account, kept separate from the other Aid income. Success bred more work: the filling of the many orders received, a task which fell to selling committee member Mrs. Anfin Odland. She apparently had the job of wrapping and sending out the books that were ordered. Readers of the minutes learn how much work this turned out to be when in August of 1952 the minutes describe how Mrs. Elias Rasmussen, the pastor's wife, used the occasion of Mrs. Odland's birthday for a formal thank you from the Aid for her hard work and presented her with a Norwegian bracelet. Both Mrs. Rasmussen and Mrs. Odland, who thanked her colleagues for the gift, emphasized how much work it was to pack and send out so many cookbooks.[25]

Almost before the money had been taken in, the suggestions for how to spend it began. Some elite members of the Aid wanted the money to go to redecorate the church, while other members, perhaps including those who did much of the cooking, wanted new stoves and an improved church kitchen in which to cook the many meals they prepared to raise money for the congregation. Those who argued for the latter use of the money clearly saw a relationship between the cookbook and the church's other fundraising events. In this instance, the women members sold enough cookbooks so that the church could be painted *and* new ovens purchased. The minutes report: "After the church is redecorated, some of the money will be used for remodeling the kitchen, so in the future it will be easier to cook and serve large dinners."[26]

CUISINE FOR TWO CULTURES

Taking a leaf from the book of contemporary scholars who proclaim that Native American cultures will not survive unless their languages continue to be spoken, I brought to this inquiry the hypothesis that the cookbooks of *Mindekirken*'s congregation would focus entirely, or at least primarily, on recipes brought from Norway. That this is not the case suggests to me that the women who produced these cookbooks did not do so primarily in order to retain or preserve their ethnicity. They recognized, however, that some of the culinary aspects of that ethnicity could be marketed to an American, as well as a Norwegian-American audience, just as the food itself could be. The design of the cookbook covers in both 1942 and 1950 reflected this awareness, although this initially led me to expect a far greater proportion of Norwegian recipes than are actually represented in the books. The study of these cookbooks suggests that like other Norwegian-Americans the women who published them were by this time very much engaged in becoming American and defining their particular positions in a multi-ethnic society. They did not see their use of the Norwegian language as an impediment to those goals, but they did think it important to eat American as well as Norwegian food, even while they continued to worship God in the Norwegian language on Sunday mornings.

Recent scholarship on ethnic foodways and community cookbooks has emphasized the two-way evolution of immigrant recipes and eating patterns. Scandinavian-American women learned to make Chop Suey and Glorified Rice to feed their families, but in 1961 *Ann Pillsbury's Baking Book* also included recipes for *sandbakelse, krumkaker,* and *fattigman* [*sic*], all Norwegian varieties of what Americans call "cookies."[27] Church cookbooks reflect the same bicultural reality with respect to that most important of human realities, food.

With their changing collections of Norwegian and American recipes, they point to ways in which Norwegians were becoming Americans. They also illustrate how certain foods were retained as treasured parts of Norwegian-American life, often for several generations. The foodways reflected in these cookbooks thus reflect a strong interest in how to become American, and the pressures immigrant women and their descendants felt to do so. At the same time these cookbooks also give evidence of sustained interest in cultural roots that seem to go very deep among those seated around Norwegian-American tables.

NOTES

[1]Alice Ross, "Ella Smith's Unfinished Community Cookbook: A Social History of Women and Work in Smithtown, New York, 1884–1922," in *Recipes for Reading: Community Cookbooks, Stories, Histories,* ed. Anne L. Bower (Amherst, MA, 1997), 167.

[2]Odd Sverre Lovoll, *A Folk Epic: The* Bygdelag *in America* (Boston, 1975), 32–33.

[3]Research on Norwegian-American Lutheran women and on the Ladies Aids in particular has provided some essential background for this article. See L. DeAne Lagerquist, "That It May Be Done Also Among Us: Norwegian-American Lutheran Women" (Ph.D. diss., University of Chicago Divinity School, 1986), and Erik Luther Williamson, "Norwegian-American Lutheran Churchwomen in North Dakota: The Ladies Aid Societies" (M.A. thesis, University of North Dakota, 1987). The collection of Norwegian-origin Lutheran congregational histories in the Luther Seminary Archives, St. Paul, Minnesota, provided a variety of perspectives on the contributions of Ladies Aids to their congregations.

[4]Papers of the Lyngblomsten Home and the Josephine Brack Papers, Archives of Norwegian-American Historical Association, Northfield, Minnesota.

[5]Immigrants from Norway did have access to Norwegian-language cookbooks published in the United States before churches and other organizations began publishing them. One example, for which I thank Kathleen Stokker, is *Minneapolis Tidende's norske-amerikanske kogebog: en samling af opskrifter paa gamle og nye retter,* published in Minneapolis by the T. Guldbrandsen Publishing Company in 1907. Some immigrants brought cookbooks

from home, such as Hanna Winsnes, *Kogebog* eller *Lærebog i de forskellige Grene af Husholdingen,* 12th ed. (Christiania, 1888).

[6]Orm Øverland helped me to think of cookbooks in this way in a paper he gave about letters as public texts. See his "Religion and Church in Early Immigrant Letters: A Preliminary Investigation," in *Crossings: Norwegian-American Lutheranism as a Transatlantic Tradition,* ed. Todd W. Nichol (Northfield, MN, forthcoming).

[7]Barbara Kirshenblatt-Gimblett, "The Moral Sublime: The Temple Emanuel Fair and Its Cookbook, Denver, 1888," in Bower, *Recipes for Reading,* 151.

[8]Janice Bluestein Longone, "'Tried Receipts': An Overview of America's Charitable Cookbooks," in Bower, *Recipes for Reading,* 28.

[9]Anne L. Bower, "Cooking Up Stories: Narrative Elements in Community Cookbooks," in Bower, *Recipes for Reading,* 47.

[10]Agnes Gunderson Olness and Elisabeth Olness Emerson, *Family Recipes and Stories,* privately printed (Minneapolis, 1994).

[11]Lydia Society, Medo Lutheran Church, *Cook Book of the Lydia Society* (Pemberton, MN, 1940), 9. Copy in collection of Steve Trimble, St. Paul.

[12]*Phi Kappa Phi Cook Book,* 2d ed. (Northfield, MN, 1908), preface.

[13]Anonymous typescript, "History of the Ladies Aid of Our Savior's Lutheran Church, 1870–1937," in Archives of the Evangelical Lutheran Church, Luther Seminary, St. Paul, Minnesota.

[14]Ladies Aid minutes, *Mindekirken* records, Minneapolis Lutheran Memorial Church, Minneapolis.

[15]Ross, "Ella Smith's Unfinished Community Cookbook," 166.

[16]Ladies Aid Society of the Norwegian Lutheran Memorial Church, *Cook Book of Tested Recipes* (Minneapolis, 1942), preface. Hereafter, Mindekirken *Cook Book* 1942.

[17]Mindekirken *Cook Book,* 1942, 96. My translation.

[18]Here and three paragraphs below, Mindekirken *Cook Book* 1942.

[19]Ann Romines, "Growing Up with the Methodist Cookbooks," in Bower, *Recipes for Reading,* 84.

[20]Here and three paragraphs below, Ladies Aid Society of the Norwegian Lutheran Memorial Church, *Cook Book of Tested Recipes* (Minneapolis, 1950). My translation.

[21]Here and below, Ladies Aid minutes and annual reports, 1950–52, *Mindekirken* records, Norwegian Lutheran Memorial Church, Minneapolis.

[22]Minneapolis Directory Company, Minneapolis (Minnesota) directories, 1940–44, Minnesota Historical Society.

[23]Mindekirken *Cook Book* 1942, 81.

[24]Romines, "Methodist Cookbooks," 78.

[25]Here and two paragraphs below, Ladies Aid minutes, *Mindekirken,* 1950–52.

[26]*Mindekirken* went on to produce another completely different cookbook, *Spis og Drikk: Norwegian Recipes Old and New,* in 1980. That book, however, belongs to a chapter of the congregation's history beyond the scope of the present investigation.

[27]Ann Pillsbury, *Ann Pillsbury's Baking Book* (New York, 1961). The names of foods are given as they appear in that cookbook.

Landstad in America

Todd W. Nichol

IN NORWEGIAN AMERICA AS IN NORWAY, mention of "Landstad" most often brings to mind a hymnal rather than the clergyman who edited this famous volume.[1] Along with the Bible and the catechism, the hymnal of Magnus Brostrup Landstad (1802–1880) was a central written expression of the Christian faith for immigrants who came from Norway to the United States in the late nineteenth century. So important was Landstad's hymnal that it eventually came to be thought of as a treasure chest emblematic of the whole cultural and religious inheritance of Norwegian Americans.

This is not surprising given the role of hymnody and hymnbooks in the popular culture of Norway prior to and during the period of the great emigration. As they had done since the introduction of vernacular song into Christian worship in Norway, hymns in this era gave Norwegians not only a basic vocabulary but a poetry, a music, and a mnemonic for their faith. Hymns also provided means for ordinary folk to construe the world and tropes for autobiography.[2] More than the Bible or the catechism, the hymnbook was preeminently the people's own book. Material culture as well as documentary evidence attests to this. To this day, for example, it is common to find Norwegian hymnals preserved in Norwegian-American families. Less often do researchers find copies of the Bible or of the catechism handed down and preserved with the same care. One can hardly imagine how many times Odd Sverre Lovoll has had a cherished hymnal put into his hands by an inquiring Norwegian American with the request that he identify it and comment on its significance.

In the popular religion of Norway's rural folk, the hymnbook was also a fetish effective in both life and death.[3] During childbirth, a hymnbook might be placed on a mother's pillow to ward off the devil, and afterward one of these small volumes could be tucked into the cradle to protect the newborn until it could be baptized. At the other end of life, a hymnbook could be laid on the breast of a gravely ill or seemingly dead person to effect resuscitation. Set in a casket, a hymnbook could also be used to secure a blessed death and to prevent the dead from returning to haunt the house of sorrow.[4] None of this would have been forgotten during the ocean crossings of the earliest immigrants. Yet these practices declined in Norway during the era of the emigration, and to whatever degree such use of hymnbooks ever took root in America, it likely vanished there earlier than in Norway. The hymnbook probably did not have a long career as an amulet among Norwegian Americans. This, however, is a speculative and tentative conclusion, because few documentary traces remain of the history of folk religion in Norwegian America, due in part to the strenuous opposition of the clergy to anything that might smack of black magic or that could otherwise bring the immigrant church into disrepute.

Hymnbooks also carried across the ocean another key element of the nineteenth-century agrarian culture of Norway, its language. In this respect, Landstad's hymnbook was revolutionary. It had at last allowed Norwegians to sing in a language more like their own than the Danish of the older hymnbooks. When it arrived in the United States, a generation after the beginning of heavy Norwegian settlement, Landstad gave Norwegian-Americans the same privilege. As Odd Lovoll has noted, Norwegian-American Lutheran ministers most often spoke *Riksmaal* [official Dano-Norwegian] with a west Norwegian coloring, and sometimes ordinary folk in the congregations understood neither their pastors nor the older hymnbooks very well.[5] We can safely assume that Landstad's new book, as it had done in Norway, offered to many immigrants a welcome opportunity to sing hymns in a language more closely attuned to their own daily speech. Likewise we can hypothesize that this hymnal must have shaped and stabilized the use of the Norwegian language in the immigrant community, as ritual language invariably does. This influence may only have increased when the use of Norwegian as an everyday language declined and it became an arcane speech used primarily in worship, catechization, and devotion.

Finally, of course, we ought not to forget that the melodies of Ludvig Mathias Lindeman (1812–1887), many of them based on traditional folktunes, traveled to America with Landstad. Together Landstad and Lindeman helped Norwegian-Americans remember old music and learn new. Indeed, this pair left a durable legacy not only to Norwegian-American Lutherans but to larger circles of Lutherans in the United States as well. To this day, for example, American Lutherans sing Grundtvig's "Built on a rock" [*"Kirken den er et gammelt hus"*] only to Lindeman's tune of the same name.[6]

LANDSTAD AS A NORWEGIAN-AMERICAN HYMNBOOK

By 1890, previously fragmented Norwegian-American Lutherans had sorted themselves into three major denominations. On one wing stood the Norwegian Synod, strongly shaped by its alliance with the German-American Missouri Synod. The corresponding wing was occupied by the ardently pietistic Hauge's Synod. Between them stood the congregations of the United Norwegian Lutheran Church in America.

Landstad's hymnal had a different history in each of these bodies.[7] The leaders of the Norwegian Synod generally took a dim view of the Norwegian hymnals of the eighteenth and nineteenth centuries, which they thought of as tainted with rationalism and other objectionable tendencies. They also disliked Landstad's book, but more for its use of the modern Norwegian language and its association with the melodies of Lindeman. They preferred the irregular rhythms and syncopation familiar to many German and German-American Lutherans rather than the regular melodies and folktunes presented by their countrymen. Rather than adopting Landstad or any of the other Norwegian hymnbooks available to it, the Norwegian Synod issued its own hymnal in 1874.[8] A revision of this book appeared in 1903.[9] In the often practically conservative Hauge's Synod, on the other hand, the congregations used a variety of older and newer hymnals, with which they were little disposed to part when the definitive version of Landstad's book appeared in Norway in 1870.

The United Norwegian Lutheran Church in America was the

largest of the three major Norwegian-American Lutheran bodies on the denominational scene in 1890 and of the three it most resembled the roomy folk church of the homeland. It was the United Church and its antecedents, rather than Hauge's Synod or the Norwegian Synod, that absorbed the greater share of the immigrants from Norway who arrived in the United States in great waves at the end of the nineteenth century, well after the adoption of Landstad as an approved hymnal in the Church of Norway. These immigrants generally brought Landstad with them from Norway, and it naturally became the most often used hymnbook in the congregations of the United Church. For a time, the United Church debated the preparation of its own hymnal based on Landstad, but eventually agreed to recommend Landstad's hymnal with modest alterations and to collaborate with Hauge's Synod in the preparation of a Norwegian-American supplement to Landstad. This eventually appeared under the title, *Tilføiede Salmer* [*Additional Hymns*].[10]

Tilføiede Salmer of 1893 for the most part augmented Landstad with more hymns from the traditional treasury of Scandinavian and German Lutheran hymnody. Yet the supplement was not entirely conservative. It also included a number of more recent Scandinavian hymns and selections from several of the foreign and inner-mission songbooks published in considerable number in the nineteenth century in Europe and the United States. The supplement presented as well a selection of hymns by Norwegian-American writers and one attributed to a German-American hymnist of the colonial period.[11]

Moving farther afield in both geographical and ecumenical terms, the editors of the supplement included a mission hymn by the Anglican bishop of Calcutta, Reginald Heber (1783–1826), "From Greenland's Icy Mountains" [*"Fra Grønlands is og kulde"*].[12] The use of this hymn indicates the increasing degree to which the small Norwegian immigrant church in America had itself begun to take part in the enormous expansion of global mission that occurred in the nineteenth century. The appearance of this hymn in the American edition of Landstad also points toward future developments in the hymnody of Norwegian America. "From Greenland's Icy Mountains" had first appeared in a hymnal associated with the Oxford Movement in the Church of England, *Hymns, Ancient and Modern*.[13] In borrowing from this hymnbook, which freely mixed ancient, medieval, and modern hymnody from a variety of confessional traditions, the

Salmebog

for

Lutherske Kristne i Amerika

~~~~~~

M. B. Landstads Salmebog,

Med nogle Forandringer og et Tillæg, udarbeidet af en Komit.

✦✦◗◉◖✦✦

Minneapolis.
Den forenede Kirkes forlag
1898.

Title page of one of several editions of Landstad's Salmebog *published for the United Norwegian Lutheran Church in America. Library of Luther Seminary (Saint Paul, Minnesota).*

editors of the supplement anticipate Norwegian-American hymn-books that would in the coming century become increasingly diverse. Like *Hymns, Ancient and Modern,* these later Norwegian-American books would include an eclectic and ecumenical selection of hymns and would most often rely on harmonization rather than irregular rhythm and syncopation to create musical interest and vitality. This preference for isometric rather than rhythmic melodies would result in the increasing alignment of Norwegian-American and Anglo-American preferences with respect to rhythm and harmonization and would prepare the way for the adoption of more Anglo-American hymnody.[14] This aspect of the evolving Norwegian-American musical aesthetic would make itself strongly felt in the emerging tradition of choral composing and singing represented by Fredrik Melius Christiansen (1871–1955) and the St. Olaf College Choir founded by him in 1912.[15] In light of this, it would not perhaps have entirely surprised the makers of the supplement of 1893 to have discovered that their descendants in coming generations would often open divine worship with the singing of Heber's "Holy, Holy, Holy" rather than of a Lutheran chorale.[16]

By 1893, then, Landstad with an American supplement had become the recommended hymnbook for two-thirds of Norwegian-American Lutheran congregations. Until Norwegian had all but vanished as a living language for worship, Landstad would remain the dominant hymnal, although the Norwegian Synod's book long remained a competitor. I can recall that when I listened to Norwegian worship services broadcast from St. Olaf College during my student days in the late 1960s and early 1970s, the liturgist would often announce a hymn as number such-and-such in *"Landstads salmebog"* and number such-and-such in *"Synodens salmebog."* And in some older Norwegian-American churches one often saw the hymnboard divided into two columns, with one for numbers from Landstad and the other for numbers from the Synod's hymnbook.

The story of Landstad's rise to preeminence is, among other things, a revealing example of the dynamics of an immigrant community. It has sometimes been argued on both sides of the Atlantic that immigrant communities are inherently conservative, especially in matters of religion. Marcus Lee Hansen, for example, cited the choice of hymnbooks to illustrate his contention that immigrant religion was driven by lay conservatism enacted in retrospective practice.

Hansen reports and observes: "A bookseller in Bergen, having stocked many copies of a hymnal which had been superseded in the Norwegian churches, sent them all to his agent in the United States who quickly disposed of them to congregations that would use no other. . . . Ministers and synods of immigrant churches have always been less liberal in theology and ecclesiastical practice than the brethren they left behind."[17] While there is no reason to doubt the veracity of this anecdote, Hansen's generalization is open to question. It is, indeed, true that immigrant religion was often quite retrospective. It could also be positively revolutionary. In the matter of hymnbooks, however, Norwegian-American Lutheranism as a whole seems to have been neither reactive nor revolutionary, but rather both conservative and evolutionary. This is illustrated not only by the strong preference of the immigrant church in the late nineteenth century for Norway's most widely used contemporary hymnal, which itself evinced both conservative and developmental tendencies, but by the decision to augment this hymnal with a supplement designed to meet specifically Norwegian-American needs and wishes.

LANDSTAD AND THE EVOLUTION OF AMERICAN LUTHERAN HYMNODY

When the Norwegian Lutheran Church of America was formed in 1917 by a union of Hauge's Synod, the Norwegian Synod, and the United Norwegian Lutheran Church, the new body adopted Landstad with the supplement of 1893 as its Norwegian hymnbook. Prior to the union, a committee composed of members from all three merging groups had worked to prepare an English hymnbook as well. This had appeared in 1913 as *The Lutheran Hymnary*.[18] Not surprisingly, many of the hymns in this collection were taken from the common store of the older north European Lutheran tradition and had been included in Landstad's book. The new *Hymnary*, however, also included many hymns from the periods before the Reformation, from Anglo-American sources, and from other European traditions. Hymns were set to both isometric and rhythmic melodies, but the majority of them were isometric. Of a total of 636 texts, this book contained more than sixty Scandinavian hymns. Sixteen of these were Norwegian. Thirteen of these hymns had texts by Landstad himself, and there were no fewer than forty melodies or arrangements by Lindeman. Some of these melodies by Lindeman were used for English hymns and are evidence of the increasing fusion of Norwegian and Anglo-American hymnody. Another Norwegian-American hymnbook, the *Concordia* of 1916 and 1932, was also widely used during this era, primarily in congregations of low-church sympathies.[19] This book adopted the eclecticism and ecumenism of *The Lutheran Hymnary*, but included many of the mission and gospel songs beloved by its constituency. The *Concordia* presented six hymns by Landstad and over thirty tunes or arrangements by Lindeman.

By the early 1950s it was evident that the Norwegian Lutheran Church of America, by this time renamed the Evangelical Lutheran Church, would soon merge with German-American and Danish-American Lutherans to form still another new Lutheran denomination in the United States, the American Lutheran Church of 1960–1963. A different merger would also bring together bodies with German, Danish, Swedish, and Icelandic backgrounds to create the Lutheran Church in America in 1962. A joint committee had been formed to provide a hymnal that could be used by both of these new churches and it produced the *Service Book and Hymnal* of 1958.[20] This hymnbook contained fewer than sixty Scandinavian hymns, including three texts by Landstad himself and six melodies by Lindeman. The representation of Scandinavian hymnody was further reduced in the *Lutheran Book of Worship* of 1978.[21] This book was created to prepare the way for the merger of the American Lutheran Church and the Lutheran Church in America and one other small body which would produce the Evangelical Lutheran Church in America in 1988. Of a total of 569 texts with melodies, the *Lutheran Book of Worship* includes 32 Scandinavian hymns. Of these hymns, 17 are Danish and 9 are Norwegian. These include three texts by Landstad and seven melodies by Lindeman. Of these twenty-six Danish and Norwegian hymns, all but one had appeared in Landstad's book of 1870 or the revised edition of 1926.[22] The first edition of Landstad and the revision of 1926 thus included virtually the entire canon of Dano-Norwegian hymns still sung in the United States.

While the English Lutheran hymnals most often used by the descendants of Norwegian immigrants to the United States in the twentieth century included fewer Scandinavian hymns as book succeeded book, the remaining hymns kept their places in the canon of hymns actually sung, especially in congregations of Norwegian-American origin. Three of Landstad's own texts, in fact, appeared in all three of the major hymnals used by Norwegian-Americans in the twentieth century: "A Multitude Comes from East and West" [*"Der mange skal komme fra øst og fra vest"*], "To You, Omniscient Lord of All" [*"Jeg staar for Gud som alting ved"*], and "I Know of a Sleep in Jesus' Name" [*"Jeg ved mig en søvn i Jesus navn"*].[23]

If these three hymns fairly represent his own work as a hymnist and the spirit of his hymnbook as a whole, what can they tell us about Landstad's living legacy in the United States? All three hymns, although quite different in message, share certain formal characteristics. They are accessible and memorable. The language is simple and poetic. Meter and rhyming scheme are immediately apparent and support easy congregational singing. As presented in translation, all three conform to the modern preference for brevity. Each of them is associated with a melody that is simple and appropriate to the related text. Their common structural traits suggest that these are meant to be popular hymns.

These hymns are markedly biblical in content. The verses of "To You, Omniscient Lord of All," for example, are successively based on Ezra 9:6, Psalm 51:11, and Luke 18:14, and in "A Multitude Comes from East and West" all who sing the hymn are written directly into the biblical narrative when they are invited to sit at table with Abraham, Isaac, and Jacob. While strongly Lutheran in their exposition of Scripture these hymns are, however, more proclamatory and devotional than they are didactic. They are trinitarian, but more oriented to the work of Christ and of Creator than to that of the Spirit. They are pronouncedly penitential in certain passages, but at the same time hopeful, even confident. Prayers in these hymns are offered in the expectation that God will hear and answer them. They recall the confident opening petition of the liturgy familiar to Norwegian-American Lutherans of the nineteenth and early twentieth centuries, a prayer offered in the expectation that God will both hear and attend [*høre og bønhøre*] to the prayers of the faithful. Metaphors are mild and humane. The image of death in "I Know of a Sleep in Jesus' Name" is the kindest of all found in the New Testament, and in "A Multitude Comes from East and West" the picture of the resurrection is the comforting and familiar one of feasting at table. In both form and content, these hymns epitomize the piety of Norwegian-American Lutheranism as a whole. Did the hymns shape faith and practice or was it vice versa? The answer is, of course, yes to both questions, because in this community *lex orandi* and *lex credendi* stood in close mutual relation.

LANDSTAD AS A SYMBOL OF NORWEGIAN-AMERICAN LUTHERANISM

Landstad's hymnbook became, in time, a primary symbol for the Norwegian-American Lutheran tradition as a whole. Curious but telling documentation of this is included in copies of *Landstads reviderte kirkesalmebok* taken out of use by the only congregation in Minneapolis, Minnesota that continue to use Norwegian as the language of public worship.[24] In 1993 this congregation, *Den norsk lutherske mindekirken,* adopted the *Norsk salmebok* of 1984 for use in worship.[25] Rather than merely discarding its copies of Landstad, the congregation gave them to members and friends with the following statement placed inside the front cover of each individual book.

"This hymnbook, M. B. Landstad's *Kirkesalmebok* is the revised edition of *Landstads Salmebok* from 1869, and it is, since June 1984, no longer in use in The Church of Norway. Next to the Bible, for almost 125 years, this hymnal has been one of the most loved and important books to the Norwegian people, a jewel and a treasure of immeasurable value.

"This was also the hymnal our ancestors brought with them for comfort on their journey to America. They, together with 'Bibelen' and 'Landstad' created a solid foundation for Faith and Confession in the Norwegian settlements up to our days. Enjoy and treasure your old Hymnbook—it is unique."

This brief inscription makes Landstad a symbol of the entire Norwegian-American experience. The writer betrays no awareness of the many Norwegian hymnals used in the United States and imagines Landstad's hymnbook of 1870 in the hands of every Norwegian settler to come to the United States. The statement also places Landstad on a level with the Bible as a norm of the religious tradition. The Bible and the hymnbook together are seen not as consequences but as the foundation of both faith and confession. Thus there is no mention, for example, of Luther's *Small Catechism* or of Pontoppidan's *Explanation* of the catechism. Nor is there reference to the *Augsburg Confession*. Yet for all its confusion about history and norm, this little inscription is probably quite right about the place of Landstad's hymnbook in Norwegian-American life. It played a unique role as a symbol of Norwegian-American Lutheranism as a whole.

A somewhat more considered reflection on the role of Landstad in America was written several decades earlier by Lars Wilhelm Boe (1875–1942), president of St. Olaf College. Boe wrote this brief statement in 1938 as a foreword to a brief historical study of Landstad and Lindeman written by a member of the St. Olaf faculty.

"Ours is a mediating generation. By training and tradition we live in the spiritual and cultural land of our fathers. With our children we are steadily marching into the land of tomorrow. Ours is the riches of two cultures and often the poverty of the desert wanderer. We live between memory and reality. Ours is the agony of a divided loyalty and joy in the discovery of a new unity. Like Moses of old we see the new but cannot fully enter in. To us has been given the task of mediating a culture, of preserving and transferring to our children in a new land the cultural and spiritual values bound up in the character, art, music, literature, and Christian faith of a generation no longer found even in the land from which the fathers came.

"Insofar as these values have been preserved in a Norwegian atmosphere and in the Norwegian language it has been in the form they had when brought over. When released in the language and genius of America they have again become sources of inspiration and power, and in the hearts and minds of a far greater number than our own flesh and blood. Ours is the privilege of releasing for America values that sustained the spirit and life of our forbears [*sic*] for generations. We must become conscious of our responsibility. If we pass on without opening the treasure chest, it will not be done. Our obligation is to translate in the largest sense and to carry over."[26]

Committed to the notion that descendants of the immigrants could truly and ought properly be both Norwegian and American, Boe does not tarry for a moment over the historical account in the pamphlet he introduces. Boe instantly and implicitly coopts Landstad as a symbol for the whole of the Norwegian-American experience. For him, Landstad's hymnbook evokes the image of a "treasure chest" containing the "character, art, music, literature, and Christian faith" of Norway. But by 1938 Boe has also come to believe that Landstad in America is also a symbol of life "lived between memory and reality." He understands that not only Norwegian hymnody, but all the forms of the inherited Norwegian culture, if they are to live at all, must be transformed into modes accessible to the American people of which Norwegian-Americans have become a part. Boe sees this as the task of translation "in the largest sense."

LANDSTAD AS PIONEER

With Boe's notion of translation "in the largest sense" in mind, we may ask whether Landstad did not contribute more to the development of Norwegian-American Lutheranism than narrative history alone can demonstrate. In religious communities, the way forward in time is often found through the past. Lutheran churches, for example, have repeatedly been renewed by appeals to the origins of Lutheranism, which itself sprang from a revolution based in part on appeals to earlier authorities, Paul and Augustine. The same pattern of moving forward through the past can also be seen in densely textured cultural communities. Norwegians today, for example, must regularly explain to people from other countries that *nynorsk,* the so-called "New Norwegian," is really the old Norwegian language brought back to life. A sense of the relation between past and present in such contexts may help to explain Landstad's diachronically extended influence in the highly Americanized Lutheran churches to which the descendants of immigrants from Norway to the United States now belong. Landstad, after all, had accustomed Norwegian Christians to modernize their hymnody by searching the past for speech and poetic form adapted to their evolving language and changing cultural contexts. Is it possible that when he showed Norwegians how to revise or invent hymnic language and forms to suit new contexts, he also taught them a sense for the deepest dynamics of such transformations and thus gave them an awareness that such might happen again in the future? Can it be that Landstad had, by exposing the workings of this process, indirectly helped Norwegian Americans to learn to sing hymns in English and to learn to sing them not only to tunes inherited from Europe but also to melodies springing from the folk experience of the evolving American nation?

It is not possible to answer such questions definitely. But we may speculate. Had Magnus Brostrup Landstad ever imagined the rolling prairies of the American Midwest, he would certainly have known that Norwegians who settled there would not long be singing of fjords, coastlines, mountains, and valleys as in:

> *Fra fjord og fære,*
> *Fra fjell og dype dal,*
> *Et "Ære være!"*
> *I dag gjenlyde skal.*[27]

He might also have understood one reason why the melody *"DEILIG ER JORDEN"* ["Beautiful is the Earth"] is used with different texts in Norway and Norwegian-America. On Christmas Eve in Norway congregations often sing the hymn *"Deilig er jorden"* to the melody of the same name.[28] Norwegian-American Lutherans associate this melody with another text, known to them as "Beautiful Savior," an American Lutheran translation of the German Catholic *"Schönster Herr Jesu"* ["Most Beautiful Lord Jesus"].[29] One reason that Norwegian-American immigrants adopted this version of the German Catholic *"Schönster Herr Jesu"* is undoubtedly that an English translation was immediately available to them. Another may be that this hymn includes the following verse, which sketches a landscape instantly recognizable to settlers in the American Midwest:

> Fair are the meadows, fair are the woodlands,
> Robed in flow'rs of blooming spring;
> Jesus is fairer, Jesus is purer,
> He makes our sorrowing spirit sing.[30]

Melodies, however, were transferable where texts were not. The English version of this hymn long continued to be sung by Norwegian Americans at Christmas time to the seasonally familiar tune *DEILIG ER JORDEN*, despite the fact that neither the text nor their hymnbooks directly associate this hymn with the nativity.[31]

On the other hand, Landstad might also have appreciated the victory of poetry over geography in another instance. As a lyricist, as a folklorist, and perhaps even as a romantic cultural nationalist, Landstad could well have understood why Norwegian-Americans on their rolling land, with hardly a hill much less a mountain in sight, would in time learn to sing another Christmas hymn:

> Go tell it on the mountain,
> Over the hills and everywhere;
> Go tell it on the mountain
> That Jesus Christ is born![32]

The descendants of immigrants from Norway borrowed this jubilant Christmas hymn from African slaves who had been compelled to come to America and share their inheritance with immigrants from hundreds of other places. Groups from all these homelands brought their own languages and music to the United States and each contributed to what would become a common American hymnody from which an enormous variety of Christian communities could draw old songs and find inspiration for new ones.

Would Magnus Brostrup Landstad have understood the processes that resulted in this eclectic hymnody? He was certainly no ecumenist. As local pastor in Frederikshald in 1856 he crusaded to suppress Methodist worship. His idiom and ecclesiology were pervasively national. He was fiercely opposed to the Enlightenment tendencies that would have so free a course in the American republic. Still, precisely as a national romantic, he might have understood what was happening to church song among Norwegians across the sea. Although indisputably conservative in theology and in his longing for the uniformities of a vanishing era, he was also a poet open to both the historically given and to cultural change, to a heritage of hymns both national and catholic. Ruthless with anything he thought tainted with the rationalism of the Enlightenment, Landstad nevertheless gathered hymns from many centuries, places, and traditions. With these things in mind, we may speculate that Magnus Brostrup Landstad, the romantic who cherished the culture of his nation, the folklorist who deeply understood the living nature of oral and musical tradition, the poet who made a new hymnody out of old resources in Norway, and the hymnist of broad sympathies, would have understood what even to the present happens when descendants of Norwegian immigrants in America gather in their churches to raise their voices in song. Readers of Odd Sverre Lovoll's writings will certainly recognize a pattern here. This speaks not only of the promise of America but of its fulfillment as well.

NOTES

[1]Magnus Brostrup Landstad, ed., *Kirkesalmebog efter offentlig foranstaltning samlet og udarbeidet* (Christiania, 1870).

[2]On the use of hymns in immigrant letters, see Orm Øverland, "Letters as Links in the Chain of Migration from Hedalen, Norway to Dane County, Wisconsin, 1857–1890," in the present volume. For hymns in immigrant autobiography, see Sigrid Eielsen's untitled autobiography in Christian O. Brohaugh and Ingvald Eisteinsen, *Kortfattet Beretning om Elling Eielsens Liv og Virksomhed* (Chicago, 1883), 160–195. For a translation and annotation see "A Haugean Woman in America: The Autobiography of Sigrid Eielsen," *Norwegian-American Studies* 35 (2000), 265–300.

[3]See Arne Bugge Amundsen, "Religiøs struktur i det gamle bondesamfunnet. Momenter til et helhetsperspektiv," *Tidsskrift for Teologi og Kirke* 53 (1982), 83–84.

[4]A fictional description of this practice occurs in O. E. Rølvaag, *Peder Victorious: A Tale of the Pioneers Twenty Years Later,* trans. Nora O. Solum and O. E. Rølvaag (New York, 1929), 178.

[5]See Odd S. Lovoll, "Den norske kirke i Amerika som kulturbærer," in *Immigrantane og norsk kyrkjeliv i Amerika. Sogndalseminaret 1998, 24. og 25. september,* 38.

[6]"Built on a Rock," #365, *Lutheran Book of Worship* (Minneapolis and Philadelphia, 1978).

[7]This paragraph compresses a complex history. It relies on Verlyn Dean Anderson, "The History and Acculturation of the English Language Hymnals of the Norwegian-American Lutheran Churches, 1879–1958," (Ph.D. diss., University of Minnesota, 1972) and Gracia Grindal, "Dano-Norwegian Hymnody in America," *Lutheran Quarterly* 6 (Autumn 1992). For a brief introduction to this history in the larger context of American Lutheran hymnody as a whole, see Carl F. Schalk, *God's Song in a New Land: Lutheran Hymnals in America* (Saint Louis, 1995).

[8]The first edition of this venerable Norwegian-American hymnbook was published as *Psalmebog, udgiven af Synoden for den norsk evangelisk lutherske kirke i America* (Decorah, IA, 1874).

[9]The revision appeared as *Salmebog, udgiven af Synoden for den norsk-evang.- luth. kirke i Amerika*, rev. ed. (Decorah, IA, 1903).

[10]*Salmebog for lutherske kristne i Amerika. M. B. Landstads Salmebog med nogle forandringer og et tillæg, udarbeidet af en komite* (Minneapolis, 1895).

[11]This hymn, attributed to Justus Falckner (1672–1723), would become a part of the yet to be studied story of America in Landstad. It appeared as *"Op I kristne, ruster eder,"* #255 in Magnus Brostrup Landstad, ed., *M. B. Landstads Kirkesalmebok revidert og forøket av Stiftsprost Gustav Jensen med bistand av en komité* (Oslo, 1926).

[12]*"Fra Grønlands is og kulde,"* #547 in *Salmebog for lutherske kristne i Amerika* (1895).

[13]A copy of William Henry Monk, ed., *Hymns Ancient and Modern for Use in the Services of the Church with Accompanying Tunes* (New York, 1870) is in the library of Luther Seminary, Saint Paul, Minnesota and may have been the edition used by the hymnologists of the United Norwegian Lutheran Church in America. "From Greenland's Icy Mountains" is #217 in this edition. The editors of the *Tillæg* to *Salmebog for lutherske kristne i Amerika* also erroneously attributed their #717, *"O Jesus, kom nu til os ind"* ["O, Jesus, Now Enter in among Us"] to Heber. This hymn is probably more correctly attributed to a German author translated by Landstad, as suggested in the version of this hymn printed as #444, *Salmebog* (1903). I am grateful to Arne Dag Kvamsoe for assistance with this attribution.

[14]On the distinction between isometric and rhythmic melodies in Norwegian and Norwegian-American hymnody, see Gerhard Malling Cartford, "Music in the Norwegian Lutheran Church: A Study of Its Development in Norway and Its Transfer to America, 1825–1917," (Ph.D. diss., University of Minnesota 1961), 81–115. Grindal, "Dano-Norwegian Hymnody in America," is instructive on the effects of this distinction.

[15]A compact disk, "Great Hymns of Faith," recently recorded by the St. Olaf Choir represents this eclectic tradition in contemporary form. The recording includes Lutheran chorales, Anglo-American hymns, and African-American songs.

[16]See, for example, "Holy, Holy, Holy," #72, *The Lutheran Hymnary Including the Symbols of the Evangelical Lutheran Church* (Minneapolis, 1913).

[17]Marcus Lee Hansen, *The Immigrant in American History*, ed. Arthur M. Schlesinger (Cambridge, 1940), 83.

[18]See note 16.

[19]*Concordia: A Collection of Hymns and Spiritual Songs* (Minneapolis, 1916)

and *The Concordia Hymnal: A Hymnal for Church, School and Home* (Minneapolis, 1932).

[20]*Service Book and Hymnal* (Minneapolis and Philadelphia, 1958).

[21]*Lutheran Book of Worship* (Minneapolis and Philadelphia, 1978).

[22]The only one of these hymns not to appear in Landstad was a Norwegian-American hymn originally published as #443 in *Psalmebog* (1874), *"Al verden nu raaber for Herren med fryd,"* by Ulrik Vilhelm Koren (1826–1910). This hymn appears in an English paraphrase as "Oh, Sing Jubilee to the Lord, Ev'ry Land," #256, *Lutheran Book of Worship*.

[23]Titles are given as in *Lutheran Book of Worship*. These three hymns are respectively #239, #97, and #506 in *Lutheran Hymnary*; #333, #380, #299 in *Service Book and Hymnal*; #313, #310, #342 in *Lutheran Book of Worship*.

[24]See note 17.

[25]*Norsk salmebok* (Oslo, 1984).

[26]Foreword to P. M. Glasoe, *The Landstad-Lindeman Hymnbook*, in *The Lutheran Church: A Series of Occasional Papers of General Interest to the Entire Lutheran Church,* Vol. 1, Number 9 (Minneapolis, 1938).

[27]*"Fra fjord og fære,"* #126 in *M. B. Landstads kirkesalmebok revidert*. A literal translation that does not attempt to reproduce meter or rhyming scheme is:

> From fjord and strand,
> From mountain and deep valley,
> A "Glory be!"
> Shall today resound.

[28]#110, *M.B. Landstads Kirkesalmebok revidert* (1926).

[29]This hymn is similar to #870, *"Herrligste Jesus"* ["Most Glorious Jesus"], in the section of "Spiritual Songs for the Home" in *M.B. Landstads Kirkesalmebok revidert* (1926).

[30]Verse 2 of "Beautiful Savior," #518, *Lutheran Book of Worship*.

[31]To the present, for example, the St. Olaf Choir often concludes the college's nationally renowned Christmas festival with "Beautiful Savior."

[32]"Go Tell It on the Mountain," #70, *Lutheran Book of Worship*.

A Selected Bibliography of the Writings of Odd Sverre Lovoll

BOOKS

A Folk Epic: The Bygdelag *in America.* Boston, 1975.

The Norwegian-American Historical Association, 1925–1975. Northfield, MN, 1975. Co-authored with Kenneth O. Bjork.

Bygda i den nye verda. Dei norsk-amerikanske bygdelaga. Oslo, 1977.

Cultural Pluralism versus Assimilation: The Views of Waldemar Ager. Northfield, MN, 1977. Edited.

Makers of an American Immigrant Legacy: Essays in Honor of Kenneth O. Bjork. Northfield, MN, 1980. Edited.

Det løfterike landet. Historien om norsk-amerikanerne. Oslo, 1983.

The Promise of America: A History of the Norwegian-American People. Minneapolis, 1984.

Scandinavians and Other Immigrants in Urban America. Northfield, MN, 1985. Edited.

A Century of Urban Life: The Norwegians in Chicago before 1930. Northfield, MN, 1988.

Den store Chicagoreisen. Oslo, 1988. Co-authored with Torill Thorstad Hauger.

Nordics in America: The Future of Their Past. Northfield, MN, 1993. Edited.

Det løfterike landet. En norskamerikansk historie. Oslo, 1997. Revised edition.

The Promise Fulfilled: A Portrait of Norwegian Americans Today. Minneapolis, 1998.

Migrasjon og tilpasning. Ingrid Semmingsen, et minneseminar. Tid og Tanke. Oslo, 1998. Edited.

The Promise of America: A History of the Norwegian-American People. Minneapolis, 1999. Revised edition.

Innfridde løfter. Et norskamerikansk samtidsbilde. Oslo, 1999.

ARTICLES AND CHAPTERS

"The Norwegian Press in North Dakota." *Norwegian-American Studies* 24 (1970), 78–101.

"North Dakota's Norwegian-Language Press Views World War I, 1914–1917." *North Dakota Quarterly* (Winter 1971), 73–84.

"The *Bygdelag* Movement." *Norwegian-American Studies* 25 (1972), 3–26.

"Valdres heimkjensle." In *Tidskrift for Valdres Historielag. Årbok 1972* (1972), 55–64.

"The Great Exodus." In *They Came from Norway,* edited by Erik J. Friis, 10–15. New York, 1975.

"A Folk Rally: The *Stevne* of the American *Bygdelag.*" In *Norwegian Influence on the Upper Midwest,* edited by Harald S. Naess, 117–120. Duluth, 1976.

"Decorah-Posten: The Story of an Immigrant Newspaper." *Norwegian-American Studies* 27 (1976), 77–100.

"En utvandreragent på Ringsaker." *Heimen* 3 (1979), 149–156.

"Norwegians in America after World War II." In *Cleng Peerson Memorial Institute 1970–1980,* 21–23. Stavanger, 1980.

"Simon Johnson and the Ku Klux Klan: Impressions from His Memoirs." *North Dakota Quarterly* (Fall 1980), 9–20.

"From Norway to America: A Tradition of Emigration Fades." In *Interpretive Essays in Contemporary American Immigration,* edited by D. Cuddy, Vol. I, 86–107. Boston, 1982.

"Foreword." In Waldemar Ager, *Sons of the Old Country,* trans. by Trygve M. Ager, v-xv. Lincoln, NE, 1983.

"On Being a Norwegian-American in the 1980s." *Scandinavian Review* (Winter 1985), 80–91.

"Introduction." In Jon Leirfall, *Old Times in Norway,* trans. by C. A. Clausen, 7–11. Oslo, 1986.

"Washington-Posten: A Window on a Norwegian-American Urban Community." *Norwegian-American Studies* 31 (1986), 163–186.

"Den tidlige Chicago-kolonien og dens innflytelse på den vestnorske utvandringen." In *Eit blidare tilvere?* edited by Ståle Dyrvik and Nils Kolle, 176–193. Voss, 1986.

"Norwegian-American Historical Scholarship: A Survey of Its History." In *Essays on Norwegian-American Literature and History,* edited by Dorothy Burton Skårdal and Ingeborg R. Kongslien, 223–240. Oslo, 1986.

"A Perspective on the Life of Norwegian America: Norwegian Enclaves in Chicago in the 1920s." *Migranten/The Migrant* 1, edited by Anne Birgit Larsen and Reidar Bakken (1988), 24–37.

"*Gaa Paa:* A Scandinavian Voice of Protest." *Minnesota History* 52 (1990), 86–99.

"A Pioneer Chicago Colony from Voss, Norway: Its Impact on the Overseas Migration, 1836–1860." In *A Century of European Migrations, 1830–1930,* edited by Rudolph J. Vecoli and Suzanne M. Sinke, 182–199. Champaign, IL, 1991.

"A Scandinavian Melting-Pot in Chicago." In *Swedish-American Life in Chicago: Cultural and Urban Aspects of an Immigrant People,* edited by Philip J. Anderson and Dag Blanck, 60–67. Champaign, IL, 1992.

"Norwegians on the Land. Address for the Society for the Study of Local and Regional History." *Historical Essays on Rural Life.* Marshall, MN, 1992.

"The Danish Thingvalla Line in the Nordic Competition for Emigration Traffic." In *On Distant Shores: Proceedings of Marcus Lee Hansen Immigration Conference, Aalborg, Denmark, June 29–July 1, 1992,* edited by Birgit Flemming Larsen, Henning Bender, and Karen Veien, 83–98. Aalborg, 1993.

"Norwegian-American Mutuality in the Iron Decade: 'Nordlyset' of Chicago." In *Fin(s) de Siècle in Scandinavian Perspective: Studies in Honor of Harald Naess,* edited by Faith Ingwersen and Mary Kay Norseng, 179–191. Columbia, SC, 1993.

"'For People Who Are Not in a Hurry': The Danish Thingvalla Line and the Transportation of Scandinavian Emigrants." *Journal of American Ethnic History* (1993), 48–67.

"Swedes, Norwegians, and the Columbian Exposition of 1893." In *Swedes in America: Intercultural and Interethnic Perspectives on Contemporary Research,* edited by Ulf Beijbom, 185–194. Växjö, 1993.

"The Rural Bond of Norwegians in America." *The Norseman* 34 (1994), 16–21.

"Innvandrernes Amerika." *Heimen* 3 (1994), 147–155.

"Harro Harring und seine Vertreibung aus Norwegen." Trans. Joachim Reppmann, in *Mitteilungen der Harro-Harring-Gesellschaft,* 13–14 (1994–95), 46–56.

"Paul Hjelm-Hansen: Norwegian 'Discoverer' of the Red River Valley of Minnesota and Settlement Promoter." In *Performance in American Literature and Culture: Essays in Honor of Professor Orm Øverland on His 60th Birthday,* edited by Vidar Pedersen and Zeljka Svrljuga, 161–178. Bergen, 1995.

"Norwegian Americans." In *Gale Encyclopedia of Multicultural America,* vol. 2, edited by Judy Galens, Anna Sheets, and Robyn V. Young, 1001–1015. New York, 1995.

"Emigration and Settlement Patterns as They Relate to the Migration of Norwegian Folk Art." In *Norwegian Folk Art: The Migration of Tradition,* edited by Marion J. Nelson, 125–132. New York, 1995.

"Better than a Visit to the Old Country: The *Stevne* of the Sognalag in America." In *Norwegian-American Essays,* edited by Øyvind T. Gulliksen, David C. Mauk, and Dina Tolfsby, 3–29. Oslo, 1996. Published in Honor of Odd S. Lovoll.

"Et valdrisgjestebø i Amerika, Valdris Samband." In *Årbok for Valdres 1997* (1997), 194–200.

"Norwegian Emigration to America: A Dramatic National Experience." *The Norseman* 39 (1999), 4–15.

"Cleng Peerson." In *American Biographical Dictionary,* Vol. 17 (New York, 1999), 241–242.

Norsk biografisk leksikon (Oslo, 1998–2002), contributed the following entries:

> John Anderson (1836–1910)
> Rasmus B. Anderson (1846–1936)
> B. Anundsen (1844–1913)
> Kenneth O. Bjork (1909–1991)
> John H. Blegen (1851–1928)
> Theodore C. Blegen (1891–1969)
> O. J. Breda (1853–1916)
> Ole Evinrude (1877–1934)
> C. G. O. Hansen (1871–1960)

J. C. M. Hanson (1864–1943)
Knute Nelson (1842–1923)

"Den norske kirke i Amerika som kulturbærer." In *Immigrantane og norsk kyrkjeliv i Amerika. Sogndalseminaret 1988, 24. og 25. september* (Sogndal, 2000), 34–40.

"Norway's Children, Americans All: A Contemporary Portrait of Norwegian Americans." In *Norwegians in New York, 1825–2000: Builders of City, Community and Culture*, edited by Liv Irene Myhre, 103–112. New York, 2000.

"Immigration and Immigrants: Scandinavia and Finland." In *The Encyclopedia of the United States in the Nineteenth Century*, Vol. 2, 86–88. New York, 2001.

"Religiøse overganger på historisk bakgrunn blant nordmenn i Amerika." In *Dissentere og emigrasjonen. Rapport fra Seminar i Tysværtunet kulturhus Aksdal, Tysvær, 22.-23. september 2000*, edited by Dag Nygård and Hans Eirik Aarek, 66–75. Stavanger, 2001.

"The Changing Role of May 17 as a Norwegian-American 'Key Symbol.'" In *Nasjonaldagsfeiring i fleirkulturelle demokrati*, edited by Brit Marie Hovland and Olaf Aagedal, 65–78. Copenhagen, 2001.

"Nytt fra løftets land. Det private brev og emigrasjon." In *Amerikabrev. Sogndalseminaret 2000, 28. og 29. september* (Sogndal, 2001), 6–11.

"Leiv Eriksson som symbol i det norske Amerika." In *Leiv Eriksson, Helge Ingstad og Vinland. Kjelder og tradisjonar*, edited by Jan Ragnar Hagland and Steinar Supphellen, 119–133. Trondheim, 2001.

"The Creation of Historical Memory in a Multicultural Society." In *Norwegian-American Essays*, edited by Harry T. Cleven, Knut Djupedal, and Dina Tolfsby, 27–40. Oslo, 2001.

"Canada Fever—The Odyssey of Minnesota's Bardo Norwegians." *Minnesota History* 57 (2001), 356–367.

"Norwegians in America." In *Nordic Emigration to America*, edited by Faith C. Ingwersen, 13–22. Madison, WI, 2002.

"The Norwegian-American Old-Home Societies Viewed as a Mediating Culture between 'Consent' and 'Descent.'" In *Hembygden och världen*. Gothenburg, 2001.

"Rasmus Sunde: Vikjer på fjorden—vikjer på prærien. Ein demografisk studie med utgangspunkt i Vik i Sogn." *Historisk Tidsskrift* 81 (2002), 129–137.

"Norwegians." In *Encyclopedia of Chicago History*. Chicago, 2003.

BOOK REVIEWS

Odd Sverre Lovoll has contributed book reviews regularly to a number of scholarly journals. His reviews have appeared in:

American Historical Review
The Journal of American History
Minnesota History
Journal of American Ethnic History
Wisconsin Magazine of History
Scandinavian Studies
Scandinavian Review
International Migration Review
Western Historical Quarterly
Lotus (University of North Texas)

EDITOR OF THE NORWEGIAN-AMERICAN HISTORICAL ASSOCIATION (NAHA)

During his tenure as editor of The Norwegian-American Historical Association (1980–2000), Odd Lovoll has edited the following publications:

Norwegian-American Studies, volumes 29 (1983), 30 (1985), 31 (1986), 32 (1989), 33 (1992), 34 (1995), 35 (2000).

Odd S. Lovoll, ed., *Makers of an American Immigrant Legacy: Essays in Honor of Kenneth O. Bjork* (1980).

Svein Nilsson, *A Chronicler of Immigrant Life,* ed. and trans. Clarence A. Clausen (1982).

Carl H. Chrislock, ed., *Ethnicity Challenged* (1981).

Per Hagen, *On Both Sides of the Ocean,* trans. Kate Stafford and Harald Naess (1984).

Odd S. Lovoll, *The Promise of America* (1984). Co-published with University of Minnesota Press.

James S. Hamre, *Georg Sverdrup: Educator, Theologian, Churchman* (1986).

Terje I. Leiren, *Marcus Thrane: A Norwegian Radical in America* (1987).

Nina Draxten, *The Testing of M. Falk Gjertsen* (1988).

Odd S. Lovoll, *A Century of Urban Life: The Norwegians in Chicago before 1930* (1988).

Einar Haugen, *Immigrant Idealist: A Literary Biography of Waldemar Ager* (1989).

Herman Amberg Preus, *Vivacious Daughter: Seven Lectures on the Religious Situation among Norwegians in America,* ed. and trans. Todd W. Nichol (1990).

Solveig Zempel, ed. and trans., *In Their Own Words: Letters from Norwegian Emigrants* (1991). Co-published with University of Minnesota Press.

Lowell J. Soike, *Norwegian-Americans and the Politics of Dissent 1889–1924* (1991).

Odd S. Lovoll, ed., *Nordics in America: The Future of Their Past* (1993).

Janet E. Rasmussen, ed., *New Land, New Lives* (1993). Co-published with University of Washington Press.

Marion J. Nelson, ed., *Material Culture and People's Art of Norwegian Americans* (1994).

Millard L. Gieske and Steven J. Keillor, *Norwegian Yankee: Knute Nelson and the Failure of American Politics, 1860–1923* (1995).

Orm Øverland, *The Western Home: A Literary History of Norwegian America* (1996).

David Mauk, *The Colony that Rose from the Sea* (1997).

O. E. Rølvaag, *Concerning Our Heritage,* ed. and trans. Solveig Zempel (1998).

Odd S. Lovoll, *The Promise Fulfilled: A Portrait of Norwegian Americans Today* (1998). Co-published with University of Minnesota Press.

Odd S. Lovoll, *The Promise of America: A History of the Norwegian-American People* (revised edition, 1999). Co-published with University of Minnesota Press.

Joseph Shaw, *Bernt Julius Muus: Founder of St. Olaf College* (1999).

Waldemar Ager, *Colonel Heg and His Boys: A Norwegian Regiment in the American Civil War* (2000). Introduction by Harry T. Cleven.

Bjørn Gunnar Østgård, ed., *America-America Letters: A Norwegian-American Family Correspondence* (2001). Introduction by Brynhild Rowberg.

The Authors

Sune Åkerman is Guest Professor at Karlstad University, associated with Gothenburg University, and Professor Emeritus at Umeå University, Sweden.

H. Arnold Barton is Professor Emeritus of History at Southern Illinois University at Carbondale, Illinois.

Jorunn Bjørgum is Professor of History at the University of Oslo, Norway.

Jon Gjerde is Professor of History at the University of California, Berkeley.

Øyvind T. Gulliksen is Associate Professor of American Literature and Culture at Telemark University College, Bø i Telemark, Norway.

Jan Ragnar Hagland is Professor of Old Norse Philology at the Norwegian University of Science and Technology, Trondheim, Norway.

Terje I. Leiren is Professor of Scandinavian Studies and History at the University of Washington, Seattle.

Deborah L. Miller is Research Supervisor at the Minnesota Historical Society, Saint Paul, Minnesota.

Todd W. Nichol is King Olav V Professor of Scandinavian-American Studies at St. Olaf College, Northfield, Minnesota and Professor of Church History at Luther Seminary, Saint Paul, Minnesota.

Einar Niemi is Professor of History at the University of Tromsø, Norway.

Orm Øverland is Professor of American Literature at the University of Bergen, Norway.

Rudolph J. Vecoli is Professor of History and Director of the Immigration History Research Center at the University of Minnesota.

Interior design by Rachel Holscher
Typeset in New Baskerville
by Stanton Publication Services, Inc.
Printed on 55# Sebago 2000 Antique paper
by The Maple-Vail Manufacturing Group